UNDERSTANDING AND USING

English Grammar

FOURTH EDITION
WORKBOOK

PEARSON
Longman

Betty S. Azar
Rachel Spack Koch
Stacy A. Hagen

Understanding and Using English Grammar, Fourth Edition Workbook

Pearson Education, 10 Bank Street, White Plains, NY 10606

Staff credits: The people who made up the *Understanding and Using English Grammar, Fourth Edition, Workbook* team, representing editorial, production, design, and manufacturing, are Dave Dickey, Christine Edmonds, Ann France, Margo Grant, Amy McCormick, and Robert Ruvo.

Text composition: S4Carlisle Publishing Services
Text font: 10.5/12 Plantin

Illustrations: Don Martinetti—pages 20, 21, 42, 50 160, 162 (bottom), 195, A15, A23; Chris Pavely—pages 4, 15, 19, 47, 60, 67, 69, 72, 80, 98, 111, 123, 140, 142, 143, 151, 155, 158, 159, 162 (top), 163, 165, 174, 180, 198, 203

ISBN 10: 0-13-241543-7
ISBN 13: 978-0-13-241543-9

Printed in the United States of America
3 4 5 6 7 8 9 10—V016—14 13 12 11 10

Contents

Preface

The *Understanding and Using English Grammar Workbook* is a place for students to explore and practice English grammar on their own. It is a place where they can test and fine-tune their understandings of English structures and improve their abilities to use English meaningfully and correctly. All of the exercises have been designed for independent study, but this book is also a resource for teachers who need exercise material for additional classwork, homework, testing, or individualized instruction.

The *Workbook* is keyed to the explanatory grammar charts found in *Understanding and Using English Grammar, Fourth Edition,* a classroom teaching text for students of English as a second or foreign language, as well as in the accompanying *Chartbook,* a reference grammar with no exercises.

The answers to the practices can be found in the *Answer Key* in the back of the *Workbook.* Its pages are perforated so that they can be detached to make a separate booklet. However, if teachers want to use the *Workbook* as a classroom teaching text, the *Answer Key* can be removed at the beginning of the term.

A special *Workbook* section called *Phrasal Verbs,* not available in the main text, is included in the *Appendix.* This section provides a reference list of common phrasal verbs along with a variety of exercises for independent practice.

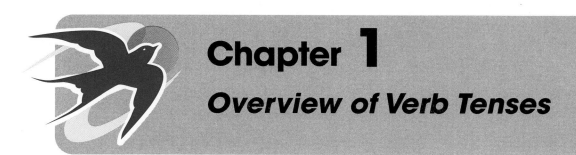

Chapter 1
Overview of Verb Tenses

▶ **Practice 1. Preview.** (Charts 1-1 → 1-5)
Write the correct form of the verbs in parentheses to complete the sentences.

1. A: I'm going to ask you some questions so that we can practice verb tenses. What do you do every day before you come to class? Name one thing.

   B: I (*eat*) _____eat_____ breakfast.

2. A: What did you do last night? Name three separate activities.

   B: Last night I (*eat*) _____ dinner. Then I (*visit*) _____ some friends, and later I (*write*) _____ a couple of letters.

3. A: What are you doing right now? What activity is in progress right now, at this exact moment?

   B: Right now I (*talk*) _____ to you. I (*answer*) _____ your questions.

4. A: Where were you at this exact time yesterday? And what activity was in progress then?

   B: Let me think. At this time yesterday, I was at the bookstore. I (*look*) _____ _____ for the books I needed to buy for this class.

5. A: How many questions have I asked since we began this exercise?

   B: I think you (*ask*) _____ me five or six questions since we began this exercise.

6. A: What have you been doing for the past five minutes? In other words, what activity began five minutes ago and has been in progress from then until now?

   B: I (*talk*) _____ to you for the past five minutes. I started talking to you five minutes ago, and I am still talking to you.

7. A: Where will you be tomorrow morning?

   B: I (*be*) _____ in class tomorrow morning.

8. A: What will you be doing at this exact time tomorrow? In other words, what activity will be in progress at this exact same time tomorrow?

   B: Right now I am sitting in the classroom. And at this exact time tomorrow, I (*sit*) _____ in the classroom.

9. A: What had you done by the time you got to class today? In other words, what is one activity that you had completed before you arrived in class today?

B: Well, for one thing, I (*eat*) _____ breakfast by the time I got to class today.

10. A: What will you have done by the time you go to bed tonight? Name one activity that you will have completed before you go to bed tonight.

B: I (*eat*) _____ dinner by the time I go to bed tonight.

▶ **Practice 2. Verb tenses: overview.** (Charts 1-1 → 1-5)
This is a calendar of the month of February. For each item, write the date or dates that the text refers to.

February						
Sun	**Mon**	**Tue**	**Wed**	**Thu**	**Fri**	**Sat**
1	**2**	**3**	**4**	**5**	**6**	**7**
8	**9**	**10**	**11**	**12**	**13**	**14**
15	**16**	**17**	**18**	**19**	**20**	**21**
22	**23**	**24**	**25**	**26**	**27**	**28**

1. Today is Wednesday, February 11th. We play tennis on Saturdays. These are the dates we play tennis in February: February __*7th*__, __*14th*__, __*21st*__, and __*28th*__ .

2. Today is Wednesday, February 4th. We're going to play tennis on Saturday. We're going to play tennis on February _____.

3. Today is Wednesday, February 4th. It rained yesterday. It rained on February _____.

4. Today is Wednesday, February 4th. It's been raining since Monday. It has rained on these days: February _____, _____, and _____.

5. Today is Friday, February 13th. It's beautiful today, but it had been raining for three days. It rained on February _____, _____, and _____.

6. Today is Friday, February 13th. It's not going to rain during the weekend. It won't rain on February _____ and _____.

7. Today is Saturday, February 21st. We've been here for exactly two weeks. We arrived here on February _____.

8. Today is Monday, February 23rd. Our singing group meets every Tuesday evening, and we sing from 7:00 to 9:00 P.M. I will be singing with my group on the evening of February _____.

▶ **Practice 3. The simple tenses and the progressive tenses.** (Charts 1-1 and 1-2)
Circle the correct verb to complete each sentence.

1. It (*is raining / rains*) every day in August.

2. Uncle Joe (*visited / visits*) us last month.

3. Our team (*will win / wins*) the soccer game tomorrow.

4. Nick (*watches / is watching*) an action movie on TV now.

5. Tomorrow at this time we (*will be flying / are flying*) over the Atlantic Ocean.

6. Tina! I (*was thinking / am thinking*) of you just a minute ago when the phone rang!

7. I know you, Aunt Martha. You're never going to retire. You (*are working / will be working*) at your computer even when you are 90 years old.

8. At 9:00 P.M. last night, all the children (*go / went*) to bed. At 10:00 P.M. they (*slept / were sleeping*).

9. Uh-oh. Look! Mr. Anton (*fell / was falling*) down on the ice. Mr. Anton! Don't move! We (*help / will help*) you!

10. A: Why is the beach closed today?

    B: There are sharks in the water! They (*swim / are swimming*) near the shore!

▶ **Practice 4. The perfect tenses.** (Chart 1-3)
Circle the correct verb to complete each sentence.

1. I (*have / had*) already seen the movie twice.

2. I (*have / had*) already seen the movie, so I didn't want to see it again.

3. Guy (*has been / was*) a professor at this university since 2001. He's going to be chairman of the English department next year.

4. Fred (*has been / was*) a judge in the Supreme Court of this state for 21 years until he retired last year.

5. On the 14th of next month, my grandparents are going to celebrate their 50th wedding anniversary. They (*will have been / had been*) married for 50 years.

6. Rafael and Sue live in Springfield. They (*lived / have lived*) there all their lives.

7. Ann and Sid moved to Chicago. Before that, they (*have / had*) lived in this town all their lives.

8. Sorry, Mr. Wu. You (*have / will have*) missed your flight! The plane left just two minutes ago.

9. Jan speaks excellent English. He (*had / has*) studied English in school for twelve years before he came here.

10. We were too late to have dinner at the restaurant. When we got there, it (*has / had*) already closed for the night.

▶ **Practice 5. The perfect progressive tenses.** (Chart 1-4)
Circle the correct verb to complete each sentence.

1. I'm thirsty, aren't you? We (*have / had*) been driving for four hours. Let's stop for a cold drink soon.

2. When is the rain going to stop? It (*has been / was*) raining for two days.

3. When Greta graduates from medical school next year, she (*will be / will have been*) studying for twenty years!

4. After Jim and Kim (*have / had*) been going out together for seven years, they finally got married last month.

5. You (*has / have*) been working in this office for only two months, and you've already gotten a raise? That's great!

6. Stan finally quit playing professional tennis after he broke his ankle two months ago. He (*has / had*) been playing for twenty years.

7. Well, it's good to be on this plane. Finally! We (*have been waiting / will have been waiting*) almost two hours!

8. Wake Maria up now. She (*had / has*) been sleeping for three hours. That's a very long nap.

9. The police officer gave Pedro a ticket because he (*has / had*) been speeding.

▶ **Practice 6. The perfect and the perfect progressive tenses.** (Charts 1-3 and 1-4)
Choose the sentence that means the same as the given sentence(s). Write the letter of the sentence.

1. We've been watching TV all night. _____
   a. We are still watching TV.
   b. We watched TV until a little while ago.

2. I've already done my homework. _____
   a. I'm still doing my homework.
   b. I've finished my homework.

3. The baby was crying when I picked him up. _____
   a. First the baby cried. Then I picked him up.
   b. First I picked up the baby. Then he cried.

4. The baby cried when I picked him up. _____
   a. First the baby cried. Then I picked him up.
   b. First I picked up the baby. Then he cried.

5. Don't wake me up when you get home at midnight. I'll be sleeping then. _____
   a. I'm going to go to sleep before midnight.
   b. I'm going to go to sleep after midnight.

6. I'm not going home for the summer break. I'll be studying. _____
   a. I have a lot of studying to do.
   b. I don't have a lot of studying to do.

7. At the beginning of the new year, I'll start a new job. _____
   a. I'll start a new job before the new year begins.
   b. I'll start a new job when the new year begins.

8. By the beginning of the new year, I will have started my new job. _____
   a. I'll start a new job before the new year begins.
   b. I'll start a new job when the new year begins.

9. Joe and his family had cleaned the whole house before his parents arrived. _____
   a. The house was already clean when his parents arrived.
   b. The house was not yet clean when his parents arrived.

► **Practice 7. Verb tenses.** (Charts 1-1 → 1-5)
Write the correct form of the verbs in parentheses to complete the sentences.

SIMPLE   **PROGRESSIVE**

PRESENT

1. Tom has regular habits. He (*eat*) _____ dinner every day. He has eaten dinner every day since he was a child. He ate dinner every day last month. He ate dinner yesterday. He will eat dinner tomorrow. He will probably eat dinner almost every day until the end of his life.

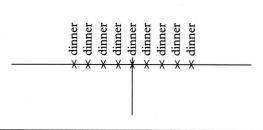

4. At 7:00 this evening, Tom started to eat dinner. It is now 7:15. Tom is on the phone because Mary called him. He says, "Can I call you back? I (*eat*) _____ dinner right now. I'll finish soon and will call you back. I don't want my dinner to get cold." Tom's dinner is in progress when Mary calls.

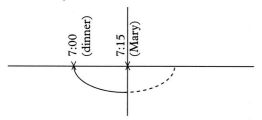

PAST

2. Tom eats dinner every day. Usually he eats at home, but yesterday, he (*eat*) _____ dinner at a restaurant.

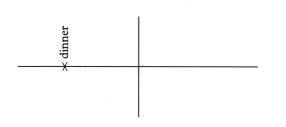

5. Last week Tom went to a restaurant. He began to eat at 7:00. At 7:15 Mary came into the restaurant, saw Tom, and walked over to say hello. Tom's dinner was still in front of him. He hadn't finished it yet. In other words, when Mary walked into the restaurant, Tom (*eat*) _____ dinner. Tom's dinner was in progress when Mary arrived.

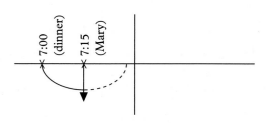

FUTURE

3. Tom ate dinner yesterday. He eats dinner every day. In all probability, he (*eat*) _____ dinner tomorrow.

6. Tom will begin his dinner at 7:00 tonight. Mary will arrive at 7:15. It takes Tom 30 minutes to eat his dinner. In other words, when Mary arrives tonight, Tom (*eat*) _____ his dinner. Tom's dinner will be in progress when Mary arrives.

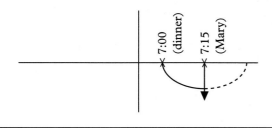

(continued on next page)

Overview of Verb Tenses **5**

| | **PERFECT** | **PERFECT PROGRESSIVE** |

PRESENT

7. Tom finished eating dinner at 7:30 tonight. It is now 8:00, and his mother has just come into the kitchen. She says, "What would you like for dinner? Can I cook something for you?" Tom says, "Thanks Mom, but I (*eat, already*) _____ dinner."

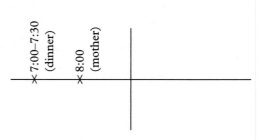

10. Tom began to eat dinner at 7:00 tonight. It is now, at this moment, 7:15. Tom (*eat*) _____ his dinner for 15 minutes, but he hasn't finished yet. In other words, his dinner has been in progress for 15 minutes.

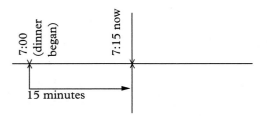

PAST

8. Yesterday Tom cooked his own dinner. He began at 7:00 and finished at 7:30. At 8:00 his mother came into the kitchen. She offered to cook some food for Tom, but he (*eat, already*) _____ _____. In other words, Tom had finished his dinner before he talked to his mother.

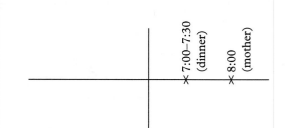

11. Last week Tom went to a restaurant. He began to eat at 7:00. At 7:15 Mary came into the restaurant, saw Tom, and walked over to say hello. Tom's dinner was still in front of him. He hadn't finished it yet. In other words, when Mary walked into the restaurant, Tom (*eat*) _____ dinner. Tom's dinner was in progress when Mary arrived.

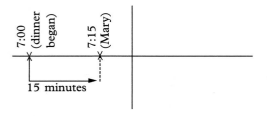

FUTURE

9. Tomorrow Tom will begin dinner at 7:00 and finish at 7:30. His mother will come into the kitchen at 8:00. In other words, Tom (*eat, already*)

    _____

    dinner by the time his mother walks into the kitchen.

12. Tonight Tom will go to a restaurant. He will begin to eat at 7:00. At 7:15 Mary will come into the restaurant, see Tom, and walk over to say hello. Tom's dinner will still be in front of him. He won't have finished it yet. In other words, when Mary walks into the restaurant, Tom (*eat*) _____ _____ dinner for 15 minutes. Tom's dinner will have been in progress for 15 minutes by the time Mary arrives.

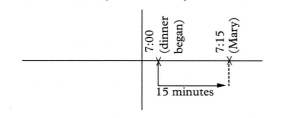

▶ **Practice 8. Verb tenses.** (Charts 1-1 → 1-5)
Circle the phrase that correctly describes each sentence.

1. He is eating dinner.   daily habit   (at this time)   in the past
2. We ate a huge dinner.   in the future   at this time   in the past
3. She doesn't eat lunch.   daily habit   at this time   in the past
4. I've been busy.   past and present   past only   only today
5. Sam spoke to Anna.   past and present   past only   daily habit
6. They were studying.   past and present   at this time   in the past
7. They're sleeping.   daily habit   at this time   in the past
8. I'll see you there.   in the future   daily habit   at this time
9. Sue plays the violin.   in the future   daily habit   at this time
10. Tina played the drums.   daily habit   at this time   in the past

▶ **Practice 9. Verb tenses.** (Charts 1-1 → 1-5)
Circle the letter of each word or phrase that can complete the sentence. More than one completion may be correct.

1. We will be there _____.
   a. now   b. soon   c. next week

2. It's raining really hard _____.
   a. right now   b. last week   c. tomorrow

3. Shhh! The movie is beginning _____.
   a. daily   b. now   c. right now

4. The newspaper hasn't come _____.
   a. tomorrow   b. all day   c. since Monday

5. We are enjoying the nice weather _____.
   a. now   b. this week   c. sometimes

6. I am going to study _____.
   a. last night   b. next month   c. this weekend

7. John has been sleeping _____.
   a. since 9:00   b. all day   c. for two hours

8. He worked hard _____.
   a. last week   b. now   c. yesterday

9. Carlos was studying _____.
   a. at midnight   b. when we came   c. in a week

10. We'll see you _____.
    a. tomorrow   b. a minute ago   c. in the morning

11. I'll be talking to you _____.
    a. soon   b. now   c. in a few days

► **Practice 10. Verb tenses.** (Charts 1-1 → 1-5)
Write the letters of all the phrases that can complete each sentence.

1. Every day I _____.
   a. memorize new vocabulary
   b. am memorizing new vocabulary
   c. was memorizing new vocabulary

2. Right now it _____.
   a. is snowing
   b. was snowing
   c. snows

3. By the time the plane lands, _____.
   a. I have finished my book
   b. I will have finished my book
   c. I had been finishing my book

4. Tomorrow at this time _____.
   a. we will have arrived home
   b. we will be arriving home
   c. we arrived home

5. Pretty soon the weather _____.
   a. will turn cold
   b. is going to turn cold
   c. will be turning cold

6. While you were sleeping, _____.
   a. your mom stopped by
   b. your mom has stopped by
   c. your mom was stopping by

7. Before you got here, _____.
   a. I had been cleaning my room
   b. I am cleaning my room
   c. I will have cleaned my room

8. They had left the restaurant _____.
   a. before we arrived
   b. after we arrived
   c. by the time we arrived

► **Practice 11. Spelling of *-ing* forms.** (Chart 1-6)
Write the *-ing* form of each verb in the correct column.

	Just add *-ing* to the simple form.	**Drop the final *-e* and add *-ing*.**	**Double the final letter and add *-ing*.**
1. arrive		*arriving*	
2. copy	*copying*		
3. cut			*cutting*
4. enjoy			
5. fill			
6. happen			
7. hope			
8. leave			
9. make			
10. rub			
11. stay			
12. stop			
13. take			
14. win			
15. work			

► **Practice 12. Spelling of _-ed_ forms.** (Chart 1-6)

Write the **_-ed_** form for each verb in the correct column.

	Just add _-ed_ to the simple form.	Add _-d_ only.	Double the final letter and add _-ed_.	Change the _-y_ to _-i_ and add _-ed_.
1. bother	bothered			
2. copy				copied
3. enjoy				
4. fasten				
5. fear				
6. occur				
7. pat				
8. play				
9. rain				
10. refer				
11. reply				
12. return				
13. scare				
14. try				
15. walk				

► **Practice 13. Spelling of *-ing* and *-ed* forms.** (Chart 1-6)
Write the *-ing* and *-ed* form for each word in the correct column.

	-ing	-ed
1. prefer	*preferring*	*preferred*
2. study		
3. work		
4. offer		
5. kiss		
6. play		
7. faint		
8. allow		
9. stop		
10. tie		
11. die		
12. fold		
13. try		
14. decide		
15. hop		

► **Practice 14. Chapter review.** (Chapter 1)
Read the conversation between a new teacher and his students on the first day of class. Write the correct form of the verbs in parentheses to complete the conversation.

Part I. The first day of the new semester.

TEACHER: Good morning, students. I'm your new music teacher, Tom Piazza.

STUDENT 1: Hello, Mr. Piazza. How (*you, spell*) _____ your name?
                                                                          1

MR. PIAZZA: I (*spell*) _____ it almost like *pizza*, but it (*have*) _____
                                2   3
an extra "A" in the middle.

STUDENT 2: Where (*you, be*) _____ from, Mr. Piazza?
                                            4

MR. PIAZZA: Well, I (*be*) _____ Italian. You can tell that by the name. I was
                                  5
born in Italy, but I (*live*) _____ there for only two years as a
                                      6
child. My parents (*move*) _____ to New York with the whole
                                          7
family when I was just two years old.

STUDENT 3: Oh, (*you, grow*) _____ up in New York then?
                                      8

MR. PIAZZA: Yes, I did. I grew up in New York City.

STUDENT 4: So when (*you, come*) _____ here to Springfield?
                                           9

MR. PIAZZA: Just two weeks ago. I (*arrive*) _____ here just two weeks ago!
                                                    10

I (*be*) _____ here for two weeks.
              11

STUDENT 5: Only two weeks! Well, (*you, like*) _____ Springfield?
                                                        12

MR. PIAZZA: I do. It seems very nice. Right now I (*stay*) _____
                                                                      13

downtown in the PriceWise Hotel. I (*look*) _____ for an
                                                          14

apartment near this school now. In fact, I (*look*) _____
                                                                15

_____ for an apartment for two weeks. I hope that I

(*find*) _____ one soon.
                16

Part II. Two weeks later.

STUDENT: (*you, find*) _____ an apartment yet, Mr. Piazza?
                                    17

MR. PIAZZA: Yes, I have. As you know, I (*look*) _____ for one for the
                                                          18

past two weeks, and then over the weekend, I found a nice one.

STUDENT: Great! When (*you, move*) _____ in?
                                                19

MR. PIAZZA: Next weekend. Usually I (*give*) _____ piano lessons all day on
                                                        20

Saturdays, but next Saturday I won't be giving lessons. Next Saturday and

Sunday — all day — I (*move*) _____ all my things
                                            21

into my new place. It will take the whole weekend, I'm sure. But next Monday at

this time, I (*move*) _____ everything into my new
                              22

apartment. I (*be*) _____ very happy here in Springfield in the
                            23

future, I know.

Chapter 2
Present and Past;
Simple and Progressive

▶ **Practice 1. The simple present and the present progressive.** (Charts 2-1 and 2-2)
Complete the sentences. Write the simple present or the present progressive form of the verbs in parentheses.

1. The sun (*set*) _____sets_____ in the west every evening.

2. Look! The sun (*set*) _____ behind the mountain now. How beautiful!

3. The football players (*practice*) _____ on the field right now.

4. The football players (*practice*) _____ on the field every afternoon.

5. I always (*listen*) _____ to the radio when I'm in my car.

6. The traffic is bad today, but it isn't bothering me. I (*listen*) _____ to
   my favorite morning talk show with Jack LaLoule, who is very funny.

7. Sam and Lara (*talk*) _____ on the phone every night.

8. Sam and Lara (*talk*) _____ on the phone right now, so I can't call
   Lara. Her line is busy.

9. I'll call you back in a little while. We (*eat*) _____ dinner right now.

10. My grandparents usually (*eat*) _____ dinner early. They often go out to
    their favorite restaurant for the early dinner special at 5:30.

▶ **Practice 2. The simple present and the present progressive.** (Charts 2-1 and 2-2)
Circle the correct verb.

1. Because of the force of gravity, objects (*fall / are falling*) down and not up.

2. It's autumn! The leaves (*fall / are falling*), and winter will soon be here.

3. Coffee (*grows / is growing*) in mountainous areas, not in deserts.

4. Oh, you (*grow / are growing*) so fast, Johnny! Soon you'll be taller than your dad.

5. Near the Arctic Circle, the sun (*shines / is shining*) for more than twenty hours a day at the
   beginning of the summer.

6. It's a beautiful day! The sun (*shines / is shining*) and the birds (*sing / are singing*).

7. Maria is a professional singer. She (*sings / is singing*) in the opera every season.

8. Olga likes mysteries. She (*reads / is reading*) one mystery book every week.

9. Hello, Sarah? I (*call / am calling*) you from my car. I'm going to be a little late for lunch.

► **Practice 3. The simple present and the present progressive.** (Charts 2-1 and 2-2)
Complete the sentences. Write either the simple present or the present progressive form of the verbs in the list. Use each verb only once.

belong	bleed	mean	shrink	try
bite	fail	✓ own	sleep	

1. The bank lent us money for a down payment, so now we _____*own*_____ the house we used to rent.

2. Shhh! I _____ to concentrate. I can't hear myself think with all that noise going on.

3. This book is mine. That one _____ to Pierre.

4. Shhh! The baby _____. We don't want to wake him up.

5. *Singular* _____ "one."

6. That sweater won't fit you if you wash it in hot water. Wool _____ in hot water.

7. Look at Joan. She _____ her fingernails. She must be nervous.

8. A: Juan! What's the matter with your hand? It _____.

   B: I just cut it when I was using a knife. It's not serious. I'll wash it and put a bandage on it.

9. A: My grades in school are terrible this term. I _____ three of my courses.

   B: Maybe you can improve them before the end of the term if you start studying.

► **Practice 4. Non-progressive verbs.** (Chart 2-3)
Write the letter of the correct completion.

1. There you are! Behind the tree! I ____ you.
   a. see   b. am seeing

2. My mother's hearing has been getting worse for several months. She ____ a specialist right now.
   a. sees   b. is seeing

3. Do you see that man? I ____ him. He was my high school English teacher.
   a. recognize   b. am recognizing

4. My favorite actor ____ at the Paramount Theater.
   a. currently appears   b. is currently appearing

5. A: Is my voice loud enough?
   B: Yes, ____.
   a. I hear you   b. I am hearing you

6. A: Aren't you having any coffee?

   B: No, _____.

      a. I prefer tea   b. I'm preferring tea

7. A: What's on your mind?

   B: I _____.

      a. think about my family   b. am thinking about my family

8. A: Did you make a decision yet?

   B: No, _____.

      a. I need your opinion   b. I'm needing your opinion

9. A: Why are you staring at me?

   B: _____.

      a. You resemble your mom so much   b. You are resembling your mom so much

10. A: There's Dr. Jones on a motorcycle! Do you believe it? _____.

    B: a. Yeah, he owns several   b. Yeah, he is owning several

▶ **Practice 5. The present progressive to describe a temporary state.** (Chart 2-3, 2nd footnote)

Circle the letter of the correct completion. If the situation describes a temporary state, choose the present progressive.

1. My husband and I are short, but our children _____.

      (a.) are tall   b. are being tall

2. Jane's an intelligent woman, but she won't see a doctor about those headaches she has. She _____ now.

      a. is foolish   (b.) is being foolish

3. The teacher spoke harshly to the children because they were too noisy, so now they _____.

      a. are quiet   b. are being quiet

4. Don't eat that chocolate dessert. It _____.

      a. is not healthy   b. is not being healthy

5. Timmy! Those are bad words you're saying to Mr. Hawkes. You _____.

      a. are not polite   b. are not being polite

6. I'm worried about Jeff. He has pneumonia. He _____.

      a. is very ill   b. is being very ill

► **Practice 6. Regular and irregular verbs.** (Charts 2-4 and 2-5)
Read the passage about *Sputnik*.

History changed on October 4th, 1957 when the Soviet Union successfully launched* *Sputnik I*. The world's first artificial satellite was about the size of a beach ball (58 cm., or 22.8 in.), weighed only 83.6 kg., or 183.9 pounds, and took about 98 minutes to orbit the Earth on its elliptical path. That launch ushered in** new political, military, technological, and scientific developments. While the *Sputnik* launch was a single event, it marked the start of the space age and the U.S.–Soviet Union space race.

Part I. Circle the eight past tense verbs in the passage.

Part II. Answer the questions according to the information in the passage. Circle "T" if the statement is true. Circle "F" if the statement is false.

1. The Soviet Union launched the first artificial satellite.   T   F
2. The first satellite was about the size of a golf ball.   T   F
3. The first orbit around the Earth took about an hour and a half.   T   F
4. *Sputnik* went into space several times.   T   F
5. This first launch was the beginning of the space age and the space race.   T   F

► **Practice 7. Regular and irregular verbs.** (Charts 2-4 and 2-5)
Complete the sentences. Write the simple past tense of the verbs in **bold**.

Part I. Regular verbs: The simple past and past participle end in *-ed*.

1. Sandy **works** at a bakery. She _____*worked*_____ there last Saturday.
2. Burt often **listens** to old Beatles songs. He _____*listened*_____ to some last night too.
3. Ana and Juan **study** English in a group on Saturday mornings. Last Saturday, they _____ the irregular past tense verbs.
4. It **rains** every afternoon in the summer. Yesterday it _____ all afternoon and all night too.

Part II. Irregular verbs: The simple past and past participle do not end in *-ed*.

5. Watch out! Those glasses **break** easily. Uh-oh . . . one glass just _____.
6. Nowadays, I occasionally **swim** for exercise when I have time, but I _____ every day when I was a child.
7. Lightning sometimes **hits** trees in this area. In the last storm, a lightning bolt _____ my neighbor's tree and caused it to fall on his house.

---

*launch = to start something, usually something big or important.
**usher in = to introduce.

▶ **Practice 8. Irregular verbs.** (Chart 2-5)
Complete the sentences. Write the simple past tense of the verbs in **bold**.

Group 1.

1. This year corn **costs** a lot more than it _____ last year.

2. Gail generally **shuts** the door very quietly, but tonight she _____ it with a loud bang because she was very angry.

3. I usually **cut** my daughter's hair myself, but last week I was sick and she went to a hairdresser. He _____ it too short, and she wasn't happy.

4. Andrew moves from job to job. Normally, he works for about a year and then **quits**, but on this last job, he _____ after only one month.

Group 2.

5. Sometimes I **forget** things. Yesterday I _____ to take my keys with me, and when I got home, I couldn't get into my house.

6. Presidents **choose** their assistants and their cabinet officers. Last week the president _____ the chief financial officer of a major bank to be the secretary of the treasury.

7. I am a history major. I **take** a lot of history courses. Last semester I _____ Medieval European History and Modern African History.

8. Jenny always **gives** generous presents. Last year she _____ me a beautiful silver picture frame from Mexico.

▶ **Practice 9. Irregular verbs.** (Chart 2-5)
Complete the sentences. Write the simple past tense of the verbs in **bold**.

Group 3.

1. The concert usually **begins** on time, but tonight it _____ ten minutes late.

2. The opera star generally **sings** beautifully, but last night he _____ poorly because he was getting a cold.

3. Joe **runs** in marathons. Last year he _____ in the New York Marathon.

4. Keisha usually **drinks** green tea. At our house, we didn't have any green tea, so she _____ decaffeinated coffee.

Group 4.

5. I always **buy** fresh vegetables on the weekend. Last Saturday I _____ fresh asparagus.

6. Mr. Joseph **teaches** Spanish in high school. He _____ my mother Spanish in the same high school 25 years ago.

7. Our basketball team doesn't **win** many games, but we _____ last Friday night.

8. The other team is an excellent team, and they rarely **lose** a game. But they _____ the game last Friday night.

9. A: Isn't Helen still here? She usually **leaves** after six, doesn't she?

   B: Not today. She _____ early for a dentist's appointment.

10. A: Don't tell this to Grandma. Bad news about the family always **upsets** her.

    B: I told her already. And it's true — the bad news _____ her. She cried.

▶ **Practice 10. Irregular verbs.** (Chart 2-5)
Complete the sentences. Write the simple past tense of the verbs in **bold**.

Group 5.

1. I **know** the whole Grant family. I know their aunts, uncles, and cousins, and I _____ their grandparents long ago.

2. Tom is a pilot. He **flies** across the Atlantic Ocean regularly. Last month he _____ to Australia for the first time.

3. I rarely **do** all of my homework. Last night I _____ about half of it before I went to bed for the night.

4. My friends and I usually **see** a movie on Friday nights. Last Friday night we _____ the new science-fiction movie, *Robot Planet.*

Group 6.

5. Joanna is an excellent runner. She **runs** in the Olympic Games. She _____ in the Olympic Games in Athens in 2004 and in Beijing in 2008.

6. Aunt Jessie rarely **comes** to our house. But last year she _____ for my brother's wedding.

7. When you mix red paint and yellow paint, it **becomes** orange paint. Yesterday I mixed yellow paint with blue paint, and it _____ green.

Group 7.

8. A: Your mother **is** an English teacher, right?

   B: Well, she _____ an English teacher until she retired. Now she writes books to teach people English.

9. A: You **go** to the math review sessions on Monday nights, don't you?

   B: Yes, I do. I _____ to the review session last night.

Group 8.

10. Some children **dream** of becoming astronauts. I didn't. I always _____ of becoming a famous writer.

11. Musicians **learn** to play instruments when they are very young. My cousin _____ to play the violin when she was only four years old.

12. Fires **burn** quickly in this dry weather. Last month a fire _____ out of control for a week in the national park.

13. Be careful! The milk is going to **spill**! Uh-oh. Too late. It _____ all over the rug.

▶ **Practice 11. Irregular verbs.** (Chart 2-5)
Write the simple past and the past participle forms of the verbs.

Simple Form	Simple Past	Past Participle
1. sell	*sold*	*sold*
2. buy		
3. begin		
4. have		
5. catch		
6. quit		
7. find		
8. make		
9. take		
10. break		
11. come		
12. lose		
13. sleep		
14. build		
15. fight		

▶ **Practice 12. Irregular verbs.** (Chart 2-5)
Complete the verb chart. Write the missing simple present, simple past, or past participle forms.

Simple Form	Simple Past	Past Participle
1. understand	*understood*	*understood*
2.	spent	
3. let		
4.		seen
5. teach		
6.	spoke	
7.		gone
8. pay		
9.		forgotten
10.	wrote	
11. fall		
12.	felt	
13.		left
14.	upset	
15.		flown

▶ **Practice 13. Irregular verbs.** (Chart 2-5)
In this exercise, a police reporter interviews the victim of a theft. The victim answers the questions, using a past tense verb. Write the victim's words.

1. REPORTER: So, a thief broke into your home last night?

   VICTIM: Yes, a thief _____ into my home last night.

2. REPORTER: Did he steal anything?

   VICTIM: Yes, he _____ some things.

3. REPORTER: Did you know he was in your apartment?

   VICTIM: Yes, I _____ he was in my apartment.

4. REPORTER: Did you hear him come in?

   VICTIM: Yes, I _____ him come in.

5. REPORTER: Did the police come?

   VICTIM: Yes, the police _____ .

6. REPORTER: Did your hands shake when you called the police?

   VICTIM: Yes, my hands _____ when I called them.

7. REPORTER: Did he hide in your garden?

    VICTIM: Yes, he _____ in my garden.

8. REPORTER: Did the police find him?

    VICTIM: Yes, the police _____ him.

9. REPORTER: Did they fight with him?

    VICTIM: Yes, they _____ with him.

10. REPORTER: Did he run away?

    VICTIM: Yes, he _____ away.

11. REPORTER: Did they shoot at him?

    VICTIM: Yes, they _____ at him.

12. REPORTER: Did they catch him?

    VICTIM: Yes, they _____ him.

▶ **Practice 14. Simple past of irregular verbs.** (Chart 2-5)
Complete the sentences. Write the simple past of the irregular verbs in the list. Pay special attention to spelling. Use each verb only once.

✓ bite	catch	hold	pay	sting
blow	feel	mean	quit	swim

1. I broke a tooth when I _____*bit*_____ into a piece of hard candy.

2. The little boy _____ his mother's hand as they walked toward the school bus.

3. Maria promised to help us. I hope she _____ what she said.

4. Arthur _____ out all of the candles on his birthday cake.

5. We both _____ eating fried foods three months ago, and we already feel much better.

6. Douglas _____ the outside of his pocket to make sure his wallet was still there.

7. A bee _____ me on the hand while I was working in the garden.

8. Matthew Webb was the first person who _____ across the English Channel.

9. Paul _____ much more for his bike than I spent for mine.

10. Rita threw the ball high in the air. Daniel _____ it when it came down.

► **Practice 15. Simple past of irregular verbs.** (Chart 2-5)
Complete the sentences. Write the simple past form of the irregular verbs in the list. Pay special attention to spelling. Use each verb only once.

bet	freeze*	sink	split
choose	lead	✓ spend	upset
fly	ring	spin	weep

1. Dr. Perez _____*spent*_____ ten hours in the operating room performing delicate surgery.

2. On my first day at the university, my English teacher _____ the class to our classroom. We all followed him.

3. Sally and I made a friendly bet. I _____ her that my grade on the math test would be higher than hers.

4. I _____ when I heard the tragic news. Everyone else cried too.

5. As she got up, Lina _____ the table, and everything on top of it fell to the floor.

6. Paul wanted to make a fire, but the logs were too big. So he _____ them with his axe.

7. When I threw a piece of wood from the shore, it floated on top of the water. When I threw a rock, it _____ immediately to the bottom of the lake.

8. In 1927, Charles Lindbergh _____ from New York to Paris in 33 hours and 30 minutes.

9. When the children _____ around and around, they became dizzy.

10. The telephone _____ several times and then stopped before I could answer it.

11. William had trouble deciding which sweater he liked best, but he finally _____ the blue one.

12. The cold temperatures _____ the water in the pond, so we can go ice-skating today.

► **Practice 16. The simple past and the past progressive.** (Charts 2-7 and 2-8)
Complete the sentences. Write the correct form of the verbs in parentheses.

1. Maria (*call*) _____ me as soon as she got the good news.

2. Last night at about nine o'clock we (*watch*) _____ TV when someone knocked at the door.

3. During the study period in class yesterday, it was hard for me to concentrate because the student next to me (*hum*) _____.

4. When Harry (*meet*) _____ Jenny, he immediately fell in love with her.

5. Jack was rushing to catch the bus when I (*see*) _____ him.

---

*freeze = stop moving completely.

6. Last Saturday while Sandy (*clean*) _____ out the attic, she found her grandmother's wedding dress.

7. It started to rain while I (*drive*) _____ to work this morning. I didn't have an umbrella with me. I (*get*) _____ very wet when I stepped out of my car.

8. When we looked outside during the storm, we saw that the wind (*blow*) _____ very hard, and the trees (*bend*) _____ over in the wind.

9. When the teacher came into the room, most of the children (*play*) _____ together nicely. But over in the corner, Bobby (*pull*) _____ Annie's hair. The teacher quickly ran over and pulled Bobby away from Annie.

▶ **Practice 17. The simple past and the past progressive.** (Charts 2-7 and 2-8)
Write "1" before the action that started first. Write "2" before the action that started second.

1. When the alarm clock rang, I was sleeping.

    _2_ The alarm clock rang.

    _1_ I was sleeping.

2. When I saw Dr. Jarvis yesterday evening, he was waving at me.

    ____ I saw Dr. Jarvis yesterday evening.

    ____ He was waving at me.

3. When I saw Dr. Jarvis yesterday evening, he waved at me.

    ____ I saw Dr. Jarvis yesterday evening.

    ____ He waved at me.

4. I closed the windows when it was raining.

    ____ I closed the windows.

    ____ It was raining.

5. I was closing the windows when it began to rain.

    ____ I was closing the windows.

    ____ It began to rain.

6. The server brought the check when we were eating our desserts.

    ____ The server brought the check.

    ____ We were eating our desserts.

7. When the doorbell rang, Sam went to the door. "Who is it?" he asked.

    ____ The doorbell rang.

    ____ Sam went to the door.

8. Sam was going to the door when the doorbell rang. "I'm coming, Bob," he said. "I saw you walking up the sidewalk."

    ____ The doorbell rang.

    ____ Sam was already going to the door.

▶ **Practice 18. The simple past and the past progressive.** (Charts 2-7 and 2-8)
Circle the correct form of the verbs in parentheses.

1. We (*had / were having*) a wonderful dinner last night to celebrate our 25th wedding anniversary.

2. We (*had / were having*) a wonderful time when suddenly the electric power went out.

3. When Richard (*stopped / was stopping*) his car suddenly, the groceries (*fell / were falling*) out of the grocery bags and (*spilled / were spilling*) all over the floor of the car.

4. When I was a child, my mother always (*served / was serving*) cookies and milk to my friends and me when they (*came / were coming*) home with me after school.

5. When we (*looked / were looking*) in on our baby last night, he (*slept / was sleeping*). I think he (*dreamt / was dreaming*) about something nice because he (*smiled / was smiling*).

6. A: Why is Henry in the hospital?

   B: He (*worked / was working*) on his car in the garage when the gas tank (*exploded / was exploding*).

   A: Oh! What (*caused / was causing*) the explosion?

   B: Henry (*dropped / was dropping*) a match too near the gas tank.

▶ **Practice 19. Simple present, present progressive, simple past, past progressive.** (Charts 2-1 → 2-4; 2-5, 2-7, and 2-8)
Underline the verbs. Decide which of the following phrases best describes the action of each sentence. Write the appropriate number.

1. actions occurring now or today
2. habitual / everyday actions
3. actions completed in the past (non-progressive)
4. one action in progress when another occurred

1. _2_ I take the bus to school when it rains.

2. _4_ I was riding the bus when I heard the news on my radio.

3. ___ I am riding the bus because my friend is repairing my bike.

4. ___ I rode the bus home yesterday because you forgot to pick me up.

5. ___ Dennis was having coffee this morning when a bird crashed into his kitchen window.

6. ___ Dennis had a big breakfast, but his wife didn't eat anything.

7. ___ Dennis is having a big breakfast this morning.

8. ___ Dennis generally has coffee with breakfast.

9. ___ My mother and I celebrate our birthdays together because they are just a few days apart.

10. ___ We were working when you called on our birthdays last week.

11. ___ One year we celebrated our birthdays apart because my mom was away on business.

▶ **Practice 20. Using progressive verbs with *always*.** (Chart 2-9)
Complete the dialogues. Write either the simple present or present progressive form of the verbs in the list and the given words in parentheses. If the speaker is expressing annoyance, use the present progressive.

| ✓ complain | leave | lose | study |
| interrupt | live | play | talk |

1. A: Why won't you go out with Carlo anymore?

    B: He (*always*) _____*is always complaining*_____ about something. It was really irritating me to hear all those complaints!

2. A: How do you like your new roommate?

    B: I don't. He (*always*) _____ loudly on his phone. I can't have any peace and quiet in the room!

3. A: Why don't you come to our Friday night get-togethers, Al?

    B: I'd like to, but I _____ on the other side of town. It's too far.

4. A: Why are you so upset with Lisa?

    B: Oh, she (*forever*) _____ the towels on the bathroom floor. She never hangs them up.

5. A: What's the matter now? Why are you angry at me?

    B: Because you (*always*) _____ me! I never get a chance to finish a sentence!

6. A: Uh-oh. I can't find the keys to the car.

    B: Again? You (*always*) _____ them! You should tie them around your neck on a string.

7. A: What radio station do you listen to when you're in your car?

    B: I don't listen to the radio. I (*usually*) _____ my English lessons in the car. It's a good way to learn.

8. A: Sorry I can't join you tonight. I have to prepare for a test tomorrow.

    B: Oh, you (*always*) _____. Can't you take a break?

▶ Practice 21. Chapter review.

Complete the crossword puzzle. Use the clues under the puzzle. Write the correct form of the verbs in parentheses.

Across

2. Shhh. I'm (*listen*) _____ to the radio.

5. Good idea! I (*think*) _____ your suggestion is great.

7. What was that? I just (*hear*) _____ a loud noise.

8. I am (*think*) _____ about going home early today.

Down

1. We (*go*) _____ to Mexico last year.

3. I was in my room (*study*) _____ when you called.

4. I (*eat*) _____ lunch with friends yesterday.

6. This is fun. I'm (*have*) _____ a great time here.

7. I only (*have*) _____ a little money right now.

Chapter 3
Perfect and Perfect Progressive Tenses

▶ **Practice 1. Preview.** (Chapter 3)
Read the graph and the passage.

Largest Cities Worldwide

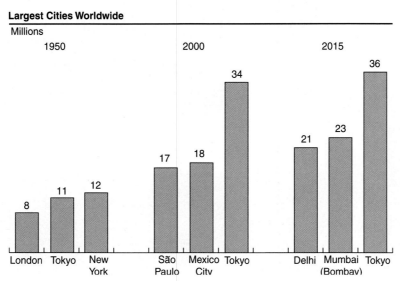

Source: United Nations, World Urbanization Projects: The 2003 Revision
(medium scenario), 2004. © 2006 Population Reference Bureau.

Tokyo has been increasing in population since 1960. In fact, Tokyo has been the only city that has remained among the world's three largest cities since 1950. New York had once been the world's largest city. By the year 2000, it had dropped from the list. São Paulo and Mexico City were once among the largest cities too. Asian cities have been growing, and experts have estimated that in 2015, the three largest cities will be in Asia.

Part I. Look at the passage.

1. Write the three verbs in the present perfect tense.

   _____

2. Write the two verbs in the present perfect progressive tense.

   _____

3. Write the two verbs in the past perfect tense.

   _____

4. Write the one verb in the simple past tense.

   _____

5. Write the one verb in the future tense.

   _____

Part II. Circle "T" if the statement is true according to the graph and the passage, and "F" if it is false.

1. New York has been the largest city in the world since 1950.   T   F
2. Tokyo has been the largest city in the world for more than 50 years.   T   F
3. London had once been one of the three largest cities of the world.   T   F
4. In 1950, one city in India was one of the top three cities in world population. T   F
5. In 2015, two cities in India will be among the three largest cities of the world. T   F

▶ **Practice 2. The present perfect.** (Chart 3-1)
Complete the sentences using the present perfect tense. Write the correct past participle of the verbs in **bold**.

1. I often **eat** Thai food. I have _____ Thai food three times this week.
2. I sometimes **visit** my cousins on weekends. I have _____ them twice this month.
3. I **work** at the Regional Bank. I have _____ there for eleven years.
4. I **like** card games. I have _____ card games since I was a child.
5. I **know** Professor Blonsky. She's my next-door neighbor. I have _____ her all my life.
6. I **wear** glasses. I have _____ glasses since I was ten years old.
7. I **take** piano lessons. I have _____ piano lessons for several years.
8. I **go** to Unisex Haircutters once a month. I have _____ to the same shop for twenty years.
9. I **ride** a bicycle for exercise. I have _____ a bicycle for about twenty years.
10. I **am** in a bicycle-riding club. I have _____ a member of this club for fifteen years.

▶ **Practice 3. The present perfect.** (Chart 3-1)
Complete each sentence with *for* or *since*.

1. I haven't seen Elvira . . .
   a. _____ several years.
   b. _____ a long time.
   c. _____ the holiday last year.
   d. _____ she was in college.
   e. _____ more than a month.
   f. _____ she got married.
   g. _____ she became famous.

2. Mehdi and Pat have been friends . . .
   a. _____ they were in college.
   b. _____ about twenty years.
   c. _____ 1990.
   d. _____ a long time.
   e. _____ they began to work together.
   f. _____ they met.
   g. _____ their entire adult lives.

▶ **Practice 4. The present perfect.** (Chart 3-1)
Complete the sentences with the present perfect tense of the appropriate verb from the list. Use each verb only once. Include any words in parentheses.

> ✓ eat   know   ride   sweep   win
>   improve   make   start   swim   write

1. A: How about more pie?

   B: No, but thanks. I can't swallow another bite. I (*already*) _____have already eaten_____ too much.

2. Our football team is having a great season. They _____ all but one of their games so far this year and will probably win the championship.

3. Jane is expecting a letter from me, but I (*not*) _____ to her yet. Maybe I'll call her instead.

4. Jack is living in Spain now. His Spanish used to be terrible, but it _____ greatly since he moved there.

5. A: Let's hurry! I think the movie is beginning!

   B: No, the movie (*not*) _____ yet. They're just showing previews of the coming attractions.

6. A: I hear your parents are coming to visit you. Is that why you're cleaning your apartment?

   B: You guessed it! I (*already*) _____ the floor, but I still need to dust the furniture. Want to help?

7. A: I understand Tom is a good friend of yours? How long (*you*) _____ him?

   B: Since we were kids.

8. Everyone makes mistakes in life. I _____ lots of mistakes in my life. The important thing is to learn from one's mistakes. Right?

9. A: I (*never*) _____ on the subways in New York City. Have you?

   B: I've never even been to New York City.

10. A: (*you, ever*) _____ in the Atlantic Ocean?

    B: No, only the Pacific — when I was in Hawaii. I even went snorkeling when I was there.

► **Practice 5. The present perfect with _since, for,_ and _ago._** (Chart 3-1)
Complete the sentences with the correct time expression.

1. Today is _____the 21st of April_____. I started this job on April 1st. I started this job
   _____three weeks_____ ago. I have had this job since _____April 1st_____.
   I have had this job for _____three weeks_____.

2. I made a New Year's resolution on January 1st: I will get up at 6:00 A.M. every day instead of
   7:00 A.M. Today is March 1st, and I have gotten up every morning at 6:00 A.M. I made this
   resolution _____ ago. I have gotten up at 6:00 A.M. since
   _____. I have gotten up at 6:00 A.M. for
   _____.

3. Today is February 28th. Valentine's Day was on February 14th. I sent my girlfriend some
   chocolates on Valentine's Day, and she phoned to say "Thank you." After that, I did not hear
   from her again. I have not heard from her for _____. I have not
   heard from her since _____.

4. Today is October 27th, 2009. Sue works for Senator Brown. She began to work for him right
   after she first met him in October, 2000. She began to work for Senator Brown
   _____ ago. Sue has worked for Senator Brown for
   _____. She has worked for Senator Brown since
   _____.

► **Practice 6. The present perfect with _since_ and _for._** (Chart 3-1)
Rewrite the sentences using _since_ and _for_.

1. We know Mrs. Jones. We met her last month.
   a. for _____We have known Mrs. Jones for one month._____
   b. since _____

2. They live in New Zealand. They moved there in 2001.
   a. for _____
   b. since _____

3. I like foreign films. I liked them five years ago.
   a. since _____
   b. for _____

4. Jack works for a software company. He started working there last year.
   a. for _____
   b. since _____

▶ **Practice 7. Is vs. has.** (Chart 3-2)
In spoken English, *is* and *has* can both be contracted to *'s*. Decide if the verb in the contraction is *is* or *has*.

Spoken English	Written English
1. He's absent.	_is_
2. Sue's been a nurse for a long time.	_____
3. Her brother's in the hospital.	_____
4. He's not happy.	_____
5. He's felt bad this past week.	_____
6. Here is a newspaper. Take one. It's free.	_____
7. The manager's taken some money.	_____
8. Mira's taking a break.	_____
9. Mira's taken a break.	_____

▶ **Practice 8. The present perfect and the simple past.** (Chart 3-3)
Circle the correct verb.

1. Botswana (*became / has become*) an independent country in 1966.

2. Botswana (*was / has been*) an independent country for more than 40 years.

3. It's raining. It (*was / has been*) raining since noon today.

4. It's raining. It's the rainy season. It (*rained / has rained*) every day since the first of the month.

5. I grew up in Scotland until I moved to Argentina with my family. I was 12 then. Now I am 21. I (*lived / have lived*) in Scotland for 12 years.

6. Now I live in Argentina. I (*lived / have lived*) in Argentina for 9 years.

7. Claude and Pierre worked together at the French restaurant for 30 years. They retired three years ago. They (*worked / have worked*) together for 30 years.

8. Claude and Pierre (*didn't work / haven't worked*) for the last three years.

▶ **Practice 9. The present perfect and the simple past.** (Chart 3-3)
Complete the sentences with the correct form of the verb in parentheses.

1. (*know*) I _____knew_____ Tim when he was a child, but I haven't seen him for many years. I _____have known_____ Larry, my best friend, for more than 20 years.

2. (*agree*) The company and the union finally _____ on salary raises two days ago. Since then, they _____ on everything, and the rest of the negotiations have gone smoothly.

3. (*take*) Mark _____ a trip to Asia last October. He _____ many trips to Asia since he started his own import-export business.

4. (*play*) Ivan _____ the violin at several concerts with the London Symphony since 1990. Last year he _____ Beethoven's violin concerto at one of the concerts.

5. (*write*) When she was in college, Julia _____ emails to her parents a few times a week. Now she has a job and is living in Chicago. In the last six months she _____ only three emails to her parents.

6. (*send*) Our university _____ 121 students to study in other countries last year. In total, we _____ 864 students abroad over the last ten years.

7. (*fly*) Masaru is a pilot for JAL. He _____ nearly 8 million miles during the last 22 years. Last year he _____ 380,000 miles.

8. (*oversleep*) Mark missed his physics examination this morning because he _____. He _____ a lot since the beginning of the semester. He'd better buy a new alarm clock.

▶ **Practice 10. The present perfect and the present perfect progressive.**
(Charts 3-1 and 3-4)

Circle the correct verb.

1. Sam and Judy began talking on the phone at 9:00 P.M. Now it is 11:00 P.M., and they are still talking. They (*have talked / have been talking*) for two hours.

2. Sam and Judy speak to each other on the phone several times a day. They are speaking on the phone now, and they might speak again later. Today they (*have spoken / have been speaking*) to each other on the phone at least seven times.

3. England (*has won / has been winning*) the World Cup only once since 1930.

4. How long (*have you sat / have you been sitting*) here in the sun? You look like burnt toast! You'd better get out of the sun.

5. The chair in the president's office is very special. Sixteen presidents (*have sat / have been sitting*) in it.

▶ **Practice 11. The present perfect and the present perfect progressive.**
(Charts 3-1 and 3-4)

Complete the sentences. Write either the present perfect or the present perfect progressive of the verbs in parentheses.

1. The children are at the park. They (*play*) _____*have been playing*_____ ball for the last two hours, but they don't seem tired yet.

2. Jim (*play*) _____*has played*_____ soccer only a couple of times, so he's not very good at it. He's much better at tennis.

3. Karl (*raise*) _____ three children to adulthood. Now they are educated and working in productive careers.

4. Sally is falling asleep at her desk. Dr. Wu (*lecture*) _____ since ten o'clock, and it's now past noon.

5. Jenna is a law student. Ever since she enrolled in law school, she (*miss, never*) _____ a class due to illness.

6. Tim (sleep) _____ in the downstairs bedroom only once. He usually sleeps upstairs in the bedroom he shares with his brother.

7. A: How much longer until we arrive at the Singapore airport?

   B: Let me see. It's about 9:15. We (fly) _____ for almost six hours. We should be there in another couple of hours.

8. A: Janice (sleep) _____ for almost eleven hours. Don't you think we should wake her up?

   B: I guess we probably should.

9. A: Is the rescue crew still looking for survivors of the plane crash?

   B: Yes, they (search) _____ the area for hours, but they haven't found anybody else. They'll keep searching until nightfall.

▶ **Practice 12. The present perfect and the present perfect progressive.**
   (Charts 3-1 and 3-4)

Write the present perfect or the present perfect progressive of the verbs in the list. Use each verb only once. Include any words in parentheses.

cook	hear	paint	stand	✓ understand
grow	meet	spend	travel	want

1. Bill and Mike have never gotten along with each other. I (never) _have never understood_ why they agreed to be roommates in the first place.

2. Al just introduced me to his sister. Now I _____ everyone in his family.

3. Ms. Erickson is a salesclerk in a large department store. It's almost closing time. Her feet hurt, as they do every day, because she _____ at the sales counter since eight o'clock this morning.

4. My uncle _____ the outside of his house for three weeks, and he's still not finished. He's being very careful. He wants his house to look just right.

5. I'm surprised that George apologized for what he said. As far as I can remember, I (never) _____ him say "I'm sorry" before.

6. The Smiths are presently in Tunisia. They _____ throughout North Africa since the middle of May. They'll return home in another month.

7. My brother's daughter _____ nearly six inches (15 cm) since I last saw her two years ago.

8. I have always _____ to travel abroad. Now the company I work for is going to send me on a sales trip to several countries.

9. A: How much money do you have to buy clothes with?

   B: Sixty dollars.

   A: I thought you had a hundred dollars.

   B: I did. But I (*already*) _____ forty.

10. A: Isn't the rice ready to eat yet? It _____ for over an hour,

    hasn't it? Are you sure you know how to cook rice?

    B: Of course I do! I've been watching the chefs on the cooking shows for years!

▶ **Practice 13. Simple past vs. the present perfect progressive.** (Charts 2-7 and 3-4)
Look at the information about Janet and write sentences with the given words. Use the simple past or present perfect progressive as necessary.

In 1998, Janet received her English teaching degree. Here is what happened to Janet after that:

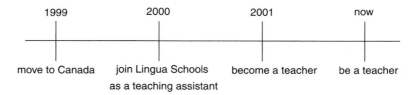

1. (move to Canada) ____*In 1999, Janet moved to Canada.*_____

2. (join Lingua Schools) _____

3. (live in Canada) _____

4. (be a teacher) _____

5. (teach her own class) _____

6. (work at Lingua Schools) _____

▶ **Practice 14. The simple past and the past perfect.** (Charts 2-6 and 3-5)
Underline each event. Write "1" over the event that happened first and "2" over the event that happened second.

1. We had driven only two miles when we got a flat tire.

2. Alan told me that he had written a book.

3. By the time we arrived at the airport, the plane had already left.

4. The dog had eaten the entire roast before anyone knew it was gone.

5. We didn't stand in line for tickets because we had already bought them by mail.

6. Carl played the guitar so well because he had studied with a famous guitarist.

7. By the time the movie ended, everyone had fallen asleep.

8. After the professor had corrected the third paper, he was exhausted from writing comments on

   the students' papers.

9. I had just placed an order at the store for a new camera when I found a cheaper one online.

► **Practice 15. The past perfect.** (Chart 3-5)
Complete the sentences. Write the correct form of the past perfect.

1. Yesterday, John got 100% on a math exam. Before yesterday, he (*get, not*) _____
   _____ 100%.

2. Last week, Sonya met her fiancé's parents. Before that, she (*meet, not*) _____
   _____ them.

3. Today, Dan used a camera phone. Before today, he (*take, not*) _____
   _____ pictures with one.

4. A few days ago, Bakir cooked a frozen dinner. Prior to that, he (*eat, not*) _____
   _____ a frozen dinner.

5. Last week, I had to have a tooth pulled. Until then, I (*have, not*) _____
   any problems with my teeth.

► **Practice 16. The simple past and the past perfect.** (Charts 2-7 and 3-5)
Complete the sentences with the simple past or past perfect form of the verb. Write the letter of
the correct verb.

1. By the time Jason arrived to help, we _____ moving everything.
   a. already finished   b. had already finished

2. The apartment was hot when I got home, so I _____ the air conditioner.
   a. turned on   b. had turned on

3. The farmer's barn caught on fire some time during the night. By the time the firefighters
   arrived, the building _____ to the ground. It was a total loss.
   a. burned   b. had burned

4. The dinner I had at that restaurant was expensive! Until then, I _____ so much on one meal.
   a. never spent   b. had never spent

5. When I saw that Mike was having trouble, I _____ him. He was very appreciative.
   a. helped   b. had helped

6. My wife and I went to Disneyland when we visited Los Angeles last spring. Prior to that time,
   we _____ such a big amusement park. It was a lot of fun.
   a. never visited   b. had never visited

7. Last year I experienced how tedious long plane trips can be. I _____ on airplanes for fairly
   long distances before, but never as long as when I went to Australia in June.
   a. traveled   b. had traveled

► **Practice 17. The simple past and the past perfect.** (Charts 2-6 and 3-5)
Write the simple past or the past perfect of the verbs in parentheses. In some cases, both forms are
correct.

1. Yesterday I (*go*) ____*went*____ to my daughter's dance recital. I
   (*be, never*) ____*had never been*____ to a dance recital before. I
   (*take, not*) ____*didn't take*____ dancing lessons when I (*be*) ____*was*____ a child.

2. Last night, I (*eat*) _____ four servings of food at the "all-you-can-eat" special dinner at The Village Restaurant. Until that time, I (*eat, never*) _____ so much in one meal. I've felt miserable all day today.

3. A: I (*see*) _____ you in the school play last night. You (*do*) _____ a terrific acting job. (*you, act, ever*) _____ in a play before this one?

   B: Yes. I (*start*) _____ acting when I was in elementary school.

▶ **Practice 18. The present perfect progressive and the past perfect progressive.** (Charts 3-4 and 3-7)
Circle the correct verb.

1. I'm studying English. I (*have been studying / had been studying*) English for several years now.

2. I came from Malaysia to live in New Zealand in 2002. I (*have been studying / had been studying*) English for three years before that.

3. Shhh! I want to see the end of this TV show! I (*have been waiting / had been waiting*) to find out who the murderer is.

4. Laura finally called me last night. I hadn't heard from her in four months. I (*have been waiting / had been waiting*) for that call for a long time!

5. Before Ada became a veterinarian last year, she (*has been working / had been working*) as a veterinarian's assistant while she was in school.

6. Li is going to quit his job. He (*has been working / had been working*) too many hours for too little money in this job. He is probably going to hand in his resignation next week.

▶ **Practice 19. The present perfect progressive and the past perfect progressive.** (Charts 3-4 and 3-7)
Complete the sentences. Write the present perfect progressive or the past perfect progressive form of the verbs in parentheses.

1. Anna (*listen*) ___*had been listening*___ to loud rock music when her friends arrived, but she turned it off so all of them could study together. When they finished, she turned it back on, and now they (*dance*) ___*have been dancing*___ and (*sing*) ___*singing*___ for two hours.

2. We (*wait*) _____ for Ali for the last two hours, but he still hasn't arrived.

3. We (*wait*) _____ for Ali for over three hours before he finally arrived yesterday.

4. Oscar (*train*) _____ for the Olympics for the last three years and wants to make the national team next year.

5. The marathon runner (*run*) _____ for almost two hours when he collapsed to the pavement. He received immediate medical attention.

6. Tom had a hard time finding a job. He (*try*) _____ to get a new job for six months before he finally found a position at a local community college. Now he has a two-year contract. He (*teach*) _____ there for only a few weeks, but he likes his new job very much.

7. Dr. Sato (*perform*) _____ specialized surgery since she began working at the university hospital ten years ago. She still does many operations each year, but now her work is so famous that she travels all over the world lecturing to other surgeons on her technique.

8. The Acme Construction Company is having problems. They (*work*) _____ _____ on a new office building for the last seven months, and everything seems to be going wrong. Earlier, they stopped work on a smaller structure that they (*build*) _____ so they could take on this job. Now both projects are in jeopardy.

▶ **Practice 20. Chapter review.**
There is one verb error in each item. Correct the error.

1. *Citizen Kane* is a great classic movie. I've been seeing it ten times.

2. *War and Peace* is a long novel. I'm reading it for two months, and I am still not finished with it!

3. Our guests have left yesterday.

4. We were studying all night. Let's take a break now.

5. Let's not leave yet. I'd been having such a wonderful time at this party.

6. By the time I got home, the rest of the family has eaten.

7. I was late for my nine o'clock class, so I had run all the way from my dorm to my class.

8. Mrs. Wang isn't in the hospital anymore. She had left early this morning.

9. I was born on February 29th in 1960, a leap year. February 29th occurs only once every four years. So by the time the 21st century began, I celebrated only ten birthdays!

10. A: Are you still on the telephone? Are you holding on for someone?

    B: Yes, I am. I am still holding for the technical help department. I am holding for more than half an hour!

Chapter 4
Future Time

▶ **Practice 1. Simple future: *will*.** (Chart 4-1)
Correct the errors with *will*. Two sentences have no errors.

1. Harry's birthday is tomorrow. He wills be fifty years old.

2. The store will stays open tomorrow night until 11:00 P.M.

3. Seventeen people will to be at the marketing meeting.

4. The new senator will make her first speech in Congress tomorrow.

5. Our teacher don't will be here tomorrow.

6. Will you call me tonight?

▶ **Practice 2. Simple future: *be going to*.** (Chart 4-1)
Complete the sentences with the correct form of *be going to* + the verb in parentheses.

1. Ben (*visit*) _____ his roommate's home for the holidays.

2. Delfina is a great tennis player. She (*win*) _____ the tennis tournament.

3. Which history course (*you, take*) _____ next semester?

4. The weather forecasters are saying it (*not, be*) _____ a cold winter this year.

5. What about Marta and Bob? (*they, join*) _____ us Saturday night?

6. I (*not, lie*) _____ to you. I (*tell*) _____ _____ you the truth.

▶ **Practice 3. Simple future: *will* and *be going to.*** (Chart 4-1)
Complete the sentences in two ways. Write sentence a. with ***will*** and sentence b. with ***be going to.*** Use the correct verb from the list.

arrive	buy	rain	take
bloom	end	set	

1. a. The sun rose at 5:46 this morning, and it _____ at 6:52 tonight.

   b. The sun rose at 5:46 this morning, and it _____ at 6:52 tonight.

2. a. The flight left Bangkok at noon today, and it _____ in Mumbai at midnight.

   b. The flight left Bangkok at noon today, and it _____ in Mumbai at midnight.

3. a. There are dark clouds over the mountain. It _____ later today.

   b. There are dark clouds over the mountain. It _____ later today.

4. a. We planted the flowers in March, and they _____ in June.

   b. We planted the flowers in March, and they _____ in June.

5. a. Our semester began in January, and it _____ in May.

   b. Our semester began in January, and it _____ in May.

6. a. When _____ you _____ a new computer?

   b. When _____ you _____ a new computer?

7. a. I _____ not _____ a vacation this year. Maybe next year.

   b. I _____ not _____ a vacation this year. Maybe next year.

▶ **Practice 4. *Will* vs. *be going to.*** (Chart 4-2)
Read the sentences. Then check the box that describes the sentence.

	Prediction	Prior Plan	Willingness
1. I'll help you change your tire, Ms. Olsen.			
2. It's going to rain tomorrow.			
3. It will rain tomorrow.			
4. Louise is going to help us next week.			
5. Wait. I'll help you carry your luggage.			
6. We're going to see a movie tonight.			
7. The moon will rise at 8:10 this evening.			

► **Practice 5. _Will_ vs. _be going to._** (Chart 4-2)
Circle a. if the meaning describes a prior plan. Circle b. if the meaning describes a decision of the moment.

1. I can't have lunch with you on Friday because I'm going to give a speech at noon to the Chamber of Commerce.
   a. prior plan   b. decision of the moment

2. My computer just crashed. I'll call the technical department to fix it right now.
   a. prior plan   b. decision of the moment

3. It's very icy and slippery on my street this morning. I'll go out and clear the sidewalk.
   a. prior plan   b. decision of the moment

4. Roberto and Sandy are going to get married next Saturday.
   a. prior plan   b. decision of the moment

5. Jimmy is going to have a tonsillectomy on Monday. The doctors are going to take out his tonsils because they are infected.
   a. prior plan   b. decision of the moment

6. Look at the price of the airport limo. It's too much money. We'll go to the airport by bus.
   a. prior plan   b. decision of the moment

► **Practice 6. _Will_ vs. _be going to._** (Chart 4-2)
Circle the correct response(s) to the questions or statements. More than one response may be correct.

1. A: What about Dominick? Doesn't he want to come with us?
   B: Nobody knows! (_I'll call him / I'm going to call him_) tonight to find out.

2. A: Jessica practices her violin for ten hours a day!
   B: I know! (_She's going to be / She'll be_) a famous violinist some day.

3. A: How about dinner and a movie on Friday?
   B: Sorry, I can't. (_I'm going to fly / I'll fly_) to London on Friday evening.

4. A: Do you and Paul have tickets for any of the hockey games this season?
   B: Yes, we do. (_We're going to the game / We'll go to the game_) tomorrow night.

5. A: I can't open this jar!
   B: Give it to me. (_I'm going to open it / I'll open it_) for you.

6. A: So you're leaving to go to another university, Professor Hu!
   B: Yes, (_I'm going to teach / I will teach_) at Emory University. They've made me a great offer.

► **Practice 7. _Will_ vs. _be going to._** (Chart 4-2)
Complete the sentences with _**will**_ or _**be going to**_ as appropriate. Include any words in parentheses.

1. A: Excuse me, waiter! This isn't what I ordered. I ordered a chicken salad.
   B: Sorry, sir. I _____will_____ take this back and get your salad.
   A: Thank you.

2. A: Would you like to join Linda and me tomorrow? We _____are going to_____ visit the natural history museum.
   B: Sure. I've never been there.

3. A: Where's the mustard?

   B: In the refrigerator, on the middle shelf.

   A: I've looked there.

   B: OK. I _____ get it for you.

4. A: What's all this paint for? (*you*) _____ paint your house?

   B: No, we _____ paint my mother's house.

5. A: Paul, do you want to go to the mall with me?

   B: No thanks. I already have plans. I _____ wash my car and then clean out the basement.

6. A: Someone needs to take this report to Mr. Day's office right away, but I can't leave my desk.

   B: I _____ do it.

   A: Thanks.

7. A: Who'll pick up Uncle Jack at the airport?

   B: I _____ .

8. A: Why is Carlos wearing a suit and tie? He usually wears jeans to class.

   B: He _____ give a speech at the faculty lunch today.

9. A: Let me ask you something, Toshi.

   B: Sure. What's up, Andy?

   A: I _____ interview for a job this afternoon, and . . . well, do I need a tie? I don't have a decent one!

   B: Yes, you need a tie. I _____ lend you one of mine.

   A: Thanks.

10. A: You're going out?

    B: Yes. I _____ stop at the grocery store for some fruit and some rice. Can you think of anything else we need?

    A: How about getting some chocolate-covered nuts?

    B: Good idea! I _____ get some of those too.

▶ **Practice 8. Expressing the future in time clauses.** (Chart 4-3)
<u>Underline</u> the time clause in each sentence and circle its verb.

1. I'll see you <u>when you (return) from your trip.</u>

2. After the rain stops, we'll go out.

3. We're going to keep driving until it gets dark.

4. As soon as the baby is born, we'll let you know!

5. When he retires, Barry is going to take painting classes.

6. You will be able to vote when you are eighteen years old.

7. I'm going to go to bed as soon as the late news is over.

8. The students will return to campus when the new semester begins.

► Practice 9. Expressing the future in time clauses. (Chart 4-3)
Complete the sentences with the correct form of the verb.

1. Grandma and Grandpa are planning to travel often when they (*retire*) _____.

2. I'll wake up tomorrow morning when the alarm clock (*ring*) _____.

3. The students will relax after they (*finish*) _____ their final exams.

4. You'll feel a lot better after you (*take*) _____ this medicine.

5. The residents of the coastal areas will prepare for the hurricane before it
   (*arrive*) _____.

6. Mark will work in a law firm as soon as he (*graduate*) _____ from law
   school.

7. We'll have dinner as soon as the rice (*be*) _____ ready.

8. I'll tell you as soon I (*hear*) _____ any news.

9. Before we (*leave*) _____ on vacation, we'll stop our newspaper delivery.

10. We'll start our newspaper delivery again after we (*get*) _____ back from vacation.

► Practice 10. Expressing the future in time clauses. (Chart 4-3)
Write the letter of the clause from either Column A or Column B to complete the sentences
correctly.

	Column A	Column B
1. When I see Irina later, _*b*_.	a. I give her the news	b. I'll give her the news
2. I'll call you tomorrow _____.	a. after I talk to Rita	b. after I will talk to Rita
3. As soon as I hear from Tom, _____.	a. I call you	b. I'll call you
4. We'll all be very happy _____.	a. when you get here	b. when you will get here
5. I'll save my files _____.	a. before I shut down my computer	b. before I will shut down my computer
6. The passengers will get off the plane _____.	a. after it lands	b. after it is going to land
7. My cell phone won't work _____.	a. until I unlock it	b. until I will unlock it
8. After the party is over tonight, _____.	a. we call a taxi to go home	b. we'll call a taxi to go home
9. I'm not going to pay for the refrigerator _____.	a. until they fix the broken door	b. until they will fix the broken door
10. I'll take this new medicine _____.	a. before I go to bed tonight	b. before I will go to bed tonight

▶ **Practice 11. Expressing the future in time clauses.** (Chart 4-3)

Complete the sentences with the following: the simple present, the future with *will*, or the future with a form of *be going to*. In some sentences, both *will* and *be going to* may be possible.

1. The strike has been going on for over two months now. The strikers

   (*return, not*) _____ will not / are not going to return _____ to work until they (*get*) _____ get _____

   a raise and the benefits they are demanding.

2. When Rita (*get*) _____ her driver's license next week, she (*be*) _____

   _____ able to drive to school every day.

3. A: Mr. Jackson called. He'll be here at the garage to pick up his car in a few minutes. He

   (*be, not*) _____ very happy when he (*learn*) _____ about

   the bill for repairs on his car. Do you want to talk to him when he (*come*) _____

   in and (*ask*) _____ about his bill?

   B: Not especially, but I will.

4. After Ali (*return*) _____ to his country next month, he (*start*) _____

   _____ working at the Ministry of Agriculture.

5. According to the newspaper, the Department of Transportation (*build*) _____

   _____ a new four-lane highway into the city next year. In my opinion, it

   (*be*) _____ obsolete before they (*complete*) _____ it.

   It seems to me that a six-lane highway is needed to handle the heavy traffic.

6. A: Have you heard any news about Barbara since her car accident?

   B: No, I've heard nothing. As soon as I (*hear*) _____ something, I

   (*let*) _____ you know.

7. A: I see you're reading *The Silk Road.*

   B: I (*lend*) _____ it to you as soon as I (*finish*) _____ it.

   A: Really? Thanks!

8. A: Relax. The plumber is on his way. He (*be*) _____ here before

   long to fix that leak in the pipe under the kitchen sink.

   B: Oh, good. I (*be*) _____ happy to get that pipe fixed.

► **Practice 12. Using the present progressive and the simple present to express future time.** (Chart 4-4)

Complete the second sentence with a form of the present progressive to express the same meaning as the first sentence.

1. I'm going to see the dentist tomorrow.

   I _____ the dentist tomorrow.

2. She will have a baby in July.

   She _____ a baby in July.

3. The new store will open in September.

   The new store _____ in September.

4. The office staff is going to work late tonight.

   The office staff _____ late tonight.

5. We're going to have a graduation party for Miriam on Saturday.

   We _____ a graduation party for Miriam on Saturday.

6. Shelley and Sue are going to attend the conference in New York next April.

   Shelley and Sue _____ the conference in New York next April.

► **Practice 13. Using the present progressive and the simple present to express future time.** (Chart 4-4)

Circle the letter of the phrases which can complete the sentences correctly. More than one completion may be correct for each sentence.

1. We have tickets for a puppet show today. The show _____.
   a. starts at 2:00 P.M.
   b. is starting at 2:00 P.M.
   c. is going to start at 2:00 P.M.

2. Look at those black clouds! Pretty soon it _____.
   a. rains
   b. is raining
   c. is going to rain

3. This afternoon I have a lunch date with a friend. After that, we _____.
   a. are going to visit her aunt
   b. are visiting her aunt
   c. visit her aunt

4. I'm hurrying to catch a plane. It _____!
   a. leaves in an hour
   b. is going to leave in an hour
   c. is leaving in an hour

5. Sorry I can't meet with you tomorrow, Helen. I have an important appointment. _____ with the president at noon.
   a. I'm meeting
   b. I'm going to meet
   c. I will meet

6. A: Nobody has volunteered to bring the drinks for the festival Saturday night. Olga, how about you? Harry, how about you? Please . . . can somebody help us out?

   B: OK, OK. _____ it.
     a. I'll do
     b. I'm doing
     c. I'm going to do

▶ **Practice 14. Using the present progressive to express future time.** (Chart 4-4)
Change the verbs in *italics* to a form of the present progressive in the sentences that express a planned event or definite intention. For the sentences where no change is possible, write "NC."

1. A: The package has to be there tomorrow. Will it get there in time?

   B: Don't worry. *I'm going to send* it by express mail.

     I'm sending it by express mail.

2. A: What's the weather report?

   B: *It is going to rain* tomorrow morning.

     NC

3. A: Would you like to have dinner with me tonight, Pat?

   B: Thanks, but *I'm going to have* dinner with my sister and her husband.

     _____

4. A: What *are you going to do* this evening?

   B: *I'm going to study* at the library.

     _____

     _____

5. A: Oh, I spilled my coffee on the floor.

   B: *I'll help* you clean it up.

     _____

6. A: Did you know that Kathy and Paul are engaged?

   B: No. That's great! When *are they going to get* married?

   A: In September.

     _____

7. A: *You're going to laugh* when I tell you what happened to me today!

   B: Oh? What happened?

     _____

8. A: Have you lived here long?

   B: No, not long. Only about a year. But *we're going to move* again next month. My father's company has reassigned him to Atlanta, Georgia.

     _____

9. A: I tried to register for Professor Stein's economics class, but it's full. *Is he going to teach* it again next semester?

    B: I think so.

    _____

10. A: Son, *I'm not going to send* you any money this month. You're spending far too much. You need to learn to be more careful.

    _____

    B: But Dad . . . !

    A: Just do the best you can. *I am going to come* to visit you next month. We can talk about it then.

    _____

▶ **Practice 15. Future progressive.** (Chart 4-5)
Complete the sentences. Write the future progressive form of the verbs in **bold**.

1. Every night at 7:00 I **sit** down **to have** dinner. Tomorrow at 7:10, I
   _____ dinner.

2. We **fly** to Italy tomorrow night. Tomorrow night at this time, we
   _____ over the Atlantic Ocean.

3. On Sunday mornings, I **sleep** late. Next Sunday morning at 9:00 A.M., I
   _____ .

4. It always **snows** in December in Moscow. We're going to Moscow in December. At that time,
   it _____ in Moscow.

5. Ellen always **watches** late movies on TV. I'm sure that tonight she
   _____ an old movie on TV around 2:00 A.M.

▶ **Practice 16. Future progressive.** (Charts 4-3 and 4-5)
Complete the sentences with the future progressive or the simple present form of the verbs in parentheses.

1. Just relax, Antoine. As soon as your sprained ankle (*heal*) _____heals_____, you can play
   soccer again. At this time next week, you (*play*) _____will be playing_____ soccer
   again.

2. I'll meet you at the airport tomorrow. After you (*clear*) _____ customs, look for
   me just outside the gate. I (*stand*) _____ right by the door.

3. Ingrid and Ruth won't be at this school when classes (*start*) _____ next
   semester. They (*attend*) _____ a new school in Taiwan.

4. Please come and visit today when you (*have*) _____ a chance. I
   (*shop*) _____ from 1:00 to about 3:00, but I'll be home after that.

5. I won't be here next week, students. I (*attend*) _____ a seminar
   in Los Angeles. Ms. Gomez will be the substitute teacher. When I (*return*) _____,
   I will expect you to be ready for the midterm examination.

► **Practice 17. Future perfect and future perfect progressive.** (Chart 4-6)
Complete the sentences with the future perfect or the future perfect progressive form of the verbs in the list. Include any words in parentheses. Use each verb only once.

drink	land	ride	save
fly	listen	✓ rise	teach

1. By the time I get up tomorrow morning, the sun (*already*) ____will already have risen____.

2. This is a long trip! By the time we get to Miami, we _____ on this bus for over 15 hours.

3. We're going to be late meeting my brother's plane. By the time we get to the airport, it (*already*) _____.

4. He's never going to stop talking. In 15 more minutes, we _____ to him lecture for three solid hours. I don't even know what he's saying anymore.

5. I drink too much coffee. I have already had two cups this morning, and I will probably have two more cups. This means that before lunch, I _____ four cups of coffee.

6. This is the longest flight I have ever taken. By the time we get to New Zealand, we _____ for 13 hours. I'm going to be exhausted.

7. Douglas has been putting some money away every month to prepare for his trip to South America next year. By the end of this year, he _____ enough.

8. Can you believe it? According to our grammar teacher, by the end of this semester, she _____ more than 3,000 students from 42 different countries. She has been teaching for nearly 20 years — and she still loves it!

► **Practice 18. Chapter review.**
These sentences describe typical events in a day in the life of a woman named Kathy. The sentences are in the past, but all of these things will happen in Kathy's life tomorrow. Change all of the sentences to the future. Use **will**.

1. When Kathy got up yesterday morning, the sun was shining. The same thing will happen tomorrow. When Kathy ____gets____ up tomorrow morning, the sun ____will be shining____.

2. Yesterday she brushed her teeth and showered. Then she made a light breakfast. Tomorrow will be the same. She _____ her teeth and _____. Then she _____ a light breakfast.

3. After she ate breakfast yesterday, she got ready to go to work. And tomorrow after she _____ breakfast, she _____ ready to go to work.

4. By the time she got to work yesterday, she had drunk three cups of coffee. Tomorrow she'll do the same. By the time she _____ to work, she _____ three cups of coffee.

5. Between 8:00 and 9:00, Kathy answered her email and planned her day. She has the same plans for tomorrow. Between 8:00 and 9:00, Kathy _____ her e-mail and _____ her day.

6. By 10:00 yesterday, she had called three new clients. Tomorrow, by 10:00, she _____ three new clients.

7. At 11:00 yesterday, she was attending a staff meeting. She plans to do the same tomorrow. At 11:00, she _____ a staff meeting.

8. She went to lunch at noon and had a sandwich and a bowl of soup. Tomorrow she _____ to lunch at noon and _____ a sandwich and a bowl of soup.

9. After she finished eating, she took a short walk in the park before she returned to the office. Tomorrow she'll do the same. After she _____ eating, she _____ a walk in the park before she _____ to the office.

10. She worked at her desk until she went to another meeting in the middle of the afternoon. And tomorrow she _____ at her desk until she _____ to another meeting in the middle of the afternoon.

11. By the time she left the office, she had attended three meetings. Tomorrow she'll follow the same schedule. By the time she _____ the office, she _____ three meetings.

12. When Kathy got home, her children were playing in the yard, and Grandma was watching them from the porch. Tomorrow will be the same. When Kathy _____ home, her children _____ in the yard, and Grandma _____ them from the porch.

13. The children had been playing since 3:00 in the afternoon. And tomorrow they _____ since 3:00 in the afternoon.

14. The family had dinner together and talked about their day. Tomorrow will be the same. They _____ dinner together, and they _____ about their day.

15. They watched television for a while, and then Kathy and her husband put the kids to bed. The same thing will happen tomorrow. They _____ television for a while, and then they _____ the kids to bed.

16. By the time Kathy went to bed yesterday, she had had a full day and was ready for sleep. Tomorrow will be the same for Kathy. By the time she _____ to bed, she _____ a full day and _____ ready for sleep.

Chapter 5
Review of Verb Tenses

▶ **Practice 1. Verb tense review.** (Chapters 1 → 4)
Circle the correct verb.

1. My grandfather (*has never flown / had never flown*) in an airplane, and he has no intention of ever doing so.

2. Jane isn't here yet. I (*am waiting / have been waiting*) for her since noon, but she still (*didn't arrive / hasn't arrived*).

3. In all the world, there (*have been / are*) only 14 mountains that (*reach / are reaching*) above 8,000 meters (26,247 feet).

4. When my parents were teenagers, people (*hadn't owned / didn't own*) computers. By the time I was a teenager, I (*was owning / had owned*) a computer for several years.

5. Right now we (*are having / have*) a heat wave. The temperature (*is / has been*) in the upper 90s Fahrenheit (30s Celsius) for the last six days.

6. I have a long trip ahead of me tomorrow, so I think I'd better go to bed. Let me say good-bye now because I won't see you in the morning. I (*will leave / will have left*) by the time you (*get / will get*) up.

7. Last night I (*went / was going*) to a party. When I (*get / got*) there, the room was full of people. Some of them (*danced / were dancing*) and others (*talked / were talking*). One young woman (*was standing / has been standing*) by herself. I (*have never met / had never met*) her before, so I (*introduced / was introducing*) myself to her.

8. About three o'clock yesterday afternoon, Jessica (*was sitting / had sat*) in bed reading a book. Suddenly, she (*heard / was hearing*) a loud noise and (*got / was getting*) up to see what it was. She (*has looked / looked*) out the window. A truck (*has just backed / had just backed*) into her new car!

▶ **Practice 2. Verb tense review.** (Chapters 1 → 4)
Circle the correct verb.

1. Next month I have a week's vacation. I (*take / am taking*) a trip. I (*leave / left*) on Saturday, July 2nd. First, I (*'ve gone / 'm going*) to Madison, Wisconsin, to visit my brother. After I (*will leave / leave*) Madison, I (*am going to go / have gone*) to Chicago to see a friend who (*is studying / will have studied*) at the university there. She (*has lived / lives*) in Chicago for three years, so she (*knows / knew*) her way around the city. She (*has promised / will be promising*) to take me to many interesting places. I (*had never been / have never been*) to Chicago, so I (*am looking / have looked*) forward to going there.

2. The weather is beautiful today, but until this morning, it (*has been raining / had been raining*) steadily for almost a week. A week ago, the temperature suddenly (*was dropping / dropped*), and after that we had bad weather for a week. Now the weather forecaster says that tomorrow it (*is going to be / is*) very warm. The weather certainly (*was changing / changes*) quickly here. I never know what to expect. Who knows? When I (*wake / will wake*) up tomorrow morning, maybe it (*snows / will be snowing*).

▶ **Practice 3. Verb tense review.** (Chapters 1 → 4)
Complete the sentences with the verbs in parentheses. Use any appropriate tense.

On June 20th, I returned home. I (*be*) _____ away from home for two years. My family (*meet*) _____ me at the airport with kisses and tears. They (*miss*) _____
me as much as I had missed them. I (*be*) _____ very happy to see them again.

When I (*get*) _____ the chance, I (*take*) _____ a long look at them. My little brother (*be*) _____ no longer little. He (*grow*) _____ a lot. He (*be*) _____ almost as tall as my father. My little sister (*wear*) _____ a green dress. She (*change*) _____ quite a bit too, but she (*be, still*) _____ mischievous and inquisitive. She (*ask*) _____ me a thousand questions a minute, or so it seemed.

My father (*gain*) _____ some weight, and his hair (*turn*) _____ a little grayer, but otherwise he was just as I had remembered him. My mother (*look*) _____ a little older, but not much. The wrinkles on her face (*be*) _____ smile wrinkles.

▶ **Practice 4. Verb tense review.** (Chapters 1 → 4)
Complete the sentences with the verbs in parentheses. Use any appropriate tense.

On June 20th, I will return home. I (*be*) _____ away from home for two years by that time. My family (*meet*) _____ me at the airport with kisses and tears. They (*miss*) _____ me as much as I have missed them. I (*be*) _____ very happy to see them again.

When I (*get*) _____ a chance, I (*take*) _____ a long look at them. My little brother (*be, no longer*) _____ so little. He (*grow*) _____ at least a foot. He (*be*) _____ almost as tall as my father. My little sister (*wear, probably*) _____ a green dress because that's her favorite color. She (*change*) _____ quite a bit too, but she

(*be, still*) _____ mischievous and inquisitive. She (*ask*) _____ me a
              12   13
thousand questions a minute, or so it will seem.

   My father (*gain, probably*) _____ some weight, and his hair
                                            14
(*turn*) _____ a little grayer, but otherwise he will be just as I remember
              15
him. My mother (*look*) _____ a little older, but not much. The wrinkles on her face
                               16
(*be*) _____ smile wrinkles.
              17

▶ **Practice 5. Verb tense review.** (Chapters 1 → 4)
Complete the sentences in each part with verbs from the list. Use any appropriate tense.

Part I.

| be | break | do | happen | have | play | recuperate | see |

A: Where's Sonia? I (*not*) _____ her lately.
                                            1

B: She's at home _____ from an accident.
                           2

A: An accident? What _____ to her?
                                3

B: She _____ her arm while she _____ volleyball last week in the
            4   5
game against South City College.

A: Gosh, that's too bad. I'm sorry to hear that. How _____ she _____?
                                                                    6   7

B: OK, I guess. Actually, she _____ a cast on her arm, but she is not in any pain. I
                                       8
think that she _____ back in class next week.
                     9

Part II.

> function   receive   send   start   try

A: Hello. Computer Data Magazine. How can I help you?

B: Well, I _____ in my money for a subscription to your magazine, *Computer Data,* two

        1

months ago, but to date I (*not*) _____ any issues.

        2

A: I'm sorry to hear that. Unfortunately, one of our main computers (*not*) _____

        3

_____ at the moment. However, our computer specialists

_____ very hard to fix it at the present time. Your new subscription

        4

_____ as soon as possible.

        5

B: Thank you.

▶ **Practice 6. Verb tense review.** (Chapters 1 → 4)
Complete the sentences with the verbs in parentheses. Use any appropriate tense.

A: Have you ever heard of the Socratic method?

B: No, I haven't. What is it?

A: It's a method of teaching that Socrates (*use*) _____ in ancient Greece more

        1

than two thousand years ago. Some teachers still (*use*) _____ this kind of

        2

method today.

B: Really? What (*it, consist*) _____ of today? How

        3

(*teachers, use*) _____ this method now?

        4

A: Well, the teacher (*not, give*) _____ any information to the students. She

        5

or he just asks a series of questions, but (*not, make*) _____ any

        6

statements. The teacher (*know*) _____ what the important questions to ask the

        7

students are. Then the students have to think about the answers.

B: That (*sound*) _____ good to me! When I was in high school, I had a lot of

        8

teachers who just (*talk*) _____ too much. Sometimes the students even

        9

(*fall*) _____ asleep in class!

        10

A: I (*agree*) _____ with you. You will learn faster after you

        11

(*think*) _____ about something than if you just have to remember facts.

        12

B: That's true. I (take) _____ a philosophy class now with a wonderful
13

professor. She (always, ask) _____ questions! I guess she
14

(use) _____ the Socratic method for the whole semester, and I
15

(not, realize) _____ it !
16

▶ **Practice 7. Verb tense review.** (Chapters 1 → 4)
Complete the sentences with the correct form of the verb in parentheses.

1. Nora is at the hospital because her cousin is having surgery today. The surgery began at 7:00
   and is expected to end at noon. Nora arrived at the hospital at 8:00 A.M.

   a. It's 8:10 A.M. Nora (wait) _____ in the waiting room.

   b. It is now 9:00 A.M. Nora (wait) _____ for one hour.

   c. By 11:00, the surgery will still be going on, and Nora will still be waiting in the waiting
      room. At that time, Nora (wait) _____ in the waiting room
      for three hours.

2. Hundreds of passengers are in the security line at the airport. Jaime entered the security line at
   8:00 A.M.

   a. It's 8:15 A.M. Jaime (stand) _____ in the security line at the airport.

   b. It is now 9:00 A.M. Jaime (stand) _____ in the security line
      for an hour.

   c. Jaime is probably going to be standing in the security line for another hour. By 9:30 A.M.,
      he (stand) _____ in the security line for an hour and a half.

   d. Jaime is probably going to be finished standing in the security line by 10:00 A.M. If he is
      finished at 10:00 A.M., he (stand) _____ in line for a total of two
      hours!

▶ **Practice 8. Verb tense review.** (Chapters 1 → 4)
Complete the sentences. Write the letter of the correct completion.

1. A: Hurry up! We're waiting for you. What's taking you so long?

   B: I _____ for an important phone call. Go ahead and leave without me.
      a. wait   c. have waited
      b. will have waited   d. am waiting

2. A: Robert is going to be famous someday. He _____ in three movies already.

   B: I'm sure he'll be a star.
      a. has been appearing   c. has appeared
      b. had appeared   d. appeared

3. A: Where's Polly?

   B: She _____.
      a. is in her room studying   c. studies in her room
      b. in her room is studying   d. has studied in her room

4. A: What _____ of the new simplified tax law?

   B: It's more confusing than the old one.
   a. are you thinking
   c. have you thought
   b. do you think
   d. have you been thinking

5. A: When is Mr. Fields planning to retire?

   B: Soon, I think. He _____ here for a long time. He'll probably retire either next year or the

   year after that.
   a. worked
   c. has been working
   b. had been working
   d. is working

6. A: Why did you buy all this sugar and chocolate?

   B: I _____ a delicious chocolate cake for dinner tonight.
   a. make
   c. 'm going to make
   b. will make
   d. will have made

7. A: Let's go! What's taking you so long?

   B: I'll be there as soon as I _____ my keys.
   a. find
   c. 'm going to find
   b. will find
   d. am finding

8. Next week when there _____ a full moon, the ocean tides will be higher.
   a. is being
   c. is
   b. will be
   d. will have been

9. While I _____ TV last night, a mouse ran across the floor.
   a. have watched
   c. watched
   b. was watching
   d. have been watching

10. Fish were among the earliest forms of life. Fish _____ on earth for ages and ages.
    a. existed
    c. exist
    b. are existing
    d. have existed

11. The phone _____ constantly since Jack announced his candidacy for president this morning.
    a. has been ringing
    c. had rung
    b. rang
    d. had been ringing

12. The earth _____ on the sun for its heat and light.
    a. depended
    c. was depending
    b. depending
    d. depends

13. I don't feel good. I _____ home from work tomorrow.
    a. 'm staying
    c. stay
    b. will have stayed
    d. stayed

14. Today there are weather satellites that beam down information about the earth's atmosphere.
    In the last several decades, space exploration _____ great contributions to weather forecasting.
    a. is making
    c. makes
    b. has made
    d. made

15. On July 20th, 1969, astronaut Neil Armstrong _____ down onto the moon. He was the first person ever to set foot on another celestial body.
   a. was stepping
   b. has stepped
   c. stepped
   d. has been stepping

16. The plane's departure was delayed because of mechanical difficulties. When the weary passengers finally boarded the aircraft, many were annoyed and irritable because they _____ in the airport for three and a half hours.
   a. are waiting
   b. were waiting
   c. have been waiting
   d. had been waiting

17. If coastal erosion continues to take place at the present rate, in another fifty years this beach _____ anymore.
   a. doesn't exist
   b. isn't going to exist
   c. isn't existing
   d. won't be existing

18. Homestead High School's football team _____ a championship until last season when the new coach led them to win first place in their league.
   a. has never won
   b. is never winning
   c. had never been winning
   d. had never won

19. Nonnative speakers need many years of intensive language study before they can qualify as interpreters. By the end of this year, Chen _____ English for three years, but he will still need more training and experience before he masters the language.
   a. will be studying
   b. has studied
   c. will have been studying
   d. has been studying

▶ **Practice 9. Verb tense review.** (Chapters 1 → 4)
Complete the sentences. Write the letter of the correct completion.

1. A: May I speak to Dr. Paine, please?

   B: I'm sorry, he _____ a patient at the moment. Can I help you?
   a. is seeing
   b. sees
   c. was seeing
   d. has been seeing

2. A: When are you going to ask your boss for a raise?

   B: _____ to her twice already! I don't think she wants to give me one.
   a. I've talked
   b. I was talking
   c. I've been talking
   d. I'd talked

3. A: Do you think Harry will want something to eat after he gets here?

   B: I hope not. It'll probably be after midnight, and we _____.
   a. are sleeping
   b. will be sleeping
   c. have been sleeping
   d. be sleeping

4. Paul, could you please turn off the stove? The potatoes _____ for at least 30 minutes.
   a. are boiling
   b. boiling
   c. have been boiling
   d. were boiling

5. A: Is it true that spaghetti didn't originate in Italy?

   B: Yes. The Chinese _____ spaghetti dishes for a long time before Marco Polo brought it back to Italy.
   - a. have been making
   - b. have made
   - c. had been making
   - d. make

6. A: I once saw a turtle that had wings. The turtle flew into the air to catch insects.

   B: Stop kidding. I _____ you!
   - a. don't believe
   - b. am not believing
   - c. didn't believe
   - d. wasn't believing

7. A: Could someone help me lift the lawnmower into the pickup truck?

   B: I'm not busy. I _____ you.
   - a. help
   - b. 'll help
   - c. am helping
   - d. am going to help

8. My family loves this house. It _____ the family home ever since my grandfather built it 60 years ago.
   - a. was
   - b. has been
   - c. will be
   - d. is

9. Here's an interesting statistic: On a typical day, the average person _____ about 48,000 words. How many words did you speak today?
   - a. spoke
   - b. was speaking
   - c. is speaking
   - d. speaks

10. It's against the law to kill the black rhinoceros. They _____ extinct.
    - a. became
    - b. have become
    - c. are becoming
    - d. become

11. After ten unhappy years, Janice finally quit her job. She _____ along with her boss for a long time before she finally decided to look for a new position.
    - a. hadn't been getting
    - b. isn't getting
    - c. didn't get
    - d. hasn't been getting

12. The National Hurricane Center is closely watching a strong hurricane over the Atlantic Ocean. When it _____ the coast of Texas sometime tomorrow afternoon, it will bring with it great destructive force.
    - a. reaches
    - b. will reach
    - c. reaching
    - d. is reaching

13. At one time, huge prehistoric reptiles dominated the earth. This Age of Dinosaurs _____ much longer than the present Age of Mammals has lasted to date.
    - a. lasted
    - b. was lasting
    - c. had lasted
    - d. has lasted

14. Jim, why don't you take some time off? You _____ too hard lately. Take a short vacation.
    - a. worked
    - b. work
    - c. have been working
    - d. were working

15. The city is rebuilding its dilapidated waterfront, transforming it into a pleasant and fashionable outdoor mall. Next summer when the tourists arrive, they _____ 104 beautiful new shops and restaurants in the area where the old run-down waterfront properties used to stand.

    a. will found   c. will find

    b. will be finding   d. will have found

16. A minor earthquake occurred at 2:07 A.M. on January 3rd. Most of the people in the village _____ at the time and didn't even know it had occurred until the next morning.

    a. slept   c. sleep

    b. had slept   d. were sleeping

17. The little girl started to cry. She _____ her doll, and no one was able to find it for her.

    a. has lost   c. was lost

    b. had lost   d. was losing

18. According to research, people usually _____ in their sleep 25 to 30 times each night.

    a. turn   c. turned

    b. are turning   d. have turned

Chapter 6
Subject-Verb Agreement

▶ **Practice 1. Preview.** (Chapter 6)
Correct the errors in the use of singular and plural forms of nouns and verbs. Don't add any new words.

1. My mother wear~~ ~~_∧ˢ glasses.

2. Elephants is large animals.

3. Your heart beat faster when you exercise.

4. Healthy hearts needs regular exercise.

5. Every child in the class know the alphabet.

6. Some of the magazine at the dentist's office are two year old.

7. A number of the students in my class is from Mexico.

8. One of my favorite subject in school is algebra.

9. There's many different kind of insects in the world.

10. Writing compositions are difficult for me.

11. The United States have a population of over 300 million.

12. Most of the movie take place in Paris.

13. Most of the people in my factory division likes and gets along with one another, but a few of the worker doesn't fit in with the rest of us very well.

► **Practice 2. Final -s on nouns and verbs.** (Chart 6-1)

Look at the words that end in **-s**. Are they nouns or verbs? Are they singular or plural? Check the correct columns.

	Noun	Verb	Singular	Plural
1. A boat floats.		✓	✓	
2. Boats float.				
3. My friend lives in my neighborhood.				
4. My friends live in my neighborhood.				
5. Helen eats a cookie every morning.				
6. Donuts contain a lot of sugar.				
7. Babies cry when they are hungry.				
8. My baby cries every night.				

► **Practice 3. Pronunciation and spelling of final -s/-es.** (Chart 6-1)

Add **-s** or **-es** to these words to spell them correctly. Then write /s/, /z/, or /əz/ to show the pronunciation of the endings.

1. ball ___s___ ___/z/___
2. wish ___es___ ___/əz/___
3. aunt ___s___ ___/s/___
4. flower _____ _____
5. park _____ _____

6. touch _____ _____
7. month _____ _____
8. tree _____ _____
9. dress _____ _____
10. valley _____ _____

11. industry _____ _____
12. swallow _____ _____
13. cliff _____ _____
14. bath _____ _____
15. bathe _____ _____

► **Practice 4. Basic subject-verb agreement.** (Chart 6-2)

Circle the correct verb.

1. The weather (*is* / *are*) cold.
2. Vegetables (*is* / *are*) good for you.
3. Each boy (*has* / *have*) his own locker in the gym.
4. A dog (*barks* / *bark*).
5. Dogs (*barks* / *bark*).
6. Ann (*is* / *are*) at home.
7. Ann and Sue (*is* / *are*) at home.
8. Every boy and girl (*is* / *are*) here.
9. A boy and a girl (*is* / *are*) in the street.
10. Eating vegetables (*is* / *are*) good for you.

▶ **Practice 5. Subject-verb agreement: using expressions of quantity.** (Chart 6-3)
Complete the sentences with *is* or *are*.

1. Some of Highway 21 _____ closed due to flooding.

2. Some of the highways _____ closed due to flooding.

3. A lot of that movie _____ full of violence.

4. A lot of movies _____ full of violence.

5. Half of the pizza _____ for you and half _____ for me.

6. Half of the pizzas _____ vegetarian.

7. Most of my friends _____ people I met in school.

8. Every one of my friends _____ a sports fan.

9. The number of desks in that classroom _____ thirty-five.

10. A number of stores _____ closed today because of the holiday.

▶ **Practice 6. Subject-verb agreement: using expressions of quantity.** (Chart 6-3)
Circle the correct verb.

1. A large part of our town (*have / has*) been badly damaged by a big fire.

2. Most of the houses (*was / were*) destroyed by the fire.

3. Most of the house (*was / were*) destroyed by the fire.

4. One of the houses (*was / were*) destroyed by the fire.

5. Each of the houses (*is / are*) in ruins.

6. Each house (*is / are*) in ruins.

7. Every one of the houses (*has / have*) serious damage.

8. Every house (*has / have*) serious damage.

9. None of the houses (*has / have*) escaped damage.

▶ **Practice 7. Subject-verb agreement: using *there* + *be*.** (Chart 6-4)
Circle the correct verb.

1. There (*is / are*) a cup on the table.

2. There (*is / are*) some cups on the table.

3. There (*is / are*) a lot of people in the line for the movie.

4. There (*is / are*) a snack bar in the lobby of the theater.

5. There (*wasn't / weren't*) any hurricanes in Florida last year.

6. There (*was / were*) a terrible tsunami in Asia in 2004.

7. Why (*isn't / aren't*) there any windows in the classroom?

8. Why (*isn't / aren't*) there a teacher in the classroom?

9. There (*has / have*) been an ongoing problem with the color printer.

10. There (*has / have*) been a lot of problems with the color printer.

▶ **Practice 8. Subject-verb agreement: some irregularities.** (Chart 6-5)
Circle the correct verb.

1. States (*is* / *are*) political units.

2. The United States (*is* / *are*) in North America.

3. The news in that newspaper (*is* / *are*) biased.

4. Economics (*is* / *are*) an important area of study.

5. Diabetes (*is* / *are*) an illness. Mumps (*is* / *are*) another kind of illness. Rabies (*is* / *are*) a disease you can get from being bitten by an infected animal.

6. One hundred meters (*isn't* / *aren't*) a long distance to travel by car.

7. Five minutes (*isn't* / *aren't*) too long to wait.

8. Six and four (*is* / *are*) ten.

9. People (*is* / *are*) interesting.

10. English (*is* / *are*) a common language.

11. The English (*is* / *are*) friendly people.

12. The elderly in my country (*is* / *are*) given free medical care.

13. Four colorful fish (*is* / *are*) swimming in the fish tank.

14. The police (*is* / *are*) coming to investigate the accident.

▶ **Practice 9. Subject-verb agreement.** (Charts 6-2 → 6-5)
Complete the sentences with the present tense of the appropriate verb from the list. Some verbs may be used more than once.

be	contain	cost	drive	like	make	remind

1. There _____ an old barn near our town. The barn has been converted to a bookstore, and its name is The Old Barn Bookstore.

2. It's a very popular place, especially on weekends. People _____ it a lot. They _____ out to the barn on weekends.

3. It's about twenty miles from downtown. Twenty miles _____ a long drive, but the bookstore is worth the drive.

4. A lot of the books in The Old Barn Bookstore _____ not new books. There _____ a lot of used books, old books, and even valuable antique books.

5. There _____ a large number of beautiful art books too. Each one _____ excellent photographs of famous pieces of art. Most of these books _____ quite expensive.

6. I'm thinking about buying a few nice art books there. One of the books _____ over a hundred dollars because it is very valuable. It has an autograph and an inscription by Ernest Hemingway.

7. There _____ a small café in The Old Barn Bookstore too. You can sit there for hours if you want, browsing through the books you are thinking of buying. The number of food items on the menu _____ very small, but about twenty different kinds of coffee _____ served.

8. Last Sunday I was browsing through some books when suddenly I heard several people speaking French. When I looked up, I saw six people at the next table, all speaking excitedly. I used to understand French, but now French _____ very difficult for me to understand. However, hearing French always _____ me of my days as a student and _____ me feel young again.

▶ **Practice 10. Subject-verb agreement.** (Charts 6-2 → 6-5)
Circle the correct verb.

1. Each skater in the competition (*has / have*) trained since childhood.

2. A convention of English teachers from all over the world (*take / takes*) place every spring.

3. Some of the new movies (*is / are*) good, but a lot of them (*have / has*) too much violence.

4. We saw a film about India last night. Some of the movie (*was /were*) fascinating, and there (*was / were*) a lot of beautiful mountain scenes.

5. Three-fourths of the patients who (*take / takes*) this new medicine report improvement.

6. Almost three-quarters of the surface of the earth (*is / are*) covered by water.

7. There (*is / are*) 100 senators in the United States Senate. The number of votes necessary for a simple majority (*is / are*) 51.

8. There (*has / have*) been some encouraging news about pandas in recent years. There (*is / are*) more pandas living today than there (*was / were*) ten years ago.

9. The United Arab Emirates (*is / are*) a country in the Middle East.

10. The *New York Times* (*is / are*) an important newspaper.

11. Economics (*is / are*) impossible for me to understand.

12. Diabetes (*is /are*) an illness. People who (*has / have*) it must be careful with their diet.

13. Five dollars (*is / are*) too much to pay for a pencil!

14. The English (*speak / speaks*) with an accent that is different from the American accent.

15. The handicapped (*use / uses*) a special entrance in this building.

► **Practice 11. Subject-verb agreement.** (Chapters 1-6)
Complete the sentences with the correct form of the given verb. Use any appropriate tense.

1. Nearly 90 percent of the people in our town always (*vote*) _____ in local elections.

2. In recent years, a number of students (*participate*) _____ in language programs abroad.

3. The number of students who knew the answer to the last question on the exam (*be*) _____ very low.

4. Every one of the boys and girls in the school (*know*) _____ what to do if the fire alarm rings.

5. A lot of people in the United States (*speak*) _____ and (*understand*) _____ _____ Spanish.

6. Why (*be*) _____ the police standing over there right now?

7. Why (*broadcast*) _____ most of the television stations _____ news at the same hour every night?

8. Some of the most important books for my report (*be*) _____ not available in the school library, so I'll have to look for information on the internet.

9. Recently there (*be*) _____ times when I have seriously considered dropping out of school.

10. Not one of the women in my office (*receive*) _____ a promotion in the past two years. All of the promotions (*go*) _____ to men.

11. The news on the radio and TV stations (*confirm*) _____ that a serious storm is approaching our city.

12. Geography (*be*) _____ fascinating. Mathematics (*be*) _____ fascinating. I love those subjects!

13. Mathematics and geography (*be*) _____ my favorite subjects.

14. By law, every man, woman, and child (*have*) _____ the right to free speech. It is guaranteed in our constitution.

15. (*Be, not*) _____ sugar and pineapple the leading crops in Hawaii now?

16. Why (*be*) _____ there a shortage of certified school teachers at the present time?

17. How many states in the United States (*begin*) _____ with the letter "A"?★

18. The United States (*consist*) _____ of 50 states.

19. What places in the world (*have*) _____ no snakes?

20. Politics (*be*) _____ a constant source of interest to me.

21. (*Be*) _____ there ever any doubt in your mind about the outcome of the election? You were sure that Garcia was going to win, weren't you?

---

*See the Answer Key for the answer to this question.

Chapter 7
Nouns

▶ **Practice 1. Regular and irregular plural nouns.** (Chart 7-1)
Write the plural forms of the given nouns.

1. one car, two _____
2. one woman, two _____
3. one match, two _____
4. one mouse, two _____
5. one city, two _____
6. one donkey, two _____
7. one half, two _____
8. one chief, two _____

9. one class, two _____
10. one foot, two _____
11. one hero, two _____
12. one piano, two _____
13. one video, two _____
14. one basis, two _____
15. one bacterium, two _____
16. one series, two _____

▶ **Practice 2. Regular and irregular plural nouns.** (Chart 7-1)
Complete the sentences with the correct plural form of the nouns in the list. Use each word once.

belief	fish	monkey	radio	thief
child	kilo	potato	species	tooth

1. I had my favorite vegetable for dinner: delicious fried _____.
2. At the zoo, we saw a lot of _____ jumping around in the trees.
3. The police caught the two _____ who had stolen over 100 _____ from people's cars.
4. The shopping mall has a playground for _____.
5. Our baby got two new _____ this week!
6. The two families found that they hold the same _____; they believe in the same things.
7. Some people think that whales are a species of _____, but they are not; they are mammals.
8. The adult male of some _____ of bears weighs about 600 _____.

► **Practice 3. Final -s / -es.** (Chapter 6 and Chart 7-1)
Add final **-s** / **-es** where necessary. Do not change, add, or omit any other words in the sentences.

1. A bird care_∧ˢ for its feather_∧ˢ by cleaning them with its beak.

2. There are many occupation in the world. Doctor take care of sick people. Pilot fly airplane.

   Farmer raise crop. Shepherd take care of sheep.

3. An architect design building. An archeologist dig in the ground to find object from past

   civilizations.

4. The first modern computer were developed in the 1930s and 1940s. Computer were not

   commercially available until the 1950s.

5. There are several factory in my hometown. The glass factory employ many people.

6. Kangaroo are Australian animal. They are not found on any of the other continent,

   except in zoo.

7. Mosquito are found everywhere in the world, including the Arctic.

8. At one time, many people believed that tomato were poisonous.

► **Practice 4. Possessive nouns.** (Chart 7-2)
Answer the questions for each sentence.

1. My parents' house is over 100 years old.
   a. What is the possessive noun? _____
   b. How many parents are there, one or two? _____
   c. What two nouns does the possessive (s') connect? _____ + _____

2. Safety is a parent's concern.
   a. What is the possessive noun? _____
   b. How many parents are there, one or more than one? _____
   c. What two nouns does the possessive ('s) connect? _____ + _____

3. Cats' eyes shine in the dark.
   a. What is the possessive noun? _____
   b. How many cats are there, one or many? _____
   c. What two nouns does the possessive (s') connect? _____ + _____

4. My cat's eyes are big and green.
   a. What is the possessive noun? _____
   b. How many cats are there, one or several? _____
   c. What two nouns does the possessive ('s) connect? _____ + _____

5. Do you know Mary's brother?

   a. What is the possessive noun? _____

   b. What belongs to Mary? _____

   c. What two nouns does the possessive ('s) connect? _____ + _____

6. Do you know Mary's brothers?

   a. What is the possessive noun? _____

   b. What belongs to Mary? _____

   c. What two nouns does the possessive ('s) connect? _____ + _____

7. My brothers' team won the game.

   a. What is the possessive noun? _____

   b. How many brothers do I have, one or more than one? _____

   c. What two nouns does the possessive (s') connect? _____ + _____

8. My brother's team won the game.

   a. What is the possessive noun? _____

   b. How many brothers do I have, one or more than one? _____

   c. What two nouns does the possessive ('s) connect? _____ + _____

▶ **Practice 5. Possessive nouns.** (Chart 7-2)
Check the correct number for the words in **bold**.

1. The **teacher's** office is down the hall.	☐ one	☐ more than one
2. The **teachers'** office is down the hall.	☐ one	☐ more than one
3. My **sisters'** clothes are all over my bed.	☐ one	☐ more than one
4. I visited the **boy's** house.	☐ one	☐ more than one
5. I agree with the **judges'** decision.	☐ one	☐ more than one
6. The customer service representative must listen to the **customers'** complaints.	☐ one	☐ more than one
7. The professor discussed the **student's** assignment.	☐ one	☐ more than one
8. The flight attendant put the **passenger's** bags in the overhead compartment.	☐ one	☐ more than one

▶ **Practice 6. Possessive nouns.** (Chart 7-2)
Make the *italicized* nouns possessive by adding apostrophes and final *-s* / *-es*. Cross out and change a letter if necessary.

1. He put the mail in his *secretary* __'s__ mailbox.

2. There are three secretaries in our office. The *secretary* ~~y~~ _ies'_ mailboxes are in the hallway.

3. Tom has two cats. The *cat* _____ food and water dishes are on a shelf in the laundry room.

4. I have one cat. My *cat* _____ feet are white, but the rest of her is black.

5. My *supervisor* _____ names are Ms. Anderson and Mr. Gomez.

6. Your *supervisor* _____ name is Ms. Wright.

7. My twin *baby* _____ eyes are dark blue, just like their father's eyes.

8. My *baby* _____ eyes are dark blue, just like her father's eyes.

9. Olga's *child* _____ name is Olaf.

10. José and Alicia's *children* _____ names are Pablo and Gabriela.

11. I'm interested in other *people* _____ ideas.

12. All of the performers in the play did well. The audience applauded the *actor* _____ excellent performances.

13. An *actor* _____ income is uncertain.

▶ **Practice 7. Possessive nouns.** (Chart 7-2)
Circle the correct word or phrase.

1. My (*mother's / mothers'*) name is Maria.

2. Both my (*grandmother's / grandmothers'*) names were Maria too.

3. The (*teacher's / teachers'*) class is so big that the students in the back of the room can't hear her when she talks.

4. My (*bosses' / boss'*) name is Carl.

5. An (*employee's / employees'*) wallet was found under a table at the (*employee's / employees'*) cafeteria yesterday.

6. Here's the directory for the department store: the (*mens' / men's*) department is on the first floor; the (*women's / womens'*) department is on the second floor; the (*children's / childrens'*) department is on the third floor. On the third floor, the (*girl's / girls'*) clothes are on the right side, and the (*boy's / boys'*) clothes are on the left side.

▶ **Practice 8. Nouns as adjectives.** (Chart 7-3)
<u>Underline</u> the adjective. Check the sentences where a noun is used as an adjective.

1. _____ It's an *expensive ticket*.

2. _____ It's a *theater ticket*.

3. _____ It's a *small theater*.

4. _____ It's a *movie theater*.

5. _____ It's a *family movie*.

6. _____ They are *family movies*.

7. _____ It's a *computer desk*.

8. _____ It's a *hair dryer*.

9. _____ They are *window washers*.

10. _____ It's a *gas station*.

▶ **Practice 9. Nouns as adjectives.** (Chart 7-3)
Complete the sentences with the given nouns. Use the singular or plural form as appropriate.

1. They sell _____*groceries*_____ at that store. It is a _____*grocery*_____ store. (*grocery*)

2. They raise _____*chickens*_____ on their farm. It's a _____*chicken*_____ farm. (*chicken*)

3. I like _____ salads. I like salads that contain _____. (*tomato*)

4. A friend gave us a wooden frame for _____. It's a very attractive wooden _____ frame. (*picture*)

5. I have a _____ garden. I grow several different kinds of _____. (*flower*)

6. Some people are addicted to _____. They are _____ addicts. (*drug*)

7. This carton holds one dozen _____. It's an _____ carton. (*egg*)

8. We drove down an old, narrow highway that had only _____. We drove down a _____ highway. (*two + lane*)

9. I gave a _____ speech in class. My speech lasted for _____. (*five + minute*)

10. The Watkins family lives in a _____ house. Any house that is _____ usually needs a lot of repairs. (*sixty + year + old*)

11. You need a special license to drive a _____. Ed has been a _____ driver for twenty-five years. (*truck*)

12. Susan programs _____. There are good jobs for _____ programmers everywhere. (*computer*)

▶ **Practice 10. Nouns as adjectives.** (Chart 7-3)
Choose the correct completion.

1. A table in a kitchen is a _____.
   a. kitchen table   b. table kitchen   c. kitchen's table

2. The two tables in my bedroom are my _____.
   a. bedrooms tables   b. tables bedroom   c. bedroom tables

3. I have an office at home. It is my _____.
   a. office home   b. home office   c. office of home

4. A lot of people have offices in their homes. They have _____.
   a. home offices   b. homes offices   c. homes office

5. There are two phone lines in my house, one for my home and one for my office. One is my home phone and the other is my _____.
   a. phone office   b. office phone   c. offices phone

6. There is a sink in the kitchen and one in each bathroom. We have two bathrooms. So we have one kitchen sink and two _____.
   a. bathrooms sinks   b. bathroom sink   c. bathroom sinks

7. In the back of our house, we grow vegetables in a garden. It's a _____.
   a. vegetable garden   b. vegetables garden   c. garden vegetables

8. We have two trees that grow cherries. They are _____.
   a. tree cherries   b. cherry trees   c. cherries trees

▶ **Practice 11. Nouns as adjectives.** (Chart 7-3)
Complete the sentences. Write the correct phrase using the two nouns in *italics*.

1. That *handbook* is for *students*. It is a _____student handbook_____.

2. There was a *party* to celebrate Lynn's *birthday*. There was a _____ for Lynn.

3. The retirees receive *checks* from the *government* every month. They receive a

   _____ every month.

4. The *seats* in the *airplane* are very small. The _____ are very

   small.

5. The *pajamas* are made of *cotton*. They are _____.

6. There were no *rooms* in the local *hotels* that were available. There were no available

   _____.

7. Their *baby* is *ten months old*. They have a _____.

8. Our *trip* lasted for *three days*. We took a _____.

9. Their *apartment* has *three rooms*. It is a _____.

10. The professor asked us to write a *paper* of *five pages*. She asked us to write a

    _____.

11. Luigi is a *singer*. He sings in *operas*. He's a famous _____.

12. A convention for people who collect *stamps* is being held at City Center. My uncle is a *collector*.

    He has been a _____ since he was a boy.

▶ **Practice 12. Count and noncount nouns.** (Chart 7-4)
Look at the *italicized* nouns. Write "C" above the count nouns and "NC" above the noncount nouns.

                           NC   *C NC NC NC*   *C*
1. We bought a lot of *food*. We bought some *eggs, bread, milk, coffee,* and *bananas.*

2. I get a lot of *mail*. I get some *letters, magazines, catalogs,* and *bills* almost every day.

3. *Euros, pounds,* and *dollars* are different kinds of *money.*

4. Alma doesn't wear much *jewelry*. She wears a *ring* and sometimes *earrings.*

5. A *language* consists of *vocabulary* and *grammar.*

6. We need some *furniture* for the patio: a *table*, six *chairs*, and an *umbrella.*

▶ **Practice 13. Count and noncount nouns.** (Charts 7-4 → 7-6)
Circle the correct completion.

1. Every day I learn some more new (*word* / *words*) in English.

2. Olga knows (*an* / *some*) American slang.

3. There are a lot of (*car* / *cars*) on the highway at rush hour.

4. We got here so fast! There wasn't (*much* / *many*) traffic on the highway.

5. We ate a tuna (*sandwich* / *sandwiches*) for lunch.

6. We got only (*some* / *one*) good picture on our trip.

7. That website contains (*an* / *some*) excellent information.

8. That is (*a very* / *very*) good news!

▶ **Practice 14. Count and noncount nouns.** (Charts 7-4 → 7-6)

Add final *-s* / *-es* to the nouns in *italics* if necessary. Do not add, omit, or change any other words. Some sentences have no errors.

1. Jackie has brown *hair* and gray *eye*ₐ.

2. My parents gave me some good *advice*.

3. I always drink *water* when I'm hot and thirsty.

4. Do winning athletes need *luck*?

5. Our country has made a lot of *progress* in the last 25 years.

6. How many *class* are you taking this semester?

7. Yesterday we received some *fax* from our lawyer.

▶ **Practice 15. Count and noncount nouns.** (Charts 7-4 → 7-6)

Circle the correct word or phrase.

1. It takes (*courage* / *a courage*) to be an astronaut.

2. We bought (*some* / *a*) new clothing.

3. The baby needs a new pair of (*shoe* / *shoes*).

4. The garbage truck comes on Monday, Wednesday, and Friday mornings to pick up the (*garbage* / *garbages*).

5. I ordered twelve (*glass* / *glasses*) from a site on the internet. When they arrived, one (*glass* / *glasses*) was broken.

6. Many people need to wear (*glass* / *glasses*) to see better. The lenses should be made of (*glass* / *glasses*) that doesn't break easily.

7. I filled out a report for (*a lost luggage* / *some lost luggage*) at the airport, but I'm not optimistic. I wonder if they find (*much* / *many*) lost suitcases.

8. Would you like to go out tonight? I don't have (*much* / *many*) homework, and I'd like to go out and have (*some* / *a*) fun.

9. Ireland is famous for its beautiful green (*hill* / *hills*). Ireland has (*a lovely* / *lovely*) scenery, but it often has (*a damp* / *damp*) weather.

10. The four-leaf clover is a symbol of (*a good* / *good*) luck in Ireland.

▶ **Practice 16. Basic article usage.** (Chart 7-7)
Complete the sentences with **a, an,** or **Ø**. Capitalize as necessary.

1. _A_ car has wheels.
2. _An_ airplane has wings.
3. _Ø_ Energy is necessary to move cars and airplanes.
4. ____ banana has a long, narrow shape.
5. ____ apple is round.
6. ____ fruit is nutritious.
7. ____ sodium is a mineral.

8. ____ air is a gas.
9. ____ rice is a kind of grass.
10. ____ elephant lives a long time.
11. ____ zebra has black and white stripes.
12. ____ football is an international sport.
13. ____ football is oval in the United States and round in the rest of the world.
14. ____ football player has to be strong.

▶ **Practice 17. Basic article usage.** (Chart 7-7)
Complete the sentences with **a, an,** or **some**.

1. I asked _____a_____ question.
2. The students asked _____some_____ questions.
3. I got _____an_____ answer.
4. I received _____ information.
5. Chess is _____ game.
6. The children played _____ games at the party.
7. I heard _____ news about the hurricane.
8. I read _____ newspaper.
9. My professor wrote _____ letter to the newspaper.
10. I wrote _____ email to my professor.
11. I got _____ mail from the university.
12. Susan left _____ things in her car.
13. Matt bought _____ printer.
14. The printer needs _____ ink.

▶ **Practice 18. General article usage.** (Chart 7-8)
Read each conversation. Circle the letter of the sentence that explains what the speakers are talking about.

1. A: Where's the teacher? I have a question.
   B: I'm not sure.
   a. Speaker A is asking about any teacher.
   b. Speaker A is asking about a teacher Speaker B is familiar with.

2. A: I put down the phone and now I can't find it.
   B: I do that a lot!
   a. Speaker A is referring to a phone Speaker B is familiar with.
   b. Speaker A is referring to any phone.

3. A: Could you pick up some eggs and rice at the store? We'll have the rice for dinner.

    B: Sure.

    a. In the first sentence, *rice* is general. In the second sentence, *rice* is specific.
    b. In both sentences, *rice* is specific.

4. A: Bananas have a lot of potassium.

    B: They're very healthy.

    a. Speaker A is referring to a specific group of bananas.
    b. Speaker A is referring to bananas in general.

5. A: Does Saturn have a moon that orbits it?

    B: I don't know!

    a. Speaker A is talking about a specific moon.
    b. Speaker A is talking about any moon.

6. A: Have you seen the moon tonight?

    B: Yes! It's spectacular.

    a. The speakers are referring to the moon that goes around the Earth.
    b. The speakers are referring to any moon in the solar system.

▶ **Practice 19. General article usage.** (Chart 7-8)
Correct the errors.

1. It's beautiful today. Sun is shining and sky is clear.

2. There's a boy on a swing, and a girl is pushing him. Boy is about five years old, and girl is about eight years old.

3. The penguins live in Antarctica. The polar bears don't live in Antarctica.

4. Which is more important — the love or the money?

5. A: What does this word mean?

    B: Do you have dictionary? Look up word in dictionary.

6. A: Watch out! There's a bee buzzing around!

    B: Where? I don't see it. Ouch! It stung me! I didn't see bee, but I felt it!

▶ **Practice 20. Using articles.** (Charts 7-7 and 7-8)
Complete the sentences with *a* / *an* or *the*.

1. A: Let's take _____ break. Do you want to go to _____ movie?

    B: That's _____ good idea. Which movie do you want to see?

    A: _____ movie at the Rialto Theater is a comedy. Let's see that one.

2. A: So, students, who knows _____ answer to this question?

    B: I do!

3. A: Professor Li, I have _____ question about the assignment.

   B: What's your question?

4. A: There's _____ spot on my shirt!

   B: Here. Take out _____ spot with this spot remover.

5. A: Listen! I hear _____ noise! Do you hear it?

   B: Yes, I hear something.

6. A: What was _____ noise that you heard?

   B: I think it was _____ mouse.

   A: But we don't have any mice in _____ house!

   B: Well, maybe it was just _____ wind.

▶ **Practice 21. Using articles.** (Charts 7-7 and 7-8)
Complete the sentences with *a / an, the,* or **Ø**. Capitalize as necessary.

1. ___Ø___ ᴸlightning is ___a___ flash of light. It is usually followed by ___Ø___ thunder.

2. Last night we had ___a___ terrible storm. Our children were frightened by ___the___ thunder.

3. _____ circles are _____ round geometric figures.

4. _____ circle with _____ slash drawn through it is an international symbol meaning "Do not do this!" For example, _____ circle in _____ illustration means "No Smoking."

5. _____ inventor of _____ modern cell phone was Dr. Martin Cooper. He made the first call on the first portable handset in 1973 when he was _____ employee of the Motorola company.

6. Frank Lloyd Wright is _____ name of _____ famous architect. He is _____ architect who designed the Guggenheim Museum in New York. He also designed _____ hotel in Tokyo. _____ hotel was designed to withstand _____ earthquakes.

7. There was _____ small earthquake in California last year. _____ earthquake caused _____ damage to several buildings, but fortunately, no one was killed.

▶ **Practice 22. Expressions of quantity with count and noncount nouns.** (Chart 7-9)
Draw a line through the expressions that <u>cannot</u> be used to complete the sentences. Item 1 has been started for you.

1. Linda did _____ work last Saturday.
   a. ~~three~~
   b. ~~several~~
   c. some
   d. a lot of
   e. too much
   f. too many
   g. a few
   h. a little
   i. a number of
   j. a great deal of
   k. hardly any
   l. no

2. Henry is planning _____ projects for next month.
   a. three
   b. several
   c. some
   d. a lot of
   e. too much
   f. too many
   g. a few
   h. a little
   i. a number of
   j. a great deal of
   k. hardly any
   l. no

▶ **Practice 23. Expressions of quantity with count and noncount nouns.** (Chart 7-9)
Complete the sentences with *much* or *many*. Also write the plural forms of the nouns as necessary. In some sentences, you will need to circle the correct verb in parentheses.

1. How ____*many*____ ~~computer~~ *computers* are there in the language lab?

2. How ____*much*____ equipment is there in the language lab?

3. How ____*many*____ ~~child~~ *children* (is /(are)) in Ms. Thompson's class?

4. How _____ tooth do babies usually have when they're born?

5. Ellen and Rick have traveled widely. They've visited _____ country.

6. I don't know _____ American slang.

7. Enrique hasn't made _____ progress in learning to play the piano. That's because he doesn't spend _____ time practicing.

8. How _____ DVDs do you usually rent during a month?

9. My hair is all frizzy today. There (*is* / *are*) too _____ humidity in the air.

10. I haven't done _____ reading lately.

11. There (*was* / *were*) so _____ smog in Los Angeles yesterday that you couldn't see any of the hills or mountains from the city.

12. I didn't know _____ grammar before taking this course.

13. How _____ active volcano (*is / are*) there in the world today?

14. Politicians give _____ speech during their careers.

▶ **Practice 24. Expressions of quantity with count and noncount nouns.**
(Chart 7-9)

Circle the letter of all the possible completions.

1. Pat bought a few _____ at the art show.
   a. pictures
   b. photographs
   c. art
   d. ceramic bowls

2. Mike bought some _____ at the supermarket.
   a. milk
   b. orange
   c. magazines
   d. flashlight battery

3. There were several _____ on the plane.
   a. child
   b. people
   c. babies
   d. passenger

4. There was a little _____ on the table.
   a. food
   b. cream
   c. coffee
   d. sandwiches

5. We have plenty of _____ for everyone.
   a. food
   b. pizza
   c. drinks
   d. hot dog

6. Can you bring a couple of _____ with you when you come to the party?
   a. ice
   b. hamburger
   c. bottles of soda
   d. water

7. I don't have many _____ about this.
   a. thoughts
   b. knowledge
   c. ideas
   d. information

8. Do Charlie and Kate have much _____?
   a. problems
   b. children
   c. fun
   d. work

9. I know a number of _____.
   a. people
   b. things
   c. professors
   d. news

10. They don't have a great deal of _____.
    a. intelligence
    b. information
    c. facts
    d. education

▶ **Practice 25. Using *a few* and *few; a little* and *little*.** (Chart 7-10)
In each pair of sentences, check the sentence that has the *larger number or quantity* of something.

1. a. We have a little money. ✓
   b. We have little money. ___

2. a. They know few people. ___
   b. They know a few people. ___

3. a. She has very little patience. ___
   b. She has a little patience. ___

4. a. I speak some Spanish. ___
   b. I speak little Spanish. ___

5. a. Marta asked few questions. ___
   b. Marta asked a few questions. ___

▶ **Practice 26. Using *a few* and *few; a little* and *little*.** (Chart 7-10)
Complete the sentences. Write the letter of the correct completion.

1. Belinda learned to skate very quickly. At first, she fell down ____ times, but now she very rarely falls down.
   a. few   b. a few   c. a little

2. The police didn't have a good description of the bank robber. ____ witnesses actually saw his face.
   a. few   b. a few   c. little

3. Please pass the cream. I like ____ cream in my coffee. It tastes better.
   a. a few   b. a little   c. very few

4. You'd better know the answers when Professor Simpson calls on you in class tomorrow. He has ____ patience with students who are not prepared.
   a. very little   b. very few   c. a little

5. Before the hurricane, the stores were crowded with people buying supplies. By the time I got to a store, ____ flashlight batteries were left, and ____ bottled water was available.
   a. very few / very little b. very little / very little c. very little / very few

6. Come over to our house tonight. Peter is bringing his guitar. He'll play ____ folk music, and we'll sing ____ old songs.
   a. few / little   b. a few / a little   c. a little / a few

7. To make this sauce, first cook ____ onions in ____ oil.
   a. few / little   b. a few / a little   c. little / few

▶ **Practice 27. Using *a few* and *few; a little* and *little*.** (Chart 7-10)
Without changing the meaning of the sentences, replace the *italicized* words with **a few, few, a little**, or **little**.

                  a little
1. If you put ~~some~~ sugar on those berries, they will taste sweeter.
                                                        a few
2. Many people live to be more than 100 years old, but only ~~some~~ people live to be 110 years old.

3. Many cities in the world have a population of over a million, and *some* cities have a population of more than ten million.

4. You might reach your goal if you put forth *some* more effort.

5. The professor lectured very clearly. At the end of the class, *not many* students had questions.

6. I have to go to the post office because I have *some* letters to mail.

7. Every day Max goes to his mailbox, but it is usually empty. He gets *almost no* mail.

8. My friend arrived in the United States *some* months ago.

9. I think you could use *some* help. Let me give you *some* advice.

10. Margaret likes sweet tea. She usually adds *some* honey to her tea. Sometimes she adds *some* milk too.

▶ **Practice 28. Singular expressions of quantity: *one, each, every.*** (Chart 7-11)
Choose the correct word from the list. Write the correct singular or plural form. Some words may be used more than once.

child	goose	neighbor	✓ state
chimpanzee	man	puppy	woman

1. There is only one _____*state*_____ in the United States that is completely surrounded by water: Hawaii.

2. One of the _____*states*_____ in the United States that shares a border with Canada is Vermont.

3. Our dog had six puppies. I wanted to keep them all, but I couldn't. I kept one of the _____, but I gave away the other five.

4. There were six puppies. One _____ was black and white, and five were all black.

5. The children enjoyed the zoo. One of the _____ wandered away from the group, but she was quickly found at the snack bar.

6. The children particularly liked watching the chimpanzees. One _____, a boy named Kevin, seemed to be having a conversation with one of the _____.

7. One of our _____ gave a welcoming party for a new family who had just moved to our neighborhood from Ecuador.

8. There were several men riding on motorcycles together. One _____ seemed to be their leader. He was riding in front of the group.

9. The geese are flying in a V-formation. One _____ is at the point of the V, apparently leading the whole flock.

10. Our book club consists of fifteen women who have been together in the club for more than twenty years. One of the _____ was just elected mayor of our town.

► **Practice 29. One, each, every.** (Chart 7-11)
Correct the errors in the *italicized* words. Not every sentence has an error.

1. According to the Constitution of the United States, *every persons* has certain rights.

2. One of *rights* is the right to vote.

3. Each of *states* is represented by two senators in the U.S. Senate.

4. *Each of* senator is elected for a six-year term.

5. The number of representatives in the House of Representatives depends on the population of *each state*.

6. For example, Nevada, one of *the very small state*, has only three representatives, but New York, a populous state, has 29 representatives.

7. Every one of *citizen* is eligible to vote for president, but not every *citizen* exercises this right.

8. In some countries, voting is compulsory. Every *citizens* must vote.

► **Practice 30. Using *of* in expressions of quantity.** (Chart 7-12)
Complete the sentences with ***of*** or **Ø**.

1. Several _____ my colleagues are going to the lecture at the library tonight.

2. I have several _____ colleagues who have PhDs.

3. Many _____ the houses in New Orleans were lost to the floods that occurred after Hurricane Katrina.

4. These days, _____ new houses are being built with stronger materials to withstand hurricanes.

5. A few _____ children are born with exceptional musical talent.

6. Some _____ the children in Mr. McFarlane's music class are playing in a recital.

7. Most _____ people like to hear compliments.

8. My cousin won a million _____ dollars on a game show.

9. Many _____ places in the world use wind as a source of energy. Some _____ these places supply energy to thousands _____ homes and businesses.

10. There was hardly any _____ rain this spring. As a result, hardly any _____ my flowers bloomed.

11. To form the plural of most _____ the words in English, we add an *-s* or *-es* at the end. Not every word forms its plural in this way, however. Some _____ words have irregular endings.

► **Practice 31. Chapter review.**
Complete the crossword puzzle. Use the clues under the puzzle and the words in the list. All the words in the puzzle are from the charts in Chapter 7. All the sentences are well-known sayings in English.

all	every	many	mice	some
an	man	men	one	two

Across

3. _____ good things must come to an end.
4. You can't make an omelet without breaking _____ eggs.
6. A _____ is known by his friends.
8. _____ cloud has a silver lining.

Down

1. _____ heads are better than one.
2. _____ picture is worth a thousand words.
3. _____ apple a day keeps the doctor away.
5. When the cat's away, the _____ will play.
6. Too _____ cooks spoil the broth.
7. Dead _____ tell no tales.

Chapter 8
Pronouns

► **Practice 1. Personal pronouns.** (Chart 8-1)

Draw a circle around each pronoun that has an antecedent. Draw an arrow from the pronoun to its antecedent.

1. Bob works for Trans-Ocean Airlines. (He) flies cargo across the Pacific Ocean.

2. Mr. and Mrs. Nobriega are moving. They have bought a house in the suburbs.

3. There goes my English teacher. Do you know her?

4. The baby just began to walk. She is eleven months old.

5. A new kind of car is being advertised. It runs on a battery.

6. There are two hawks up there on the telephone wire. Do you see them?

7. Sorry, Mr. Frank is not in the office now. Please call him at home.

8. We have a dog and a cat. They are part of our family.

► **Practice 2. Personal pronouns.** (Chart 8-1)

Circle the words in *italics* that are grammatically correct.

1. Sarah and (*I / me*) are taking a yoga class.

2. I'm going to tell you something, but don't tell anyone. It's just between you and (*I / me*).

3. Carlos and Julia were at the movies together. I saw (*they / them*). (*They / Them*) were holding hands.

4. Where are my papers? I left (*it / them*) right here on the table.

5. I have (*my / mine*) problems, and you have (*your / yours*).

6. Jim and Helena both work from home. He works at (*he / his*) computer all day, and she works at (*her / hers*). At five o'clock sharp they both stop (*they / their*) work.

7. My aunt is only five years older than I am. (*She and I / Her and me*) are very close. We are like sisters. (*Our / Ours*) friends and relatives treat (*our / us*) like sisters.

8. I studied Latin when I was in high school. Of course, nobody speaks Latin today, but Latin was very useful to (*me / I*). Because I understand (*it / its*) grammar, I can understand grammar in other languages. And my vocabulary is bigger because of (*it / its*) too.

9. When baby giraffes are born, (*they / its*) are six feet tall, taller than the average person. (*They / It*) sometimes grow an inch a day, and they double (*its / their*) height in one year.

10. Did you know Mauna Kea in Hawaii is actually the tallest mountain in the world? If you measure it from (*its* / *it's*) base at the bottom of the Pacific Ocean to (*its* / *it's*) peak, it has a height of 33,476 feet (10,203 meters). (*Its* / *It's*) taller than Mount Everest.

▶ **Practice 3. Personal pronouns: agreement with generic nouns and indefinite pronouns.** (Chart 8-2)

Circle the letter of the correct completions. In some sentences, both choices are correct.

1. All students must bring _____ books to class every day.
   a. his   b. their

2. Each girl in the class must bring _____ books to class every day.
   a. her   b. his or her

3. Everyone on the tennis team must leave _____ cell phone number with the coach.
   a. his or her   b. their

4. Everybody on the men's bowling team brings _____ own bowling ball to the bowling alley.
   a. his   b. his or her

5. Everyone should know how to do _____ job.
   a. his or her   b. their

6. Girls, whose keys are these? Somebody left _____ keys on the table.
   a. their   b. her

7. Nobody in the Boy Scout troop failed _____ tests. Everybody passed.
   a. his   b. their

▶ **Practice 4. Personal pronouns: agreement with collective nouns.**
   (Charts 8-2 and 8-3)

Complete the sentences with a word or phrase from the list. You may use an item more than once.

her	his or her	its	them
his	it	their	they

1. Tonight's audience is special. Everyone in _____ is a member of the fire department or the police department. The show is being performed especially for _____.

2. When the play was over, the audience arose from _____ seats and applauded wildly.

3. The actors bowed to the audience's applause. The leading man took _____ bow first, and then the leading lady took _____ bow.

4. The faculty of the philosophy department is very small. In fact, _____ has only two professors. _____ share an office.

5. Well, Mia, I'm sorry you're having problems. Everyone has _____ problems, goodness knows!

6. A notice sent home with each girl on the girls' volleyball team said: "The girls' volleyball team is playing at Cliffside on Friday of this week. This will be _____ final game of the season. Each girl must have a signed consent form for a field trip from _____ mother or father."

7. Instructions on an application for admission to a university said: "Each student must submit _____ application by December 1st. The admissions committee will render _____ final decision before April 1st."

▶ **Practice 5. Reflexive pronouns.** (Chart 8-4)
Complete the sentences with appropriate reflexive pronouns.

1. In our creative writing class, we all had to write short biographies of ____*ourselves*____.

2. Anna wrote a biography of _____.

3. Tom wrote a biography of _____.

4. Larry and Harry, who are twins, wrote biographies of _____, but surprisingly, they were not similar.

5. I wrote a biography of _____.

6. After our teacher had read them all, he asked us, "Did all of you enjoy writing about _____?"

7. One student replied. He said, "Well, yes, I think we did. But now we would like to know something about you. Will you tell us about _____?"

▶ **Practice 6. Reflexive pronouns.** (Chart 8-4)
Complete the sentences with one of the words or phrases from the list, and add a reflexive pronoun.

feeling sorry for	help	✓ is angry at	pat
fix	introduce	laugh at	talks to

1. John overslept and missed his plane to San Francisco. Now he
   ____*is angry at himself*____ for not checking his alarm clock before going to bed.

2. I didn't know anyone at the party. I stood alone for a while; then I decided to walk over to an interesting-looking person and _____ to him.

3. Sue, please _____ to some more cake. And would you like some more coffee?

4. You did a great job, team. You should all _____ on the back for playing the game so well.

5. Sabrina is a lonely little girl. She doesn't have any brothers or sisters, or live near any friends. Sometimes she _____ or to an imaginary friend.

6. The sink is not going to _____. We have to call a plumber to repair it.

7. Come on, Kim. Don't be so hard on yourself. Everyone makes mistakes. We have to _____ sometimes and keep a sense of humor!

8. I told Tommy he couldn't buy a new toy today. He's mad at me. He's in his bedroom _____.

▶ **Practice 7. Using *you, one,* and *they* as impersonal pronouns.** (Chart 8-5)
Choose the correct pronoun to complete each sentence. Write the letter of the pronoun.

1. People make New Year's resolutions at the beginning of a new year. They promise ____ that they will do something to improve their well-being, or to benefit their community or the world.
   a. them   b. oneself   c. themselves

2. One should be honest with ____.
   a. one   b. oneself   c. yourself

3. Parents tell their children, "You should be polite to ____ elders."
   a. your   b. one's   c. their

4. How do ____ start this car?
   a. you   b. one   c. he

5. How does ____ make a complaint in this store? Is there a customer-service department?
   a. you   b. they   c. one

6. If you are a student, ____ can get a discount at shops in the mall.
   a. they   b. you   c. one

7. Students can get discounts at the mall. ____ just have to show their student ID.
   a. They   b. Themselves   c. One

▶ **Practice 8. Forms of *other.*** (Chart 8-6)
Complete each sentence. Write the letter of the correct form of ***other***.

1. One of the biggest problems in the world is global warming. ____ problem is AIDS.
   a. Another   b. The another   c. Other

2. Some cities have strict anti-pollution laws, but ____ cities do not.
   a. other   b. others   c. the others

3. New York is a multilingual city. In addition to English, many people speak Spanish. ____ speak French, Chinese, Portuguese, or Russian.
   a. Others   b. Other   c. Another

4. In addition to these languages, there are 40 ____ languages spoken in New York City, according to the U.S. Census Bureau.
   a. other   b. others   c. another

5. Istanbul lies on both sides of the Straits of Bosporus. One side is in Europe, and ____ side is in Asia.
   a. another   b. the other   c. other

6. There are 47 countries in Africa. Of these, 35 countries have coastlines. _____ do not have coastlines; they are landlocked.
     a. Others   b. The other   c. The others

7. There are several countries that have a king or a queen. One is Thailand. _____ is England.
     a. Another   b. The other   c. The another

8. There are a few _____ countries that have a king or a queen, but I can't remember which ones.
     a. others   b. other   c. another

9. Scandinavia consists of four countries. One is Denmark. _____ are Finland, Norway, and Sweden.
     a. The other   b. The others   c. Others

10. Canada has ten provinces. French is the official language of Quebec province. English is the language of _____ provinces.
     a. others   b. another   c. the other

11. Washington is one of the five states of the United States with borders on the Pacific Ocean. What are _____ states?*
     a. other   b. the other   c. the others

▶ **Practice 9. Forms of *other*.** (Chart 8-6)
Circle the correct word or phrase.

1. A: How much longer until we get home?
   B: We're almost there. We have (*other / another*) twenty minutes.

2. A: This road is expensive! I see we have to pay more money at the next toll booth.
   B: Right. I think we have to pay (*another / others*) three dollars.

3. A: So you didn't buy that house way out in the country?
   B: No, it's too far from work. I have to drive ten miles to work now. I don't want to add (*another / the another*) ten miles to the trip.

4. A: I heard you moved out of your apartment.
   B: That's right. They raised the rent by 100 euros. I didn't want to pay (*other / another*) 100 euros.

5. A: How was the test?
   B: I am sure that I failed. I didn't finish. I needed (*the other / another*) ten or fifteen minutes to finish.

6. A: Who won the game?
   B: The other team. In the last minute of the game, our team scored six points, not enough to win; we needed (*another / other*) eight points.

---

*See the Answer Key for the answer to this question.

▶ **Practice 10. Common expressions with *other*.** (Chart 8-7)

Complete the sentences in Column A with a phrase from Column B.

Column A

1. John loves Mary and Mary loves John. They love _____.

2. Nobody in my class understands this poem _____ Ron, who seems to understand everything.

3. The discussion group doesn't meet every week; it meets _____ week, that is, twice a month.

4. A tiger is a feline; _____, it's a cat, a big cat.

5. The children jumped into the water one by one, in a line, one _____.

6. What? The letter carrier quit his job? I saw him just _____. He seemed happy.

Column B

a. every other

b. after another

c. the other day

d. each other

e. in other words

f. other than

▶ **Practice 11. Nouns and pronouns.** (Chapters 6 → 8)

Correct the errors. The first paragraph has 4 errors. The second paragraph has 12 errors. The third paragraph has 13 errors.

(1) The potatoes are grown in most country. They are one of the most widely grown vegetable in the world. They are very versatile; they can be prepared in many different way.

(2) French fry are popular almost everywhere. Besides frying it, you can boil or bake potato. Other way people use potatoes is to make potato flour for bread and another kinds of dishes. Its also possible to make alcoholic beverages from potato. There are still others ways potatoes are used by commercial food processor to make product such as potatoes chips and freeze-dried potato.

(3) Potato originated in South America, where it were cultivated by the Incas as early as 5,000 year ago. It is believed that potatoes were the worlds first freeze-dried food. Over 4,000 years ago, the Incas carried his harvested potato up into the mountains and spread them on the ground to freeze overnight. The next day, after sun came up and heated the potatoes, the Incas squeezed the water out of them by stepping on it. This process were repeated for four or five day until almost all the moisture was gone from the potatoes. The Incas then dried the potatoes and stored it in pot. An Indians of South America still do this today.

Chapter 9
Modals, Part 1

▶ **Practice 1. Basic modal introduction.** (Chart 9-1)
Correct the errors in verb forms. Not all sentences have errors.

1. He can ~~to~~ hear it.
2. He can hear it.
3. He can heard it.
4. Can you help me?
5. Do you can help me?
6. They can't help me.

7. He oughts to help you.
8. He is able to help you.
9. He supposed to help you.
10. They have to do it.
11. We have got to do it.
12. She should to tell the truth.

▶ **Practice 2. Polite requests with "*I*" as the subject; polite requests with "*you*" as the subject.** (Charts 9-2 and 9-3)
Complete the sentences with a phrase from the list. Write the letter of the phrase that fits the sentence.

a. Can I help you
b. Can you hurry
c. could you help me

d. Could you please repeat
e. May I borrow
f. Would you please give me

1. A: Omigosh! I've lost my passport. Rick, _____ find it?

   B: OK. I'll be right there.

2. A: Omigosh! I've lost my passport.

   B: _____, Jenny? Maybe I can find it for you.

3. A: I'm sorry. Mr. Robbins isn't in today. Do you want to leave a message on his voice mail?

   B: Well, it's very important. _____ his cell phone number?

4. A: _____ your dictionary, please?

   B: Sure.

5. A: OK, sir. I'll be there some time today to fix your refrigerator.

   B: _____, please? All the food is melting fast!

6. A: Students, do you understand the assignment?

   B: Not really, Dr. Johnson. _____ what you said?

▶ **Practice 3. Polite requests with _Would you mind._** (Chart 9-4)

Complete the sentences with _if I_ + the present tense or the _-ing_ form of the verb.

1. a. I want you to cook dinner.   Would you mind _____cooking_____ dinner?

   b. I want to cook dinner.   Would you mind _____if I cooked_____ dinner?

2. a. We want you to take us to the airport.   Would you mind _____ us to the airport?

   b. We want to take you to the airport.   Would you mind _____ you to the airport?

3. a. I want to open the windows.   Would you mind _____ the windows?

   b. I want you to open the windows.   Would you mind _____ the windows?

4. a. We want you to join us for lunch.   Would you mind _____ us for lunch?

   b. We want to join you for lunch.   Would you mind _____ you for lunch?

5. a. I want you to write a letter to the boss.   Would you mind _____ a letter to the boss?

   b. I want to write a letter to the boss.   Would you mind _____ a letter to the boss?

▶ **Practice 4. Polite requests with _Would you mind._** (Chart 9-4)

Complete the sentences with the verbs in parentheses. Write _if I_ + the past tense or the _-ing_ form of the verb. In some sentences, either response is possible, but the meaning is different.

1. A: It's cold in here. Would you mind (close) _____closing_____ the window?
   B: Not at all. I'd be glad to.

2. A: It's cold in here. Would you mind (close) _____if I closed_____ the window?
   B: Not at all. Go right ahead. I think it's cold in here too.

3. A: You're going to the library? Would you mind (take) _____ this book back to the library for me?
   B: Not at all.

4. A: I'm not feeling well at all. Would you mind (go) _____ home now?
   B: Oh, I'm sorry. I hope you can come back when you feel better.

5. A: I'm not feeling well at all. Would you mind (leave) _____ now before the visiting hours are over?
   B: Oh, of course not. We shouldn't stay more than a short time for a hospital visit anyway.

6. A: I'll be working late tonight, honey. Would you mind (cook) _____ dinner tonight? I'll clean up after dinner.
   B: I'd be happy to. About what time do you think you'll be home?

7. A: We have a lot of chicken left over from dinner last night. Would you mind
     (*make*) _____ a chicken salad from the leftovers for dinner tonight?
   B: No, that'll be good. You make a great chicken salad.

8. A: I'm feeling kind of worn out. Chopping wood in the hot sun is hard on me. Would you
     mind (*finish*) _____ the work yourself?
   B: No problem, Grandpa. Why don't you go in and rest? I'll finish up.

9. A: Would you mind (*use*) _____ your name as a reference on this job
     application?
   B: Not at all. In fact, ask them to call me.

10. A: I'd like to apply for the job as department manager. Would you mind
     (*recommend*) _____ me to the boss?
    B: No. As a matter of fact, I was thinking of recommending you myself.

▶ **Practice 5. Expressing necessity, lack of necessity, and prohibition.**
   (Charts 9-5 and 9-6)
Read the statements. Then check the box that describes each item.

	Necessity	Lack of Necessity	Prohibition
1. Taxpayers must pay their taxes by April 15th.			
2. You must not touch electrical wires.			
3. Students don't have to register on campus. They can register by computer.			
4. We've got to hurry! We don't want to miss our flight!			
5. You don't have to pay for the car all at once. You can pay month by month.			
6. Passengers must show their boarding passes and their IDs when they go through security.			
7. A person has to be seventeen years old to obtain a driver's license in many states.			
8. Doctors have to graduate from medical school and pass special exams before they can practice medicine.			
9. Soldiers must not disobey a superior officer.			
10. Nobody has to come to work tomorrow! The company has given everybody a day off.			

▶ **Practice 6. Past tense of *must* and *have to*.** (Chart 9-5)
Rewrite the sentences using the past tense.

1. I must be on time for my job interview.

   _____

2. The students have to memorize 100 new words a week.

   _____

3. Sylvia has to cancel her summer vacation. She has too much work to do.

   _____

4. Who do you have to call?

   _____

5. The children must get vaccinations.

   _____

6. The passengers have to fasten their seat belts because of the turbulent weather.

   _____

▶ **Practice 7. Expressing necessity and prohibition.** (Charts 9-5 and 9-6)
Write the letter of the correct word or phrase.

1. Plants _____ have water in order to live.
   a. must   b. don't have to   c. must not

2. A lot of people _____ leave their homes to go to work. They can work from their home offices.
   a. must   b. don't have to   c. must not

3. To stay alive, people _____ breathe oxygen.
   a. must   b. don't have to   c. must not

4. People who have diabetes will have serious health problems if they eat foods with a lot of sugar.
   They _____ eat foods with a lot of sugar.
   a. must   b. don't have to   c. must not

5. A salesperson _____ motivate people to buy his/her product.
   a. has to   b. doesn't have to   c. must not

6. You _____ finish your work on this project before you go on vacation. Your job is at risk.
   a. must   b. must not   c. don't have to

7. My room is a mess, but I _____ clean it before I go out tonight. I can do it in the morning.
   a. have got to   b. must not   c. don't have to

8. I _____ get some help with my statistics course. If I don't, I won't pass it.
   a. have got to   b. must not   c. don't have to

9. Yoko _____ study for her English tests. She understands everything without studying.
   a. has to   b. must not   c. doesn't have to

10. Everywhere in the world, stealing is against the law. People _____ steal.
    a. must   b. must not   c. don't have to

▶ **Practice 8. Verb form review: *have to*.** (Charts 9-5 and 9-6)
Complete the sentences with an appropriate form of *have to*. Include any words in parentheses.

1. Richard travels to Russia on business frequently. Luckily, he speaks Russian, so he

   (*not*) _____ rely on an interpreter when he's there.

2. Jackie _____ go to an important meeting in Sydney last month.

3. I (*not*) _____ water the garden later today. Joe has agreed to do it for me.

4. I _____ write three term papers for my history class last semester.

5. Matt has been nearsighted all his life. He _____ wear glasses even when he was

   a child.

6. In your country, _____ children _____ attend school?

7. Years ago, there weren't laws to keep children in school. If poor families needed the money,

   children _____ work to contribute income to the family. Children

   (*not*) _____ stay in school in those days.

8. High school graduates (*not*) _____ attend college, but of course,

   many want to.

9. Anyone who wants to drive a truck _____ get a special truck driver's license.

10. A: You're leaving so early!

    B: Yes. I'm sorry. I _____ finish some work for tomorrow before I go to bed

    tonight.

▶ **Practice 9. Advisability: *should, ought to, had better*.** (Chart 9-7)
Which sentence in each pair has a stronger meaning? Circle the letter.

1. a. I should study.
   b. I'd better study.

2. a. You must turn right here.
   b. You should turn right here.

3. a. He's got to get a warmer jacket.
   b. He ought to get a warmer jacket.

4. a. You should get new tires for your car.
   b. You'd better get new tires for your car.

5. a. They shouldn't say those words.
   b. They must not say those words.

6. a. Jane had better not tell anyone about this.
   b. Jane shouldn't tell anyone about this.

7. a. You must not drink the water here.
   b. You shouldn't drink the water here.

8. a. We don't have to vote for John Turner.
   b. We shouldn't vote for John Turner.

▶ **Practice 10. Advisability: *should, ought to, had better*.** (Chart 9-7)
Cross out the ideas that are not good advice for each situation, or are not relevant to the situation.

1. José wants to lose weight.
   a. He should exercise regularly.
   b. ~~He should eat a lot of sweets.~~
   c. He should go on a diet.

2. Ludmila wants to go to medical school in a few years.

    a. She should study poetry now.
    b. She should take science and math courses now.
    c. She should start saving money for tuition.

3. Ikira is a concert pianist.

    a. He should take good care of his hands.
    b. He should go bowling often.
    c. He should visit his grandmother often.

4. Mia is failing her math class.

    a. She should drink a lot of black coffee.
    b. She should get a tutor to help her.
    c. She should study more.

5. Beth wants her flowers to grow.

    a. She should water them.
    b. She should take any weeds out of her garden.
    c. She should give the flowers plant food as directed.

6. Ira sprained his ankle.

    a. He should practice standing on it.
    b. He should rest his ankle.
    c. He should put ice on it.

▶ **Practice 11. *Should, ought to, had better.*** (Chart 9-7)
Give advice to the people in the following situations. Write the letter of the piece of advice that fits each situation.

    a. call home and talk to his family quite often
    b. change his clothes before he goes
    c. clean it up right away
    d. get his roommate a set of earphones
    e. join some clubs to meet people with similar interests
    f. make her own decisions about her career
    g. stop for gas as soon as we see a station
    h. take it back now so you won't have to pay any more money

1. Ann would like to make some new friends. She should ____.

2. We're running out of gas! We had better ____.

3. Sam and Tim, both teenagers, have messed up the house, and their parents are coming home soon. They had better ____.

4. You are going to have to pay a fine because your library book is overdue. You ought to ____.

5. Ron is wearing jeans. He has to go to a formal reception this evening. He had better ____.

6. Mary's parents expect her to work in the family business, a shoe store, but she is an adult and wants to be an architect. She should ____.

7. Richard's roommate, Charlie, stays up very late studying. While Charlie is studying, he listens to loud music, and Richard can't get to sleep. Richard ought to ____.

8. Pierre is feeling really homesick these days. He should ____.

► **Practice 12. The past form of *should*.** (Chart 9-8)
Give advice about the situation using the past form of *should*. Complete each sentence with a verb from the list. Use any words in parentheses.

buy	come	order	take	visit
change	keep	stay	turn	watch

1. A: We're having hamburgers? I thought you were cooking a turkey for the holiday.

   B: Well, I did, but I cooked it for too long. It burned up in the oven! I
   _____ it out after three hours, but I forgot.

2. A: Where are we? Are we lost?

   B: I think we are. We _____ left instead of right at the last
   intersection.

3. A: I'm tired this morning! What time did we finally go to bed last night?

   B: Around 2:00 A.M. We (*not*) _____ that late movie.

4. A: Is Lionel angry at you?

   B: He is. I _____ his mother when she was so sick, but I didn't.

5. A: Beautiful shoes! Where did you buy them?

   B: I bought them at Norwalk's, but I _____ them at Pansy's
   Discount Store. They were a lot cheaper there.

6. A: How was dinner at Henri's?

   B: Not so good. I had the fish, but it didn't taste fresh. I _____
   something else.

7. A: Why are you upset with Frank?

   B: He came to work today with his terrible cold, coughing and sneezing all over us! He
   (*not*) _____ to work today. He _____
   home.

8. A: Are you glad you took the new job?

   B: No, actually, I'm not. I (*not*) _____ jobs. I
   _____ my old job.

► **Practice 13. Present and past forms of *should*.** (Charts 9-7 and 9-8)
Give advice in each situation. Complete each sentence with the present or past form of *should* and the verb in parentheses.

1. Travel broadens one's horizons. Everyone (*travel*) _____.

2. We did not travel to Africa when we had the opportunity last year. We (*go*) _____
   _____ at that time.

3. Our house will look much better with a fresh coat of paint. It will look good in a yellow color. I think we (*paint*) _____ our house, and the color (*be*) _____ yellow.

4. We painted our house. Now it's white and has beige shutters. It doesn't look good. We (*not, paint*) _____ our house in such dull colors.

5. Ernie is allergic to shellfish. Last night he ate shellfish, and he broke out with terrible hives. Ernie (*not, eat*) _____ that shellfish.

6. Some people are sensitive to caffeine. They cannot fall asleep at night if they drink coffee in the afternoon. These people (*not, drink*) _____ coffee after 12:00 P.M. They (*drink*) _____ decaffeinated coffee or tea instead.

7. Years ago, people did not realize that some species were dying off because of human activity. For example, many buffalo in North America were killed because of human thoughtlessness. As a result, there are few buffalo left in North America. People (*not, kill*) _____ _____ those buffalo.

8. Today, people are making efforts to save the environment and to save endangered species. We (*make*) _____ strong efforts to recycle, conserve our resources, and nourish endangered species.

▶ **Practice 14. Obligation: *be supposed to.*** (Chart 9-9)
Rewrite the sentences. Use a form of ***be supposed to*** + verb.

1. Allen is expected to arrive at seven o'clock. Will he?
   Allen _____ at seven o'clock. Will he?

2. I'm expected to go hiking with Beth on Saturday, but I'd really rather sleep late.
   I _____ hiking with Beth on Saturday, but I'd really rather sleep late.

3. The weather is expected to be nice over the weekend.
   It _____ nice over the weekend.

4. The plane was expected to arrive at 6:35, but it didn't.
   The plane _____ at 6:35, but it didn't.

5. I was expecting my friends to come over tonight, but they didn't.
   They _____ tonight, but they didn't.

6. Our dog is very independent. We expect him to run to us when we call his name, but he completely ignores us.
   Our dog _____ to us when we call his name, but he completely ignores us.

► **Practice 15. Unfulfilled intentions: *was / were going to.*** (Chart 9-10)
Circle *yes* if the sentence expresses intention. Circle *no* if not.

		Expresses Intention	
1.	We are going to visit our cousins on Saturday.	yes	no
2.	We were going to visit our cousins on Saturday, but Jack got sick.	yes	no
3.	Ann was going down the stairs when she fell down and sprained her ankle.	yes	no
4.	I had planned to finish writing this document tonight, but I couldn't.	yes	no
5.	I was going to finish writing this document tonight, but I can't.	yes	no
6.	I was just finishing the document when my computer crashed.	yes	no
7.	I had planned to wash my car, but it rained.	yes	no
8.	I was going to wash my car, but it rained.	yes	no
9.	I was washing my car when it began to rain.	yes	no
10.	I was going to the car wash when it began to rain.	yes	no

► **Practice 16. Obligation: *be supposed to* and unfulfilled intentions: *was / were going to.*** (Charts 9-9 and 9-10)
Complete the sentences with a logical phrase from the list. Write the letter of the phrase.

a. he'll be late
b. I didn't want to upset you
c. I fell asleep
d. it's already two hours late
e. she lost her voice

f. the audience was applauding wildly
g. the bus broke down
h. the weather report was terrible
i. there was no lettuce in the fridge
j. they saw a train wreck

1. The plane was supposed to arrive at noon, but _____.
2. The students were going to go by bus to the TV station, but _____.
3. Tim was supposed to be here by 6:00, but _____.
4. The students were going by bus to the TV station when _____.
5. I was going to tell you the bad news, but _____.
6. Elena was going to sing at the concert, but _____.
7. Jenny was singing at the concert, and _____.
8. I was planning to watch the movie from beginning to end, but _____.
9. Dan was going to make a salad, but _____.
10. We were going to go sailing last weekend, but _____.

► **Practice 17. Making suggestions: *could* vs. *should.*** (Chart 9-12)
Write *could* or *should* as appropriate.

1. PATIENT: I don't know what to do about my noisy neighbors. They play their music so loud that it's driving me crazy.

   PSYCHOLOGIST: Well, you _____ play your own music louder, or you _____ call the police.

   PATIENT: No, seriously. I don't like those ideas. I want you to give me some good advice.

PSYCHOLOGIST: OK, if you insist. Then I think you _____ try to talk to them about the situation in a nonthreatening manner. That's the best way.

PATIENT: I agree. That's exactly what I _____ do, and I will.

2. WAITER: Good evening. My name is Walter, and I'll be your server tonight.

CARL: Good evening. What kind of fish is fresh tonight?

WAITER: The snapper is excellent. It's the best.

CARL: Well, I _____ order snapper, but . . . do you have wild salmon? I _____ order that, perhaps, or . . . .

WAITER: The snapper is out of this world. You _____ have the snapper.

CARL: OK, if you say that I _____ have the snapper, I will take your advice. I'll have the snapper with lemon and garlic.

3. SAM: The bridge is closed for repairs. How can we get across the lake into the city?

MARY: Well, you _____ take the Lincoln Bridge — that's five miles south of here, or you _____ drive north about fifteen miles and take the Longman Tunnel.

BOB: No, no, those routes are too long and not scenic. Here's what you _____ do, Sam: You _____ drive north for about thirty miles, and head east. You'll be entirely north of the lake then, and you won't need a bridge.

▶ Practice 18. Chapter review.
Correct the modal verb errors.

1. Our teacher can to speak five languages.

2. Oh, this table is heavy! Jim, may you help me move it?

3. We come to class on weekdays. We are not have to come to class on weekends.

4. Park here. It's free. You must not pay anything.

5. When you speak in court, you must to tell the truth. You must not tell lies.

6. Pat looks tired. She should gets some rest.

7. I wanted tickets for the concert, but they were all sold out. I should ordered them sooner.

8. The children are suppose to be in bed by nine o'clock.

9. The Garcias supposed to be here at 7:00, but I think they will be late, as usual.

10. We're going to make chicken for dinner. Why you don't join us?

11. Here's my advice about your diet, Mr. Jackson. You could not eat a lot of sugar and salt.

12. A: This is wonderful music. Will we dance?

    B: No, let's don't dance. Let's just sit here and talk.

Chapter 10
Modals, Part 2

▶ **Practice 1. Degrees of certainty: _must_ and _may / might / could._** (Chart 10-1)
How certain is the speaker when making each of the following remarks? Check the appropriate box.

	100%	About 95%	About 50% or less
1. Charlotte might be home by now.			
2. Phil must be home now.			
3. Mr. Brown's at home now.			
4. Lilly must know the answer to this question.			
5. Fred might have the answer.			
6. Shelley knows the answer.			
7. Those people must have a lot of money.			
8. You may remember me from high school.			
9. We could be related!			
10. Traffic might be heavy on the interstate.			

▶ **Practice 2. Degrees of certainty: _must_ and _may / might / could._** (Chart 10-1)
Circle the letter of the correct word to complete each sentence. In some sentences, both are correct.

1. A: Drive slowly! This is a school zone. Children are crossing the street here.

   B: It ____ be three o'clock. That's the time that school is out.

       a. must   b. might

2. A: Professor McKeon says that we're going to have a very high inflation rate next year.

   B: He ____ be right. He knows more about economics than anyone I know.

       a. must   b. could

3. A: Have you heard anything from Ed? Is he still on safari in Africa?

   B: He ____ be, or he ____ already be on his way home. I'm just not sure.

       a. must . . . must   b. may . . . may

4. A: Is that a famous celebrity over there in the middle of that crowd?

   B: It _____ be. She's signing autographs.

      a. must   b. might

5. A: Isn't Peter Reeves a banker?

   B: Yes. Why don't you talk to him? He _____ be able to help you with your loan.

      a. must   b. may

6. A: Is Margaret's daughter sixteen yet?

   B: She _____ be. I saw her driving a car, and you have to be at least sixteen to get a driver's license.

      a. must   b. might

7. A: Overall, don't you think the possibility of world peace is greater now than ever before?

   B: It _____ be. I don't know. Political relationships can be fragile.

      a. must   b. may

8. A: What's the matter with my son, doctor? Why does he cough and sneeze every day?

   B: He's allergic to something. It _____ dust in the house, or certain foods, or pollen in the air, or something else. It's hard to know, so we'll do some tests to find out.

      a. must be   b. may be

9. A: The speedometer on my car is broken. Do you think I'm driving over the speed limit?

   B: I can't tell. It doesn't seem like it, but you _____.

      a. must be   b. could be

10. A: You've been on the go all day. Aren't you exhausted?

    B: Yes, I _____. I can't remember when I've ever been this worn out.

       a. am   b. must be

11. A: I thought this movie was a comedy!

    B: Me too, but it _____ sad. Look at the people leaving the theater. A lot of them are crying.

       a. might be   b. must be

12. A: How old do you think Roger is?

    B: I just saw his driver's license. He _____ 33.

       a. could be   b. is

▶ **Practice 3. Degrees of certainty: present time negative.** (Chart 10-2)
Complete the sentences with the correct phrase from the list. Write the letter of the phrase.

    a. can't be him   d. may not speak
    b. can't be true   e. must not get
    c. may not be   f. must not like

1. A: I can't hear the singers! That man sitting behind us is snoring in his sleep!

   B: I hear him! He _____ opera.

2. A: Look! Isn't that our history professor over there? In the yellow sweater!

   B: No, that _____. He's in Tokyo this week, giving a presentation.

3. A: This coffee doesn't taste very good. It's supposed to be 100 percent Arabica.

   B: It _____ 100 percent Arabica. Maybe they mixed it with something else. Maybe it's a blend.

4. A: Who is that woman standing alone over there? She isn't talking to anyone.

   B: Well, she _____ any English. Or maybe she's very shy. Anyway, let's go over and try to talk to her.

5. A: Jane has been accepted at Harvard, I heard.

   B: No way! That _____. She isn't even a good student.

6. A: Did you see the new pickup truck that Mario's driving?

   B: I sure did. It's very big. It _____ good gas mileage.

▶ **Practice 4. Degrees of certainty: past time.** (Chart 10-3)
Which sentence describes the given sentences? Circle the correct letter.

1. The little boy is crying. His knees are scraped and bleeding.
   a. He may have fallen down.
   b. He must have fallen down.

2. Someone called, but I don't know who it was. Maybe it was Alice, but I'm not sure.
   a. It may have been Alice.
   b. It must have been Alice.

3. Nobody's answering the phone at Juan's apartment. I guess he has already left for the airport. He always likes to get to the airport early, you know.
   a. He might have already left for the airport.
   b. He must have already left for the airport.

4. I've lost track of my old friend Lola from high school. Maybe she moved away. Maybe she got married and has a different last name.
   a. She could have moved away.
   b. She must have moved away.

5. Irv looks unhappy today. Maybe his boss criticized him. Maybe he had an argument with his girlfriend. Maybe he lost a lot of money in the stock market.
   a. Irv might have had an argument with his girlfriend.
   b. Irv must have had an argument with his girlfriend.

6. I told Charles — only Charles — about my secret engagement, but now everyone is congratulating me! It's clear that Charles can't keep a secret.
   a. Charles may have told everyone.
   b. Charles must have told everyone.

► **Practice 5. Degrees of certainty: past time negative.** (Chart 10-3)
Write the past negative of an appropriate modal and the verb in parentheses.

1. ANN: I've called Howard ten times, I'm sure. He doesn't answer his cell phone.

   SAM: He (*remember*) _____ you were going to call him.
   He's a little forgetful, you know. I'll bet he forgot to turn his phone on.

2. LAWYER: Mr. Jones, where were you on the night of June 24th?

   MR. JONES: I was at home. I was at home all night.

   LAWYER: You (*be*) _____ at home on that night, Mr.
   Jones. Four witnesses saw you at the victim's apartment.

3. JIM: Look! There are lights on in the Thompsons' house. Didn't they go away on vacation?

   ANN: They (*leave*) _____ yet. Or maybe they left the
   automatic timer on to deter burglars.

4. BOB: Hey, you guys! You are not supposed to ride your bikes on the sidewalk! You could
   crash into someone!

   SUE: They (*hear*) _____ you, Bob. Look! They just kept
   going.

5. Scientists are not sure why the Mayan civilization collapsed. The Mayans (*have*)
   _____ enough to eat, or perhaps their enemies became too
   strong for them.

6. After his voyage on the *Kon Tiki*, Thor Heyerdahl set forth the theory that modern Polynesians
   descended from ancient South Americans. However, later scientists believe this (*happen*)
   _____. They believe it was impossible because of recent
   DNA evidence to the contrary.

► **Practice 6. Degrees of certainty: present and past time.** (Charts 10-1 → 10-3)
Complete the dialogues with ***must*** and the verb in parentheses. Use the correct present or past
form. Use ***not*** if necessary.

1. A: You got here in twenty minutes! You (*drive*) _____ really fast.
   Normally it's a forty-minute drive.

   B: No faster than usual.

2. A: Sally gave a speech at her graduation. I think I saw tears in her parents' eyes.

   B: Oh, that is touching. They (*be*) _____ very proud of her.

3. A: That's strange. Oscar didn't come to the meeting. He never misses a meeting.

   B: He (*know*) _____ about it. He was out of town all last week, and probably no one told him.

4. A: How old do you think our teacher is?

   B: Well, she was a couple of years ahead of my father in college, so she (*be*) _____ _____ around 55 now.

5. A: Uh-oh! I can't find my credit card.

   B: You (*leave*) _____ it at the cash register at the grocery store.

6. A: Have you seen Clark? I can't find him anywhere.

   B: He was feeling terrible. He (*go*) _____ home a while ago.

7. A: Look! Do you see that big bird on top of the tree?

   B: What big bird?

   A: You can't see that? You (*need*) _____ stronger glasses.

8. A: What happened to your knee?

   B: I twisted it very badly in the tennis match.

   A: Oh! That (*hurt*) _____ a lot!

▶ **Practice 7. *Must have* vs. *had to*.** (Charts 9-5 and 10-3)
Circle the letter of the correct response.

1. ANN: Why didn't you come to the party?
   BOB: a. I had to study.   b. I must have studied.

2. SAM: Where's Sally? She's still not here?
   DAN: a. She must have overslept.   b. She had to oversleep.

3. IRA: Thomas missed an important meeting this morning.
   JAN: I just spoke with him and he's very sick. He told me he . . .
          a. had to go to the doctor's.   b. must have gone to the doctor's.

4. BUD: We're out of coffee again.
   TOM: a. Jane must have forgotten to   b. Jane had to forget to get
             get some.   some.

5. PAT: How were you able to stay awake during that long, boring lecture?
   ONA: It was difficult!
          a. I must have drunk a lot of coffee! b. I had to drink a lot of coffee!

6. LIL: I can't sleep again!
   MAX: a. You must have drunk too   b. You had to drink too
             much coffee today.   much coffee today.

► **Practice 8. Degrees of certainty: future time.** (Chart 10-4)
Complete the sentences in Column A with a phrase from Column B.

Column A

1. Keiko has always loved animals. She's in veterinary school now. She should _____.
2. Most apple trees bear fruit about five years after planting. Our apple tree is four years old. It should _____ next year.
3. Aunt Ella's plane arrived an hour ago. She's taking a taxi, so she should _____.
4. We could invest this money in a conservative stock fund. If we do that, we should _____ at the end of a year.
5. Ali should _____. He's been studying hard for it all semester.
6. The little horse is growing very fast. He should _____ in a year.
7. Bake the fish in the oven at 350 degrees. It should _____ in about ten minutes.
8. Take this medicine every morning. You should _____ in about two weeks.
9. Luis is taking a heavy course load. He wants to finish school quickly. He should _____.
10. The mechanic is fixing the car now. It should _____.

Column B

a. be here just in time for dinner
b. do very well on the final exam
c. feel better
d. double his weight
e. make a great veterinarian
f. have about 5 percent more
g. be fixed before five o'clock
h. graduate next June
i. be moist and tender
j. give us some apples

► **Practice 9. Degrees of certainty: future time.** (Charts 4-2, 10-1, and 10-4)
Circle the correct word.

1. Today is Monday. Tomorrow (*should / will*) be Tuesday.

2. Hello, Jack. This is Arturo in the tech department. I'm working on your computer now. Good news — I can fix it pretty easily and it (*should / must*) be ready by 5:00 P.M. today.

3. My son's birthday is next month. He (*should / will*) be two years old.

4. It's ten minutes to four. The next bus (*must / should*) arrive at four o'clock. The buses usually stop here every hour on the hour.

5. A: Don't be late! They won't let you into the theater after the play begins.

   B: OK. I (*will / should*) be at the theater at 7:15. I promise.

6. Your husband is resting comfortably, Ms. Robbins. I'm giving him some antibiotics, so the infection (*must / should*) be cleared up by next week.

7. A: Look up there. Is that Mars?

   B: I don't think so. Mars isn't visible right now. It (*should / must*) be Venus. Venus is visible now.

8. A: Who's going to win the tennis tournament?

   B: Well, the Australian is highly rated, and she (*must / should*) win, but the Serbian is good too. Maybe she'll surprise us and win.

► **Practice 10. Progressive forms of modals.** (Chart 10-5)

Complete the sentences. Use the appropriate progressive forms of *must*, *should*, or *may* / *might* / *could* and a verb from the list. You may use a verb more than once.

date	fly	hike	kid	sleep	work

1. A: Call Phil. He's at his office now.

   B: Let's email him instead. He _____ on something important at the moment. Or maybe he's with a client.

2. A: When will Betty be back from Italy?

   B: Tonight. She _____ over the Atlantic at this very moment.

3. A: Helga must know the answer to this problem. Shall we call her?

   B: Not now. It's 11:00 P.M. She _____.

4. A: Listen, I just heard this. Mr. Milner isn't going to be our teacher anymore. He has joined the navy.

   B: You _____! That can't be true. Who told you that?

5. A: Sara told me that she had won the lottery, and so she invited us all to dinner at Henri's French restaurant.

   B: Oh, she _____ when she said that. She never plays the lottery!

6. A: What do you think Ann's doing now on her vacation?

   B: Oh, she _____ in the mountains. Or maybe she's relaxing at the pool.

7. A: I was hoping to go out with John, but I heard he's dating Julia.

   B: Well, he (*not*) _____ Julia anymore. I think that they may have broken up.

► **Practice 11. Modals and modal phrases.** (Charts 10-1 → 10-5)
Circle the letter of the correct completion.

1. A: Where's Angie? Didn't she come back after lunch?

   B: I'm not sure where she is. But she _____ the presentation that Human Resources is giving right now.

       a. is attending   b. could attend   c. could be attending

2. A: You're taking Spanish at 8:00 A.M. every day? Why did you choose such an early class?

   B: Because Ms. Cardenas is the teacher. She _____ excellent. I've been in the class for a month now, and I don't mind the early hour.

       a. should be   b. must be   c. is

3. A: The meteorologists predicted five major hurricanes for this hurricane season.

   B: They _____ wrong, you know. Sometimes they make mistakes.

       a. must be   b. might be   c. are

4. A: Is this chicken in the refrigerator still good?

   B: I don't think so. It's been in there for over a month! It _____ spoiled by now.

       a. may be   b. must be   c. could be

5. A: Can you tell me if Flight 86 is on time?

   B: It is on time, sir. It _____ at Gate B21 in about five minutes.

       a. might arrive   b. might be arriving   c. should be arriving

6. A: Did you know that Mike got a scholarship to State School of Engineering?

   B: Yes, I know that! I was the first one he told about it. He _____ very happy.

       a. might be   b. must be   c. is

7. A: Did you know that Li received a scholarship to the City School of Music?

   B: No, I didn't. That's great news! He _____ very happy.

       a. might be   b. must be   c. is

8. A: Who's going to win the election?

   B: It's a close call. The senator _____ with all his experience, but the opposition candidate is stronger than anyone expected.

       a. must win   b. must be winning   c. should win

9. A: Where's Harold? He's supposed to be at this meeting. Didn't Jim tell him about it?

   B: Jim _____ to tell him.

       a. must forget   b. must have forgotten   c. should have forgotten

10. A: This soup has an interesting flavor, but there's too much salt in it.

    B: Yes, it is too salty. I _____ so much salt in it.

        a. must not have put   b. shouldn't have put   c. may not have put

► **Practice 12. Review of modals.** (Charts 10-1 → 10-5)
Write modal sentences for the situations.

1. The plane is late, and we didn't call the airport.

    a. I expect it will arrive soon. _____It should arrive soon._____

    b. Maybe it took off late. _____It may / might / could have taken off late._____

    c. It was a good idea to call the airport, but we didn't. _We should have called the airport._

2. There's a package in the mail.

    a. Maybe it's for me. _____

    b. I'm sure it's for me. _____

    c. It's impossible that it's for me. _____

3. Tom didn't respond to my email.

    a. I expected him to respond. _____

    b. Maybe he didn't get it. _____

    c. I'm pretty sure he didn't get it. _____

    d. His email isn't working. It was impossible for him to get it. _____
    _____

4. There's water all over the kitchen floor.

    a. Perhaps the dishwasher is leaking. _____

    b. The dishwasher is new. It's impossible that it's the dishwasher. _____

    c. I'm pretty sure a pipe is broken. _____

    d. It's a good idea for you to call a plumber. _____

    e. It isn't necessary for us to call a plumber. _____

► **Practice 13. Ability: *can* and *could*.** (Chart 10-6)
Complete the sentences with *can*, *can't*, *could*, or *couldn't*.

1. Fish _____ talk.

2. My uncle was a wonderful craftsman. He made beautiful things out of wood. But he
    _____ read or write because he never went to school.

3. An illiterate person is someone who _____ neither read nor write.

4. I _____ get to sleep last night because it was too hot in my room.

5. Why _____ all the nations of the world just get along in peace? Why are there
    always wars somewhere on earth?

6. When I was younger, I _____ stay up past midnight and get up at dawn feeling
    refreshed and ready to go. I _____ do that any longer now that I'm middle-
    aged.

▶ **Practice 14. Repeated action in the past.** (Chart 10-7)
Complete the sentences with *would* and a verb from the list. Use the words in parentheses.

bring	fall	sleep	tell	wipe
come	listen	stay	throw	yell

1. I'll always remember Miss Emerson, my fifth-grade teacher. Sometimes a student
   _____ asleep in her class. Whenever that happened, Miss Emerson
   _____ a piece of chalk at the student!

2. My father never liked to talk on the phone. Whenever it rang, he *(always)* _____
   _____, "I'm not here!" Usually, he was only joking and _____
   to the phone when it was for him.

3. I have fond childhood memories of my Aunt Betsy. Whenever she came to visit, she
   (always) _____ me a little present.

4. Some people have strange habits. For example, my Uncle Oscar, who lived with us when I was
   a child, *(always)* _____ his plate with his napkin whenever he sat down to
   a meal.

5. When I was in college, I acquired some bad habits. I didn't study until the night before a test,
   and then I _____ up all night studying. Then the next day after the test, I
   _____ all afternoon.

6. I'll never forget the wonderful evenings I spent with my grandparents when I was a child. My
   grandmother _____ stories of her childhood seventy years ago, and we
   _____ intently and question her for every detail.

▶ **Practice 15. Expressing preference: *would rather.*** (Chart 10-8)
Complete the sentences with a form of *would rather* and a verb from the list. Use the words in
parentheses.

eat	go	have	sail	say	study

1. I know you want to know, but I *(not)* _____ anything more
   about this topic. I told Marge that I'd keep it a secret.

2. Last night, I _____ home right after dinner at the
   restaurant, but my friends insisted on going back to John's apartment to listen to some music
   and talk.

3. I _____ history and literature in college than study
   business as I did. I majored in business, and now that's all I know. I might never again have
   the opportunity to learn about history and literature.

4. If you insist, we'll go to the pizza place after the movie, but I *(not)* _____
_____ pizza again. I'm tired of it.

5. Do you think that young people _____ a choice about whom to
marry, or do you think that they prefer their parents to choose a mate for them?

6. I like my work a lot, but my favorite thing is sailing. I love sailing. At this moment, even
though I have just been promoted to vice-president of my company, I
_____ right now instead of sitting here in my office.

▶ **Practice 16. Combining modals with phrasal modals.** (Chart 10-9)
Complete each sentence with the given words in its list. Write the words in their correct order in
the sentences.

1. to \ get \ have

   You _____ a passport if you are going to travel in other countries.

2. be \ should \ to \ able \ complete

   Everyone _____ this form easily.

3. have \ to \ won't \ stand

   People _____ in the line for a long time. The line is
   moving quickly.

4. you \ be \ able \ leave \ to \ will

   When _____ here?

5. not \ able \ to \ graduate \ to \ going \ am \ be

   I _____ with my class. I lost a complete
   semester when I was sick.

6. been \ must \ to \ get \ have \ not \ able

   Mike and Helen haven't arrived yet. They were going to try to get on an earlier flight. They
   _____ on the earlier flight.

Chapter **11**
The Passive

▶ **Practice 1. Forming the passive.** (Charts 11-1 and 11-2)
Change the active to the passive by writing the correct form of **be**. Use the same tense for **be** in the passive sentence that is used in the active sentence.

Example: Mrs. Bell answered my question. My question ___was___ **answered** by Mrs. Bell.

1. *simple present:*

   Authors write books. .... Books _____ **written** by authors.

2. *present progressive:*

   Mr. Brown is writing that book. .... That book _____ **written** by Mr. Brown.

3. *present perfect:*

   Ms. Lee has written the report. .... The report _____ **written** by Ms. Lee.

4. *simple past:*

   Bob wrote that letter. .... That letter _____ **written** by Bob.

5. *past progressive:*

   A student was writing the report. ..... The report _____ **written** by a student.

6. *past perfect:*

   Lucy had written a memo. .... A memo _____ **written** by Lucy.

7. *simple future:*

   Your teacher will write a report. .... A report _____ **written** by your teacher.

8. *be going to:*

   Tom is going to write a letter. .... The letter _____ **written** by Tom.

9. *future perfect:*

   Alice will have written the report. ..... The report _____ **written** by Alice.

10. The judges have made a decision. ..... A decision _____ **made** by the judges.

11. Several people saw the accident. ... The accident _____ **seen** by several people.

12. Ann is sending the letters. .... The letters _____ **sent** by Ann.

13. Fred will plan the party. .... The party _____ **planned** by Fred.

14. The medicine had cured my illness. .. My illness _____ **cured** by the medicine.

15. The cat will have caught the mouse. ..The mouse _____ **caught** by the cat.

16. Engineers design bridges. .... Bridges _____ **designed** by engineers.

17. The city is going to build a bridge. ...... A bridge _____ **built** by the city.

18. A guard was protecting the jewels. .... The jewels _____ **protected** by a guard.

▶ **Practice 2. Active vs. passive.** (Charts 11-1 and 11-2)

Underline the subject of each sentence. Circle the complete verb. Then identify the sentences as active (A) or passive (P).

1. _A_ <u>Henry</u> ⟨visited⟩ a national park.

2. _P_ <u>The park</u> ⟨was visited⟩ by over 10,000 people last month.

3. _____ Olga was reading the comics.

4. _____ Philippe has read all of Tolstoy's novels.

5. _____ *Bambi* has been read by children all over the world.

6. _____ Whales swim in the ocean.

7. _____ Whales were hunted by fishermen until recently.

8. _____ The answer won't be known for several months.

9. _____ I know the answer.

10. _____ Two new houses were built on our street.

11. _____ A famous architect designed the new bank on First Street.

12. _____ Television was invented before I was born.

13. _____ The World Cup is seen on television all over the world.

14. _____ Television has expanded the knowledge of people everywhere.

▶ **Practice 3. Forming the passive.** (Chart 11-2)

Complete the sentences. Change the verbs in *italics* from active to passive.

1. Sue *writes* the book. → The book ___is written___ by Sue.

2. Sue *is writing* the book. → The book _____ by Sue.

3. Sue *has written* the book. → The book _____ by Sue.

4. Sue *wrote* the book. → The book _____ by Sue.

5. Sue *was writing* the book. → The book _____ by Sue.

6. Sue *had written* the book. → The book _____ by Sue.

7. Sue *will write* the book. → The book _____ by Sue.

8. Sue *is going to write* the book. → The book _____ by Sue.

9. Sue *will have written* the book. → The book _____ by Sue.

10. *Did* Sue *write* the book? → _____ the book _____ by Sue?

11. *Will* Sue *write* the book? → _____ the book _____ by Sue?

12. *Has* Sue *written* the book? → _____ the book _____ by Sue?

▶ **Practice 4. Forming the passive.** (Chart 11-2)

Part I. Complete the sentences. Change the verbs from active to passive.

1. Picasso painted that picture.

   That picture ___was painted by Picasso___.

2. Experienced pilots fly these planes.

   These planes _____.

3. A famous singer is going to sing the national anthem.

    The national anthem _____ .

4. Yale University has accepted my cousin.

    My cousin _____ .

5. The doctor will examine the patient.

    The patient _____ .

6. The defense attorney is questioning a witness.

    A witness _____ .

7. A dog bit our mail carrier.

    Our mail carrier _____ .

8. The mother bird was feeding the baby bird.

    The baby bird _____ .

9. His words won't persuade me.

    I _____ .

10. I didn't paint this picture. Did Laura paint it?

    The picture _____ . Was it _____ ?

11. Does Mrs. Crane own this restaurant? I know that her father doesn't own it anymore.

    Is this restaurant _____ ?

    I know that it _____ .

12. I didn't sign these papers. Someone else signed my name.

    These papers _____ .

    My name _____ .

Part II. Change each sentence to the active voice. The subject of the new sentence is given. Keep the same tense of the verb.

13. My teeth are going to be cleaned by the dental assistant.

    The dental assistant _____ .

14. Was that email sent by Mr. Tyrol?

    _____ Mr. Tyrol _____ ?

15. The Fourth of July isn't celebrated by the British.

    The British _____ .

16. Has your house been sold by the realtor yet?

    _____ the realtor _____ ?

17. The thief hasn't been caught by the police.

    The police _____ .

18. The carpets are being cleaned by the carpet cleaners.

    The carpet cleaners _____ .

► **Practice 5. Active vs. passive.** (Charts 11-1 and 11-2)
In these sentences, some of the verbs are transitive and some are intransitive. <u>Underline</u> the verb in each sentence. Then identify the object of the verb if there is one. If the verb has an object, change the sentence to the passive. If not, write Ø.

	Verb	Object Of Verb	Passive Sentence
1. Al <u>will pay</u> the bill.	*will pay*	*the bill*	*The bill will be paid by Al.*
2. Jane <u>will arrive</u> tomorrow.	*will arrive*	*Ø*	*Ø*
3. The hotel supplies towels.			
4. Accidents happen every day.			
5. Everyone noticed my error.			
6. The train arrived at three.			
7. The news didn't surprise me.			
8. Did the news surprise you?			
9. Do ghosts exist?			
10. Mr. Lee died last year.			
11. An old man told the story.			
12. It hasn't rained lately.			

► **Practice 6. Active vs. passive.** (Charts 11-1 and 11-2)
Complete the sentences. Write the letter of the correct verb.

1. We'll let you know about the job. You _____ by my secretary next week.
   a. will notify   b. will be notified   c. will have notified

2. Last night I _____ to lock my front door.
   a. wasn't remembered   b. didn't remember   c. hadn't been remembered

3. This old wooden chest _____ by my grandfather over 40 years ago.
   a. built   b. had built   c. was built

4. Disneyland is a world-famous amusement park in Southern California. It _____ by millions of people every year.
   a. is visited   b. visited   c. has visited

5. I _____ with people who say space exploration is a waste of money. What do you think?
   a. not agree   b. don't agree   c. am not agree

6. Do you really think that we _____ by creatures from outer space in the near future?
   a. will invade   b. be invaded   c. will be invaded

7. Had you already _____ by this university when you heard about the scholarship offer from the other school?
   a. were accepted   b. accepted   c. been accepted

8. When Alex was only ten, his father _____ .
   a. was died   b. died   c. dead

9. Elephants _____ a long time, sometimes for 70 years.
   a. live   b. were lived   c. have been lived

10. The impact of the earthquake yesterday _____ by people who lived hundreds of kilometers from the epicenter.
    a. felt   b. has felt   c. was felt

11. At one time, the entire world _____ by dinosaurs.
    a. ruled   b. was ruled   c. been ruled

12. Some dinosaurs _____ on their hind legs and were as tall as palm trees.
    a. walked   b. were walked   c. have stood

▶ **Practice 7. Using the passive.** (Chart 11-3)
Circle the letter of the sentence that has the same meaning as the given sentence.

1. In my dream, the monster is being chased.
    a. The monster is chasing someone in my dream.
    b. Someone is chasing the monster in my dream.

2. An airplane was delivered to a cargo facility last week.
    a. The airplane delivered some cargo.
    b. Someone delivered the airplane.

3. Witnesses are going to be asked for information.
    a. Someone will request information from witnesses.
    b. Witnesses will request information from someone.

4. Internet access will be provided free of charge.
    a. The internet will provide access.
    b. Someone will provide internet access.

5. All of the participants have been counted.
    a. Someone has finished counting the participants.
    b. The participants have finished counting.

▶ **Practice 8. Using the passive.** (Chart 11-3)
Complete each passage with the given verbs. Write the correct form of the verb, active or passive.

1. *invent, tell*

   The sandwich _____ by John Montagu, an Englishman with the title of

   the Earl of Sandwich. In about 1762, he is reputed to have been too busy to sit down at a

   regular meal, so he _____ his cook to pack his meat inside some bread in

   order to save him time.

2. *attend, establish, give*

   Al-Azhar University in Cairo, Egypt, is one of the oldest universities in the world. It

   _____ at about the same time as the city of Cairo, in 969 A.D. The

   first lecture _____ in 975 A.D. Students (*still*) _____ the

   university today.

3. *become, kill, know, live, relate, save*

One animal that is famous in the history of the American West is actually a bison, but it _____ by the name of *buffalo*. The American buffalo _____ to a similar animal in Asia, the water buffalo. Buffaloes _____ in parks and flat grasslands. At the end of the nineteenth century, they almost _____ extinct because thousands of them _____ by hunters. Fortunately, they _____ by the efforts of naturalists and the government.

4. *believe, give, like, originate, treat, use, value*

Garlic _____ in Asia over 6,000 years ago, and it spread throughout Europe and Africa. Today, people _____ to use garlic not only for its strong flavor, but because it _____ them physical strength and good health. In ancient times, garlic _____ so highly that it _____ as money. Injuries and illnesses _____ with garlic by the ancient Greeks. Even today, garlic _____ to be effective by some people in lowering cholesterol and in treating other digestive disorders.

▶ **Practice 9. Active vs. passive.** (Charts 11-1 → 11-3)
Write complete sentences with the given words. Use the simple past.

1. the chefs \ prepare \ the food _____.
2. the food \ prepare \ yesterday _____.
3. the rain \ stop _____.
4. a rainbow \ appear \ in the sky _____.
5. the documents \ send \ to you \ yesterday _____.
6. my lawyer \ send \ the documents to me _____.
7. the winner of the election \ announce \ on TV _____.
8. I \ not agree \ with you about this _____.
9. what \ happen \ yesterday _____?
10. something wonderful \ happen \ to me _____.
11. the trees \ die \ of a disease _____.
12. the trees \ kill \ by a disease _____.
13. a disease \ kill \ the trees _____.
14. I \ accept \ at the University of Chicago _____.
15. I \ recommend \ for a scholarship _____.

▶ **Practice 10. The passive form of modals and phrasal modals.** (Chart 11-4)
Circle the correct verb.

1. A language (*can't be* / *couldn't have been*) learned only by reading about it. You have to practice speaking it.

2. These jeans (*should be washed* / *should have been washed*) before you wear them. The material will be softer and more comfortable.

3. This shirt was washed in hot water, and it shrank. It (*should have washed* / *should have been washed*) in cold water.

4. The road is still being fixed. It is supposed (*to be finished* / *to finish*) by next month, but I'm not so sure it will be.

5. There's an old house for sale on Route 411. They say that George Washington visited it, so it (*must be built* / *must have been built*) in the 1700s.

6. Taxes (*have to pay* / *have to be paid*) on or before April 15th. Payments (*must be sent* / *must have been sent*) to the government on or before April 15th.

7. The senator has made a good point, but I disagree. May I (*permit* / *be permitted*) to speak now?

8. Our kitchen is old and dark. We're going to renovate it. It (*ought to be painted* / *ought to paint*) a light shade of green or white to make it look brighter.

▶ **Practice 11. The passive form of modals and phrasal modals.** (Chart 11-4)
Complete the sentences with the given words. Write the appropriate form, active or passive.

1. The decision (*should + make*) _____ as soon as possible.

2. We (*should + make*) _____ our decision right now, without further discussion.

3. A decision (*should + make*) _____ before now.

4. They say that Einstein (*couldn't + talk*) _____ until he was four years old.

5. I (*couldn't + talk*) _____ to Mr. Forth this morning even if I had wanted to. It would have been impossible. He is in Europe on business all this week.

6. All vehicles (*must + register*) _____ with the Department of Motor Vehicles of this state.

7. You (*must + register*) _____ your car with the Department of Motor Vehicles.

8. This bill (*have to + pay*) _____ by tomorrow. I (*had better not + send*) _____ a check by mail. It won't get there on time.

9. A: Who called?
   B: I don't know who it was. They hung up. It (*must + be*) _____ a wrong number.

10. A: Was Yuri at the party? Did you see him?

    B: I didn't see him, but he (*may + be*) _____ there. There was a

    huge crowd, and I didn't get to talk to many people.

▶ **Practice 12. Non-progressive passive.** (Chart 11-5)
Complete the sentences in Column A with a verb from Column B.

Column A

1. Uh-oh. I forgot my key, and the door is ____.
2. The museum isn't open today. It's ____.
3. Finally! The report I've been writing for a week is ____.
4. The TV doesn't work. It's ____.
5. Do you know where we are? I think we're ____.
6. Let's go to another restaurant. This one is too ____.
7. What happened to the cookies? They're all ____.
8. It's freezing in this room! I guess the heat isn't ____.

Column B

a. finished
b. lost
c. crowded
d. turned on
e. closed
f. gone
g. locked
h. broken

▶ **Practice 13. Non-progressive passive.** (Charts 11-5 and 11-6)
Complete each sentence with a verb from the list. Use the present tense, active or passive. Add a preposition if necessary.

bore	do	locate	marry
compose	interest	make	scare
depend			

1. Ismael _____ the history of languages. He is studying linguistics.

2. We may have a picnic on Saturday. It _____ the weather.

3. Sam _____ Salma. They have been married for 24 years.

4. Our son _____ the dark, so we keep a night light on in his room.

5. Golf _____ me. There isn't any action, and it is too slow.

6. These jeans _____ cotton. They're 100 percent organic cotton.

7. Our class is diverse. It _____ people from nine countries.

8. The Hague _____ the Netherlands.

9. We _____ this exercise now.

▶ **Practice 14. Common non-progressive passive verbs + prepositions.**
    (Chart 11-6)
Circle the correct preposition.

1. Professor Wills is deeply involved (*by / in*) campus politics.

2. Who is qualified (*for / in*) this job?

3. Are you worried (*for / about*) your grade in this class?

4. A lot of people are interested (*in / about*) the astronauts in space.

5. Your last name is Mason? Are you related (*with / to*) Tony Mason?

6. Ann doesn't travel on planes. She's terrified (*from / of*) flying.

7. Mrs. Redmond? No, I'm not acquainted *(to / with)* her.

8. This is a wonderful book. I'll give it to you when I'm finished *(with / for)* it.

9. I'm bored *(in / with)* this movie. Can we leave?

10. Are you satisfied *(for / with)* our service? Let us know by email.

11. We are tired *(from / of)* paying rent, so we are going to buy an apartment.

12. Do you recycle? Are you committed *(to / by)* helping the environment?

▶ **Practice 15. Passive vs. active.** (Charts 11-1 → 11-6)
Correct the errors. One item doesn't need to be changed.

1. The plane was arrived very late.

2. Four people injured in the accident.

3. Bella is married with José.

4. People are worried with global warming.

5. Astronomers are interesting in several new meteors.

6. We were surprise by Harold's announcement.

7. Spanish is spoken by people in Mexico.

8. This road is not the right one. We lost.

9. Pat should try that new medicine. He might helped.

10. Lunch is been served in the cafeteria right now.

11. Something unusual was happened yesterday.

12. Will be fixed the refrigerator today?

13. Nobody knows how old my grandfather was when he died last year, but he must been over 100

    years old. He remembers the flu epidemic of 1918.

▶ **Practice 16. The passive with *get*.** (Chart 11-7)
Complete the sentences with the correct word from the list.

crowded	elected	hungry	invited	scared
dressed	fat	hurt	lost	stopped

1. At first, we were the only people in the restaurant, but it quickly got _____.

2. We can eat soon if you're getting _____.

3. Stan followed the map closely and didn't get _____.

4. When I heard those strange sounds last night, I got _____.

5. Wake up and get _____! We have to leave in five minutes.

6. Be careful on these old steps. You could fall and get _____.

7. Lola is disappointed because she didn't get _____ to the party.

8. If children don't get any exercise, they might get _____.

9. Don't drive so fast! You could get _____ for speeding!

10. Dr. Sousa is going to get _____ to the city government.

▶ **Practice 17. Participial adjectives.** (Chart 11-8)
Circle the correct word.

1. When their team scored the winning point, the fans were (*exciting* / *excited*).

2. The football game was very (*exciting* / *excited*).

3. The news I just heard was (*shocking* / *shocked*).

4. Everyone was (*shocking* / *shocked*) by the news.

5. Our forty-mile bike ride was (*exhausting* / *exhausted*). I was (*exhausting* / *exhausted*) at the end of it.

6. This work is so (*boring* / *bored*). I'm very (*boring* / *bored*) with my work.

7. I'm really (*confusing* / *confused*). Professor Eng's explanation was (*confusing* / *confused*).

8. The ruins of the old city are very (*interesting* / *interested*).

9. Archeologists are (*interesting* / *interested*) in the ruins of the old city.

10. The experience of climbing Mount Kilimanjaro was (*thrilling* / *thrilled*). The climber's family was (*thrilling* / *thrilled*) when she returned safely.

▶ **Practice 18. Participial adjectives.** (Chart 11-8)
Write one of the given words to complete each sentence.

1. *fascinating, fascinated*

    a. Your lecture was _____.

    b. I was _____ by your lecture.

2. *exhausting, exhausted*

    a. Listening to Mrs. Wilson complain is _____.

    b. I am _____ by Mrs. Wilson's complaints.

3. *disappointing, disappointed*

    a. Your parents are _____ in your behavior.

    b. Your behavior is _____.

▶ **Practice 19. Participial adjectives.** (Chart 11-8)
Circle the letters of all the correct sentences in each group.

1. a. I am confused by these instructions.

    b. I am confusing by these instructions.

    c. These instructions are confused me.

    d. These instructions confuse me.

2. a. The history of civilization interests Professor Davis.

    b. The history of civilization is interesting to Professor Davis.

    c. The history of civilization is interested to Professor Davis.

    d. Professor Davis is interesting in the history of civilization.

3. a. I was embarrassing by all the attention.

    b. I was embarrassed by all the attention.

    c. All the attention embarrassed me.

    d. All the attention was embarrassed to me.

4. a. This is shocked news about your family.

    b. This is shocking news about your family.

    c. I was shocking by the news about your family.

    d. I was shocked by the news about your family.

5. a. Fred is boring by spectator sports.

    b. Spectator sports are boring to Fred.

    c. Fred is bored by spectator sports.

    d. Spectator sports are bored to Fred.

▶ **Practice 20. Participial adjectives.** (Chart 11-8)
Complete each sentence with the present or past participle of the given verbs.

1. There was an emergency on campus. We were not allowed to leave the buildings. The
    situation was very (*frustrate*) _____ .

2. As a little boy, Tom's jokes were cute, but as a (*grow*) _____ man, his jokes
    irritate people. Both Tom and his jokes are (*irritate*) _____ .

3. The invention of the (*wash*) _____ machine was a great help to households
    everywhere.

4. The pencil is a simple (*write*) _____ instrument.

5. The history of these people is not a (*write*) _____ one. The only history is oral.

6. This weather is (*depress*) _____ . I've been (*depress*) _____
    all day.

7. You're going to laugh a lot when you see that movie. The critics say that it is the most
    (*entertain*) _____ movie of the year.

8. Here's a well-(*know*) _____ saying: "Don't cry over (*spill*) _____
    milk." It means that you shouldn't worry about mistakes that you've made in the past.

9. Here's a (*comfort*) _____ saying: "(*Bark*) _____ dogs
    seldom bite." It means that things that seem dangerous often turn out not to be dangerous.

10. Here's an (*inspire*) _____ saying: "(*Unite*) _____ we stand,
    (*divide*) _____ we fall." It means that we must stand together against an enemy
    in order to survive.

Chapter 12
Noun Clauses

▶ **Practice 1. Introduction.** (Chart 12-1)
<u>Underline</u> the noun clauses. Some sentences don't have one.

1. I couldn't hear what he said.
2. What did he say?
3. I don't know what happened.
4. Why are you calling me?
5. I wonder why Dora is calling me.
6. Do you know who that man is?
7. Do you know where Hank lives?
8. What are they doing?
9. What they are doing is wrong.
10. What should I say?
11. I don't know what I should say.
12. Where will she live?

▶ **Practice 2. Questions and noun clauses beginning with a question word.**
(Chart 12-2)
Complete the sentences with the given words.

1. they \ do \ want

   What _____?

2. want \ they \ what

   I don't know _____.

3. Stacy \ live \ does

   Where _____?

4. lives \ where \ Stacy

   Can you tell me _____?

5. what \ Carl \ likes

   Do you know _____?

6. Carl \ does \ like

   What _____?

7. is \ Lina \ going

   Where _____?

8. is \ where \ going \ Lina

   I wonder _____.

► **Practice 3. Questions and noun clauses beginning with a question word.**
(Chart 12-2)

Add punctuation and capitalization. <u>Underline</u> the noun clause if there is one.

1. Where does Lee live does he live downtown

   Where does Lee live**?** **D**oes he live downtown**?**

2. I don't know where he lives

   I don't know <u>where he lives</u>.

3. What does Sandra want do you know

4. Do you know what Sandra wants

5. What Yoko knows is important to us

6. We talked about what Yoko knows

7. What do you think did you tell your professor what you think

8. My professor knows what I think

9. Where is the bus stop do you know where the bus stop is

10. What did he report what he reported is important

► **Practice 4. Noun clauses beginning with a question word.** (Chart 12-2)
Change each question in parentheses to a noun clause.

1. (*How far is it?*) I don't know _____how far it is_____.

2. (*What is that on the table?*) I don't know _____.

3. (*How much did it cost?*) Ask her _____.

4. (*What did he say?*) _____ is very interesting.

5. (*When are they leaving?*) Do you know _____?

6. (*Which road should we take?*) Can you tell us _____?

7. (*Who called?*) Please tell me _____.

8. (*What's happening?*) Do you know _____?

9. (*Why do they work at night?*) Nobody knows _____.

10. (*What are they trying to do?*) _____ is difficult.

11. (*What kind of insects are these?*) I don't know _____.

12. (*Whose keys are these?*) I wonder _____.

► **Practice 5. Questions and noun clauses beginning with a question word.**
(Charts 12-1 and 12-2; Appendix Charts B-1 and B-2)

Make a question from the given sentence. The words in parentheses should be the answer to the question you make. Use a question word (**who, what, how,** etc.). Then change the question to a noun clause.

1. That man is (*Mr. Robertson*).

   QUESTION: _____Who is that man?_____

   NOUN CLAUSE: I want to know _____who that man is._____

2. George lives (*in Los Angeles*).

   QUESTION: _____

   NOUN CLAUSE: I want to know _____

3. Ann bought (*a new dictionary*).

   QUESTION: _____

   NOUN CLAUSE: Do you know _____

4. It is (*350 miles*) to Denver from here.

   QUESTION: _____

   NOUN CLAUSE: I need to know _____

5. Jack was late for class (*because he missed the bus*).

   QUESTION: _____

   NOUN CLAUSE: The teacher wants to know _____

6. That is (*Ann's*) pen.

   QUESTION: _____

   NOUN CLAUSE: Tom wants to know _____

7. Alex saw (*Ms. Frost*) at the meeting.

   QUESTION: _____

   NOUN CLAUSE: I don't know _____

8. (*Jack*) saw Ms. Frost at the meeting.

   QUESTION: _____

   NOUN CLAUSE: Do you know _____

9. Alice likes (*this*) book best, (*not that one*).

   QUESTION: _____

   NOUN CLAUSE: I want to know _____

10. The plane is supposed to land (*at 7:14 P.M.*).

   QUESTION: _____

   NOUN CLAUSE: Could you tell me _____

▶ **Practice 6. Noun clauses beginning with a question word.** (Chart 12-2)
Write the letter of the phrase in the list to complete each conversation.

   a. what did he say
   b. what he said
   c. where are you going
   d. where you are going

   e. which bus should we take to the stadium
   f. which bus we should take to the stadium
   g. why did she do that
   h. why she did that

1. A: What did the professor just say?

   B: I don't know _____. I couldn't understand anything.

2. A: Hey, Kim, _____?

   B: Downtown. We're going to the new show at the art museum.

3. A: Hello, there! You look lost. Can I help you?

   B: Yes, ____? We want to go to the football stadium in Fairfield.

4. A: Turn the TV up, please. I can't hear the weather reporter. Linda, ____ ?

   B: He said that there will be a lot of rain tomorrow.

5. A: Hello! Can you please tell us ____?

   B: Sorry, I don't know. I'm a stranger here myself.

6. A: I told you that we are going to Bermuda for a vacation, didn't I?

   B: Well, you told us about the vacation, but you didn't say ____.

7. A: Ms. Holsum just quit her job at the university.

   B: Oh, ____? That was such a good job!

   A: Nobody knows ____. It's a mystery.

▶ **Practice 7. Noun clauses beginning with *whether* or *if.*** (Chart 12-3)
Circle the letters of all the correct completions for each sentence.

1. We don't know ____.
   - a. whether it will snow
   - b. whether or not it will snow
   - c. whether it will snow or not
   - d. if it will snow
   - e. if or not it will snow
   - f. if it will snow or not

2. ____ doesn't matter to me.
   - a. Whether or not it snows
   - b. Whether it snows or not
   - c. Whether does it snow or not
   - d. If or not it snows
   - e. If snows or not
   - f. If does it snow

3. I wonder ____.
   - a. whether or not does she know
   - b. whether she knows or not
   - c. whether does she know
   - d. if does she know
   - e. if she knows or not
   - f. if or not she does know

▶ **Practice 8. Review.** (Charts 12-2 and 12-3)
Complete the questions using *Do you know.*

Do you know . . .

1. How much does this book cost? _____

2. When is Flight 62 expected? _____

3. Where is the nearest phone? _____

4. Is this word spelled correctly? _____

5. What time is it? _____

6. Is this information correct? _____

7. How much does it cost to fly from Toronto to London? _____

8. Where is the bus station? _____

9. Whose pen is this? _____

10. Does this bus go downtown? _____

▶ **Practice 9. Question words followed by infinitives.** (Chart 12-4)
Complete the sentences in Column A with a phrase from Column B.

Column A

1. Where can I find fresh fish?
   I don't know __*g*__ .
2. Which person will be a better president?
   I don't know ____ .
3. Who can I get to repair the TV?
   I don't know ____ .
4. Should I get another job?
   I don't know ____ .
5. What's good to eat here?
   I don't know ____ .
6. How far is the airport from here?
   I don't know ____ .
7. What should it cost?
   I don't know ____ .
8. Do we need a lot of sandwiches for the party?
   I don't know ____ .

Column B

a. who to vote for
b. how far the airport is from here
c. whether to look for one
d. how much to spend
e. how to fix it
f. what to order
✓g. where to buy it
h. how many to prepare

▶ **Practice 10. Noun clauses beginning with *that*.** (Chart 12-5)
Complete the sentences. Choose a word from the list. More than one word may be appropriate.

angry	confident	lucky	relieved
aware	disappointed	proud	worried

1. We are _____ that our son graduated first in his class. We are not surprised — he is an excellent student.

2. I am _____ that the store owner cheated me. That was awful!

3. Our teacher is _____ that all the students did poorly on the test. However, she is encouraging them to do well on the next test.

4. I was not _____ that our boss hired a new assistant. When did this happen?

5. It was _____ that we got off the elevator when we did. Just after we got off, it got stuck between floors, and the other passengers were inside for three hours!

6. Lee always wins the Ping-Pong tournaments at our community center. He is _____ that he will win the one next weekend.

7. We were very _____ that the hurricane was coming our way. But it changed course and went out to sea instead. Now we are _____ that the hurricane didn't hit us.

► **Practice 11. Noun clauses beginning with *that*.** (Chart 12-5)
Rewrite the sentences in *italics* in two ways. Use the words from the original sentence.

1. *Nobody stopped to help Sam on the road. That is surprising.*

   a. It _____*is surprising that*_____ nobody stopped to help Sam on the road.

   b. The fact that _____*nobody stopped to help Sam*_____ on the road

      _____*is surprising*_____ .

2. *People in modern cities are distrustful of each other. That is unfortunate.*

   a. It _____ people in modern cities are distrustful of each other.

   b. That _____

      distrustful of each other _____ .

3. *People in my village always help each other. That is still true.*

   a. It _____

      in my village always help each other.

   b. That _____ always

      _____ each other _____ .

4. *People need each other and need to help each other. That is undeniably true.*

   a. It _____ people need each other and need to help each other.

   b. That _____ and need to help each other

      _____ .

5. *People in cities live in densely populated areas but don't know their neighbors. That seems strange to me.*

   a. It _____ me _____ in

      densely populated areas but don't know their neighbors.

   b. The fact that _____ live in densely populated areas but

      _____ seems strange to me.

► **Practice 12. Quoted speech.** (Chart 12-6)
Add punctuation and capitalization.

1. Millie said   there's an important meeting at three o'clock today

2. There's an important meeting at three o'clock today   she said

3. There is   said Millie   an important meeting at three o'clock today

4. There is an important meeting today   it's about the new rules   said Millie

5. Where is the meeting   Carl asked

6. Robert replied   it's in the conference room

7. How long will it last   asked Ali

8. I don't know how long it will last   replied Millie

9. I'll be a little late   said Robert   I have another meeting until 3:00 P.M. today

10. Who is speaking at the meeting   asked Robert

11. I am not sure who is speaking   said Millie   but you'd better be there   everybody is supposed to be there

▶ **Practice 13. Quoted speech.** (Chart 12-6)
Read this familiar story about the rabbit and the turtle. Punctuate the quoted speech in the numbered sections.

One day a rabbit laughed at a turtle because the turtle was very slow.

(1) You are so slow Mr turtle   said the rabbit   and I am very fast.

(2) I don't know about that   said the turtle   let's have a race   we will run for five miles and see who wins

(3) I agree   said the rabbit

They started off, and the rabbit was so far ahead that he laughed and laughed. He said to himself:

(4) I am so far ahead of the turtle   I am going to take a little nap right here   it is going to take a long time before that turtle can catch up with me

And so, while the rabbit was taking his nap, the turtle came along slowly but steadily. The turtle passed by the sleeping rabbit and won the race.

(5) The turtle looked back at the rabbit and exclaimed   slow but steady wins the race   who's laughing now mr rabbit

▶ **Practice 14. Reported speech.** (Chart 12-7)
Complete the sentences with the correct form of the verb.

1. Tom said, "I am busy."   Tom said that he ____was____ busy.
2. Tom said, "I need some help."   Tom said that he _____ some help.
3. Tom said, "I am having a good time."   Tom said that he _____ a good time.
4. Tom said, "I have finished my work."   Tom said that he _____ his work.
5. Tom said, "I finished it."   Tom said that he _____ it.
6. Tom said, "I will arrive at noon."   Tom said that he _____ at noon.
7. Tom said, "I am going to be there."   Tom said that he _____ there.

8. Tom said, "I can solve that problem."   Tom said that he _____ that problem.

9. Tom said, "I may come early."   Tom said that he _____ early.

10. Tom said, "I might come early."   Tom said that he _____ early.

11. Tom said, "I must leave at eight."   Tom said that he _____ at eight.

12. Tom said, "I have to leave at eight."   Tom said that he _____ at eight.

13. Tom said, "I should go to the library."   Tom said that he _____ to the library.

14. Tom said, "Stay here."   Tom told me _____ here.

▶ **Practice 15. Reported speech.** (Chart 12-7)
Complete the sentences by changing the quoted speech to reported speech. Use formal sequence of tenses as appropriate. Pay attention to whether the reporting verb is past or present.

1. I asked Martha, "Are you planning to enter law school?"

   I asked Martha _____*if / whether she was planning*_____ to enter law school.

2. Ed just asked me, "What time does the movie begin?"

   Ed wants to know _____.

3. Fred asked, "Can we still get tickets for the concert?"

   Fred asked _____ tickets for the concert.

4. Thomas said to us, "How can I help you?"

   Thomas wants to know _____ us.

5. Eva asked, "Can you help me, Mario?"

   Eva asked Mario _____ her.

6. Charles said, "When will the final decision be made?"

   Charles wanted to know _____.

7. Frank asked Carla, "Where have you been all afternoon?"

   Frank asked Carla _____ all afternoon.

8. Jaime just asked, "What is Kim's native language?"

   Jaime wants to know _____.

9. I asked myself, "Am I doing the right thing?"

   I wondered _____ the right thing.

10. George asked me, "What time do I have to be at the lab in the morning?"

    George asked me _____ to be at the lab in the morning.

11. Yuki asked, "Who should I give this message to?"

    Yuki asked me _____ to.

12. Nancy asked, "Why didn't you call me?"

    Nancy wanted to know _____ her.

► **Practice 16. Reported speech.** (Chart 12-7)
Complete the sentences using the information in the conversation. Use past verb forms in the noun clauses if appropriate and possible.

Conversation 1.

"Where are you going, Ann?" I asked.

"I'm on my way to the market," she replied. "Do you want to come with me?"

"I'd like to, but I have to stay home. I have a lot of work to do."

"OK," Ann said. "Is there anything I can pick up for you at the market?"

"How about a few bananas? And some apples if they're fresh?"

"Sure. I'd be happy to."

When I asked Ann where she _____ , she said she _____
                                          1   2
on her way to the market and _____ me to come with her. I said I
                                          3
_____ to, but that I _____ to stay home because I
                  4   5
_____ a lot of work to do. Ann kindly asked me if there _____ anything she
          6   7
_____ pick up for me at the market. I asked her to pick up a few bananas and some
                  8
apples if they _____ fresh. She said she'd be happy to.
                          9

Conversation 2.

"Where are you from?" asked the passenger sitting next to me on the plane.

"Chicago," I said.

"That's nice. I'm from Mapleton. It's a small town in northern Michigan. Have you heard of it?"

"Oh yes, I have," I said. "Michigan is a beautiful state. I've been there on vacation many times."

"Were you in Michigan on vacation this year?"

"No. I went far away from home this year. I went to India," I replied.

"Oh, that's nice. Is it a long drive from Chicago to India?" she asked me. My mouth fell open.
I didn't know how to respond. Some people certainly need to study geography.

The passenger sitting next to me on the plane _____ me where I _____
                                                                      1   2
from. I _____ her I _____ from Chicago. She _____ that she
                  3   4   5
_____ from Mapleton, a small town in northern Michigan. She wondered if I
          6
_____ of it, and I told her that I _____ . I went on to say that I
                  7   8
thought Michigan _____ a beautiful state and explained that I _____
                          9   10
there on vacation many times. She _____ me if I _____ in
                                                11   12
Michigan on vacation this year. I replied that I _____ and _____ her that I
                                                              13   14
_____ far away, to India. Then she asked me if it _____ a long drive
          15   16
from Chicago to India! My mouth fell open. I didn't know how to respond. Some people certainly

need to study geography.

► **Practice 17. Using -ever words.** (Chart 12-8)
Complete each sentence with the correct **-ever** word.

1. As vice-president of international sales, Robert has complete control over his travel schedule.
He can travel _____*whenever*_____ he wants.

2. Robert is free to decide which countries he will visit during his overseas trips. He can travel
_____ he wants.

3. The English professor told us that we could write our papers on _____ subject
we wanted as long as it related to the topics we discussed in class this semester.

4. I understand that the planes aren't flying because of the weather, but you have to come
anyway. Get here _____ you can: take the train, take a bus, or drive. Just get
here fast.

5. There are several appointment times available. You may select _____ one you
prefer.

6. Linda is very amiable and gregarious. She makes friends with _____ she meets.

7. It doesn't matter what class you take to fulfill this requirement. Just take _____
one fits best into your schedule.

8. _____ is the last to leave the room should turn off the lights and lock the door.

9. I know that Norman will succeed. He'll do _____ is required to succeed.

10. My wife and I are going to ride our bicycles across the country. We will ride for six to seven
hours a day, and then we'll stop _____ we happen to be at the end of the day.

Chapter 13
Adjective Clauses

▶ **Practice 1. Adjective clause pronouns used as the subject.** (Chart 13-1)
Underline the adjective clause in each sentence. Draw an arrow to the word it modifies.

1. We are looking for a person who fixes computers.

2. I know a man who lives on a boat.

3. In our office, there is a woman who speaks four languages.

4. There are several people who are bilingual in the office.

5. I work in an office that is in an old building.

6. The building which we work in was built in 1890.

7. Two trees that were over two hundred years old were struck by lightning last night.

8. Two other trees which were nearby were not harmed.

9. The traffic jam was caused by one truck that had broken down.

10. The truck which caused the problem was in the middle of the highway.

▶ **Practice 2. Adjective clause pronouns used as the subject.** (Chart 13-1)
Circle the letter of all the possible completions for each sentence. Do not add any commas or capital letters.

1. I thanked the woman _____ brought back our lost cat.
   a. who   b. that   c. which   d. she

2. The aquarium is looking for new employees _____ know a lot about dolphins.
   a. who   b. that   c. which   d. they

3. What is the TV channel _____ has stories about animals?
   a. who   b. it   c. which   d. that

4. On my flight, there was a weight-lifter _____ didn't fit into the airplane seat.
   a. who   b. that   c. he   d. which

5. None of the houses _____ have protective shutters were damaged in the typhoon.
   a. who   b. that   c. which   d. they

6. I'm transferring to a school _____ has a well-known program in cinematography.
   a. who   b. that   c. which   d. it

► **Practice 3. Adjective clause pronouns as the object of a verb.** (Chart 13-2)
Underline the adjective clause in each sentence. Draw an arrow to the word it modifies.

1. There's the man that I met last night.

2. There's the woman that Sandro is going to marry.

3. All the people whom we invited have accepted the invitation.

4. The book which I just read is going to be made into a movie.

5. I can't figure out how to use the software program that Jason installed.

6. We are still living in the house we built in 1987.

7. What happened to the cake I left on the table?

8. I bought the book my professor wrote.

► **Practice 4. Adjective clause pronouns as the object of a verb.** (Chart 13-2)
Circle the letter of all the possible completions for each sentence.

1. That's the woman _____ the people elected.
   a. who   b. whom   c. that   d. which   e. she   f. Ø

2. The man _____ the police arrested was not the thief.
   a. whom   b. he   c. that   d. which   e. who   f. Ø

3. I'd already seen the movie _____ we rented last night
   a. who   b. it   c. Ø   d. which   e. that   f. whom

4. Ms. McCarthy is a teacher _____ everyone loves.
   a. who   b. whom   c. Ø   d. which   e. that   f. her

5. Many of the people _____ we met on our vacation were very friendly.
   a. who   b. which   c. that   d. whom   e. Ø   f. they

6. A man _____ I know is going to be interviewed on a morning TV program.
   a. who   b. that   c. whom   d. which   e. him   f. Ø

► **Practice 5. Adjective clause pronouns used as the subject or object of the verb.** (Charts 13-1 and 13-2)
Complete the sentences with the correct adjective clause.

1. The book was good. I read it.

   The book that ___I read was good___ .

2. The movie was very sad. I saw it.

   The movie that _____ .

3. Elephants are animals. They can live a long time.

   Elephants are animals that _____ .

4. At the zoo, there were two fifty-year-old elephants. We photographed them.

   At the zoo, there were two fifty-year-old elephants which _____ .

5. Sarah is a person. She does many things at the same time.

Sarah is a person who _____.

6. Bill is a person. You can trust him.

Bill is a person you _____.

7. The painting was valuable. The thieves stole it.

The painting _____.

▶ **Practice 6. Adjective clause pronouns used as the object of a preposition.**
(Chart 13-3)

Circle the letter of all possible completions.

1. The person _____ was Bob Jones in the customer service department.

   a. which I spoke to   f. to who I spoke
   b. to which I spoke   g. that I spoke to
   c. whom I spoke to   h. to that I spoke
   d. to whom I spoke   i. I spoke to
   e. who I spoke to him   j. I spoke to him

2. This is the explanation _____ .

   a. which I was referring to   f. that I was referring to
   b. to which I was referring   g. to that I was referring
   c. whom I was referring to   h. I was referring to
   d. to whom I was referring   i. I was referring to it
   e. which I was referring to it

▶ **Practice 7. Adjective clauses.** (Charts 13-1 → 13-3)
Write all the possible completions for each sentence.

1. Mr. Green is the man ⬚ I was talking about.

2. She is the woman ⬚ sits next to me in class.

3. The hat ⬚ Tom is wearing is unusual.

4. Hunger and poverty are worldwide problems to ⬚ solutions must be found.

5. I enjoyed talking with the man ☐ I sat next to on the plane.

6. People ☐ fear flying avoid traveling by plane.

7. The people about ☐ the novelist wrote were factory workers and their families.

8. A barrel is a large container ☐ is made of wood or metal.

▶ **Practice 8. Adjective clauses.** (Charts 13-1 → 13-3)
Correct the errors in the adjective clauses. Do not change any punctuation.

1. That's a subject I don't want to talk about it.

2. A person who he writes with his left hand is called a lefty.

3. Our family brought home a new kitten that we found it at the animal shelter.

4. What is the name of the radio program to that many people listen on Saturday nights?

5. The candidate for who you vote should be honest.

6. Here's a picture of Nancy who I took with my cell phone.

7. People have high cholesterol should watch their diets.

8. Suzie is going to marry the man she has always loved him.

9. There's an article in today's newspaper about a woman that she is 7 feet tall.

10. Passengers which have children may board the plane first.

▶ **Practice 9. Whose vs. Who's.** (Chart 13-4)
Complete the sentences. Write the letter of the correct pronoun.

1. This class is for students _____ English needs improvement.
   a. who's   b. whose

2. Belinda is a student _____ good in both math and languages.
   a. who's   b. whose

3. Will the student _____ cell phone is ringing please turn it off?
   a. who's   b. whose

4. A customer _____ dissatisfied is not good for a business.
   a. who's   b. whose

5. The customer _____ young son was crying tried to comfort him.
   a. who's   b. whose

6. Life is sometimes difficult for a child _____ parents are divorced.
   a. who's   b. whose

7. And now, I'd like to introduce the man _____ going to be our next senator . . .
   a. who's   b. whose

   . . . and his wife, _____ his greatest asset.
   c. who's   d. whose

▶ **Practice 10. Using *whose*.** (Chart 13-4)

1. Circle the possessive pronoun.
2. Draw an arrow from the possessive pronoun to the noun it refers to.
3. Replace the possessive pronoun with *whose*.
4. Combine the two sentences into one.

1. Do you know the man? His car is parked over there.

   _____

2. I know a skin doctor. His name is Dr. Skinner.

   _____

3. The people were very hospitable. We visited their home.

   _____

4. Mrs. Lake is the teacher. I enjoy her class the most.

   _____

5. The teacher asked the parents to confer with her. Their children were failing.

   _____

▶ **Practice 11. Understanding adjective clauses.** (Charts 13-1 and 13-4)
Choose the correct meanings for each sentence.

1. The secretary that trained my office assistant was arrested for ID theft.
   a. _____ My office assistant was arrested for ID theft.
   b. _____ A secretary trained my office assistant.
   c. _____ A secretary was arrested for ID theft.

2. The nurse who gave the patient her medication was unusually talkative.
   a. _____ The nurse was unusually talkative.
   b. _____ The patient was unusually talkative.
   c. _____ The patient received medication.

3. The taxi driver who turned in a lost wallet to the police received a large reward.
   a. _____ The taxi driver lost a wallet.
   b. _____ The police received a reward.
   c. _____ The taxi driver received a reward.

4. The math teacher whose methods include memorization and a focus on basic skills is very popular with parents.

    a. _____ The parents like the math teacher.

    b. _____ The parents focus on basic skills.

    c. _____ The math teacher requires memorization.

5. The computer that couldn't read your files had a virus.

    a. _____ The computer couldn't read your files.

    b. _____ The computer had a virus.

    c. _____ Your files had a virus.

6. A friend of mine whose husband is a firefighter accidentally started a fire in their kitchen.

    a. _____ My friend is a firefighter.

    b. _____ My friend started a fire.

    c. _____ The firefighter started a fire.

7. The surgeon who operated on my mother is undergoing surgery today.

    a. _____ The surgeon is having surgery today.

    b. _____ My mother is having surgery today.

    c. _____ My mother already had surgery.

▶ **Practice 12. Using *where* in adjective clauses.** (Chart 13-5)
Complete the sentences in two different ways with the given words.

1. *grew up, in, I, which, where,*

    a. The town _____ has changed.

    b. The town _____ has changed.

2. *I, where, lived, in,*

    a. The house _____ isn't there anymore.

    b. The house _____ isn't there anymore.

3. *on, lived, which, where, I*

    a. The street _____ is now a parking lot.

    b. The street _____ is now a parking lot.

4. *where, which, I, played, in*

    a. The park _____ is now a mall.

    b. The park _____ is now a mall.

▶ **Practice 13. Using *when* in adjective clauses.** (Chart 13-6)
Complete the sentences in three different ways with the given words.

1. *on, which, when, I, go, that*

    a. Saturday is the day _____ to the movies with my grandmother.

    b. Saturday is the day _____ to the movies with my grandmother.

    c. Saturday is the day _____ to the movies with my grandmother.

2. *when,   that,   which,   on,   I play tennis*

   a. Sunday is the day _____ with my friend.

   b. Sunday is the day _____ with my friend.

   c. Sunday is the day _____ with my friend.

▶ **Practice 14. Using *where* and *when* in adjective clauses.** (Charts 13-5 and 13-6)
Write the letter of the clause in the list to complete each conversation correctly.

   a. that George Washington slept in   f. which I start my new job

   b. when I spend time with my family   g. which people here celebrate their

   c. when they were really in love   independence

   d. where I was born   h. which you can do all the things you never

   e. where we can sit and talk   could before

  1. A: Where do you want to go after the movie?

     B: Let's go to a place _____.

  2. A: Sal and Lil broke up? That's impossible!

     B: There was a time _____, but not anymore.

  3. A: See you Monday!

     B: No. Don't you remember? Monday is the day on _____.

  4. A: Are you new in town?

     B: New? Are you kidding? This is the place _____.

  5. A: Is there something special about that house? It looks historic.

     B: Yes. They say it's a house _____ when he was on his way to Philadelphia.

  6. A: Grandma is never home. Since she's retired, she's always doing something.

     B: Right. She says that retirement is the time in _____.

  7. A: What's the celebration here? Is it a holiday?

     B: Yes. It's the day on _____.

  8. A: Would you like to go out this weekend?

     B: No, thanks. Saturdays and Sundays are the days _____.

▶ **Practice 15. Adjective clauses.** (Charts 13-1 → 13-6)
Circle the letter of all the words that can complete each sentence correctly.

  1. Yoko told me about students _____ have taken the entrance exam 13 times.
     a. who   b. whom   c. which   d. that

  2. Is this the room _____ the meeting is going to be?
     a. which   b. where   c. that   d. Ø

  3. Judge Savitt is a judge _____ people respect.
     a. whose   b. which   c. whom   d. Ø

  4. I'll never forget the day _____ I met Bobbi.
     a. Ø   b. that   c. when   d. which

5. We're looking for a teacher _____ specialty is teaching dyslexic children.
   a. who   b. his   c. that   d. whose

6. I'm looking for an electric can opener _____ also can sharpen knives.
   a. who   b. which   c. that   d. Ø

7. The problems _____ Tony has seem insurmountable.
   a. what   b. whom   c. that   d. Ø

8. People _____ live in glass houses shouldn't throw stones.
   a. who   b. whom   c. which   d. Ø

▶ **Practice 16. Using adjective clauses to modify pronouns.** (Chart 13-7)
Complete the sentences in Column A with a clause from Column B.

Column A

1. May I ask you a question? There is something _____.
2. I don't have any more money. This is all _____.
3. Anyone _____ must be a genius.
4. He's a spoiled child. His parents give him everything _____.
5. I'm sorry I can't help you. There's nothing _____.
6. We need to hire someone _____.
7. The charity organization invited everyone _____.
8. Students _____ can take the advanced course.

Column B

a. who can understand Einstein's theory of relativity
b. who doesn't mind working long hours and on weekends
c. I've been wanting to ask you
d. who have taken the basic course
e. who had donated money to their cause
f. that he asks for
g. that I can do about the situation
h. I have with me today

▶ **Practice 17. Punctuating adjective clauses.** (Chart 13-8)
Circle *yes* if the adjective clause requires commas and add them in the appropriate places. Circle *no* if the adjective clause does not require commas.

1. I made an appointment with a doctor who is an expert on eye disorders.   yes   (no)

2. I made an appointment with Dr. Raven, who is an expert on eye disorders.   (yes)   no

3. Bogota which is the capital of Colombia is a cosmopolitan city.   yes   no

4. The city that is the capital of Colombia is a large, cosmopolitan city.   yes   no

5. South Beach which is clean, pleasant, and fun is known as a party town.   yes   no

6. The name Bogota comes from the word *Bacata* which was the Indian name for the site.   yes   no

7. The person who writes the best essay will win a prize.   yes   no

8. The first prize was given to Belinda Jones who wrote a touching essay about being an adopted child.   yes   no

9. On our trip to Africa we visited Nairobi which is near several fascinating game reserves and then traveled to Egypt to see the pyramids.   yes   no

10. To see wild animals, you have to fly to a city that is near a game reserve and then take a small plane to the reserve itself.   yes   no

11. Someone who understands physics better than I do is going to have to help you.   yes   no

12. Violent tropical storms that occur in western Asia are called typhoons.   yes   no

13. Similar storms that occur on the Atlantic side of the Americas are called hurricanes rather than typhoons.   yes   no

14. A typhoon which is a violent tropical storm can cause great destruction.   yes   no

15. According to the news report, the typhoon that threatened to strike the Indonesian coast has moved away from land and toward open water.   yes   no

16. Hurricane Katrina which destroyed parts of New Orleans occurred in 2005.   yes   no

▶ **Practice 18. Punctuating adjective clauses.** (Chart 13-8)
Circle the letter of the sentence that gives the correct meaning of the given sentence.

1. The students, who attend class five hours per day, have become quite proficient in their new language.
   a. All of the students attend class five hours per day.
   b. Some of the students attend class five hours per day.

2. The students who attend class five hours per day have become quite proficient in their new language.
   a. All of the students attend class five hours per day.
   b. Some of the students attend class five hours per day.

3. The orchestra conductor signaled the violinists, who were to begin playing.
   a. All of the violinists were to begin playing.
   b. Some of the violinists were to begin playing.

4. The orchestra conductor signaled the violinists who were to begin playing.
   a. All of the violinists were to begin playing.
   b. Some of the violinists were to begin playing.

5. I put the vase on top of the TV set, which is in the living room.
   a. I have more than one TV set.
   b. I have only one TV set.

6. I put the vase on top of the TV set that is in the living room.
   a. I have more than one TV set.
   b. I have only one TV set.

7. Trees which lose their leaves in winter are called deciduous trees.
   a. All trees lose their leaves in winter.
   b. Some trees lose their leaves in winter.

8. Pine trees, which are evergreen, grow well in a cold climate.
   a. All pine trees are evergreen.
   b. Some pine trees are evergreen.

▶ **Practice 19. Using expressions of quantity in adjective clauses.** (Chart 13-9)
Combine the sentences. Use the second sentence as an adjective clause. Add commas where necessary.

1. I received two job offers. I accepted neither of them.

   _____I received two job offers, neither of which I accepted._____

2. I have three brothers. Two of them are professional athletes.

   _____

3. Jerry is engaged in several business ventures. Only one of them is profitable.

   _____

4. The two women have almost completed law school. Both of them began their studies at age 40.

   _____

5. Eric is proud of his success. Much of it has been due to hard work, but some of it has been due to good luck.

   _____

   _____

6. We ordered an extra-large pizza. Half of it contained meat and half of it didn't.

   _____

7. The scientist won the Nobel Prize for his groundbreaking work. Most of his work was on genomes.

   _____

   _____

8. The audience gave a tremendous ovation to the Nobel Prize winners. Most of them were scientists.

   _____

   _____

▶ **Practice 20. Using *which* to modify a whole sentence.** (Chart 13-10)
Combine the sentences. Include an adjective clause that begins with *which* in the new sentence.

1. Mike was accepted at the state university. This is surprising.

   _____

2. Mike did not do well in high school. This is unfortunate.

   _____

3. The university accepts a few students each year with a low grade-point average. This is lucky for Mike.

   _____

4. The university hopes to motivate these low-performing students. This is a fine idea.

   _____

5. Mike might actually be a college graduate one day. This would be a miracle!

   _____

► **Practice 21. Reducing adjective clauses to adjective phrases.** (Chart 13-11)
Change the adjective clauses to adjective phrases. Cross out the adjective clause and write the adjective phrase above it.

                              wearing a green hat
1. Do you see that man ~~who is wearing a green hat?~~

2. The person who is in charge of this department is out to lunch.

3. The picture which was painted by Picasso is extremely valuable.

4. The professors who are doing research will not teach classes next year.

5. The students' research projects which are in progress must be finished by the end of the year.

6. The students' research projects which are scheduled to begin in September will have to be completed by the middle of next year.

7. Toronto, which is the largest city in Canada, is not the capital.

8. In our solar system, there are eight planets that orbit the sun.

9. Pluto, which was formerly known as a planet, was reclassified as a dwarf planet in 2006.

10. Now there is a slang verb, *to pluto*, which means "to devalue someone or something."

► **Practice 22. Reducing adjective clauses to adjective phrases.** (Chart 13-11)
Combine the sentences. Cross out the second sentence. Use it instead as an adjective phrase. Place the phrase in the sentence with a caret (∧). Add commas as necessary.

                   ,officially inaugurated in 1960,
1. Brasilia∧ is the capital of Brazil. ~~It was officially inaugurated in 1960.~~

2. Rio de Janeiro used to be its capital. It is the second largest city in Brazil.

3. Two languages, Finnish and Swedish, are spoken in Helsinki. It is the capital of Finland.

4. In Canada, you see signs. They are written in both English and French.

5. Libya is a leading producer of oil. It is a country in North Africa.

6. Simon Bolivar led the fight for independence early in the nineteenth century. He was a great South American general.

7. Five South American countries are Venezuela, Colombia, Ecuador, Panama, and Peru. They were liberated by Bolivar.

8. We need someone to design this project. He or she holds a degree in electrical engineering.

9. The project will be finished next year. It is being built in Beijing.

10. A lot of new buildings were constructed in Beijing in 2008. Beijing was the site of the summer Olympics that year.

▶ Practice 23. Chapter review.

All of the following sentences contain one or two errors in adjective clauses, adjective phrases, or punctuation. Find the errors and correct them, using a correct adjective clause or adjective phrase, and the correct punctuation.

1. When we walked past the theater, we saw a lot of people waited in a long line outside the box office.

2. Students who living on campus are close to their classrooms and the library.

3. If you need any information, see the librarian sits at the central desk on the main floor.

4. My best friend is Anna who her birthday is the same day as mine.

5. Hiroko was born in Sapporo that is a city in Japan.

6. Patrick who is my oldest brother. He is married and has one child.

7. The person sits next to me is someone I've never met him.

8. My favorite place in the world is a small city is located on the southern coast of Thailand.

9. Dr. Darnell was the only person to that I wanted to speak.

10. There are eighty students, are from all over the world, study English at this school.

11. The people who we met them on our trip last May are going to visit us in October.

12. Dianne Baxter that used to teach Spanish has organized a tour of Central America for senior citizens.

13. I've met many people since I came here who some of them are from my country.

14. People can speak English can be understood in many countries.

15. Grandpa is getting married again. This is a big surprise.

Chapter 14
Gerunds and Infinitives, Part 1

▶ **Practice 1. Gerunds: introduction.** (Chart 14-1)
Circle the gerunds. Some sentences have no gerund.

1. Driving a car is not difficult.

2. We were tired of driving, so we stopped for a rest.

3. When I saw Bob, he was driving around and looking for a parking space.

4. I enjoy singing.

5. Singing songs is a good way to learn a language.

6. Who's singing? It sounds wonderful.

▶ **Practice 2. Using gerunds as the objects of prepositions.** (Chart 14-2)
Complete the sentences with a verb from the list. Write the verb in its gerund form.

buy	fly	hear	lower
drink	go	improve	take

1. Thank you for _____ care of my plants while I was in the hospital.

2. The children are excited about _____ to the circus tomorrow.

3. Students who are interested in _____ their English conversation skills can sign up for special private classes.

4. Psychiatrists say that dreaming about _____ in the sky is quite common.

5. The candidate says he is committed to _____ taxes.

6. We are thinking about not _____ tickets for the opera this year. They have become so expensive.

7. I'm used to _____ tea with my meals. I never drink coffee.

8. We look forward to _____ from you soon.

▶ **Practice 3. Using gerunds as the objects of prepositions.** (Chart 14-2)
Complete the sentences with the correct preposition.

Part I. **Honest Henry . . .**

1. believes _____ telling the truth.

2. is not capable _____ lying.

3. never thinks _____ cheating.

4. would never forgive himself _____ cheating.

5. prohibits his children _____ lying.

Part II. **Devious Dan . . .**

6. is often guilty _____ cheating his friends.

7. never apologizes _____ cheating.

8. is accustomed _____ cheating.

9. is used _____ stealing.

10. has been accused _____ stealing.

▶ **Practice 4. Using gerunds as the objects of prepositions.** (Chart 14-2)
Write the letter of the correct preposition.

1. We are talking _____ opening a vegetarian restaurant in our neighborhood.
   a. to   b. about   c. with

2. Don't worry _____ being on time today. Everybody's going to be late because of the weather.
   a. to   b. about   c. with

3. Aren't you tired _____ studying? Let's take a break.
   a. with   b. about   c. of

4. Beth is a chocoholic. Nothing can stop her _____ eating chocolate whenever she feels like it.
   a. of   b. for   c. from

5. We are looking forward _____ seeing you again.
   a. to   b. of   c. from

6. Let's go dancing instead _____ going to the movies.
   a. with   b. about   c. of

7. Andy is still angry at me. He accused me _____ misplacing his iPod.
   a. of   b. for   c. in

8. He blames me _____ being too careless.
   a. of   b. about   c. for

9. I apologized _____ losing it, and I offered to replace it.
   a. of   b. in   c. for

10. Believe it or not, Andy is not interested _____ being my friend anymore.
    a. about   b. in   c. of

▶ **Practice 5. Using gerunds as the objects of prepositions.** (Chart 14-2)

Write the correct preposition and the correct form of the verb in parentheses.

1. Henry is excited _____ (*leave*) _____ for India.

2. I have no excuse _____ (*be*) _____ late.

3. The rain prevented us _____ (*complete*) _____ the work.

4. Fred is always complaining _____ (*have*) _____ a headache.

5. Instead _____ (*study*) _____, Margaret went to a ballgame with some of her friends.

6. The weather is terrible tonight. I don't blame you _____ (*want, not*) _____ _____ to go to the meeting.

7. Who is responsible _____ (*wash*) _____ and (*dry*) _____ the dishes after dinner?

8. The thief was accused _____ (*steal*) _____ a woman's purse.

9. I'm going to visit my family during the school vacation. I'm looking forward _____ (*eat*) _____ my mother's cooking and (*sleep*) _____ in my own bed.

10. I thanked my friend _____ (*lend*) _____ me lunch money.

▶ **Practice 6. Using gerunds as the objects of prepositions.** (Chart 14-2)

Complete the sentences with a preposition and a verb from the list. Write the verb in its gerund form.

answer	change	live	waste
arrive	clean	save	write
buy	fail	✓ take	

1. I'm thinking ____*about taking*____ a class in digital photography.

2. Are you interested _____ a new computer?

3. Brrr! I don't like this cold weather. I'm used _____ in warmer climates.

4. Please forgive me (*not*) _____ your email until now. I've been very busy.

5. If you are worried _____ this class, why don't you get a tutor?

6. Everybody talks _____ the situation, but nobody does anything about it.

7. This room is a mess! Isn't anyone responsible _____ it up?

8. Bad weather prevented the plane _____ on time.

9. Thank you _____ a letter of recommendation for me.

10. The environmental group believes _____ energy. They want to stop people _____ electricity.

▶ **Practice 7. Verbs followed by gerunds.** (Chart 14-3)
Complete the sentences with a verb from the list. Write the verb in its gerund form.

argue	have	play	sell
drive	pay	read	smoke

1. Boris' hobby is chess. He enjoys _____ chess.

2. Leon's asthma is better now. He is breathing easier since he quit _____ a year

   ago.

3. I don't mind _____ an hour to work every day. I always listen to a good audio

   book in my car.

4. I put off _____ my taxes for too long; I missed the deadline and had to pay a

   penalty.

5. You should avoid _____ with your boss.

6. Would you consider _____ your house at a lower price than you are asking?

7. Our teacher is so great! We really appreciate _____ a teacher like her.

8. When you finish _____ that book, may I borrow it?

▶ **Practice 8. Go + gerund.** (Chart 14-4)
Look at the pictures of the activities that the Green family and the Evans family enjoy. Use
expressions in Chart 14-4 to describe the activities. Write the correct tense of **go** + a gerund.

Part I. The Green family enjoys the outdoors.

1.   2.   3.   4.

1. Every weekend they _____ on the trails near their home.

2. In the summers they _____ on the lake. They like to go out in boats

   that have no motors.

3. In the winters they _____ in the mountains.

4. Last year they took a trip to Costa Rica, where they saw many colorful birds. They

   _____ .

5. On that trip, they also _____ on a river.

5.

Part II. The Evans family enjoys different kinds of activities.

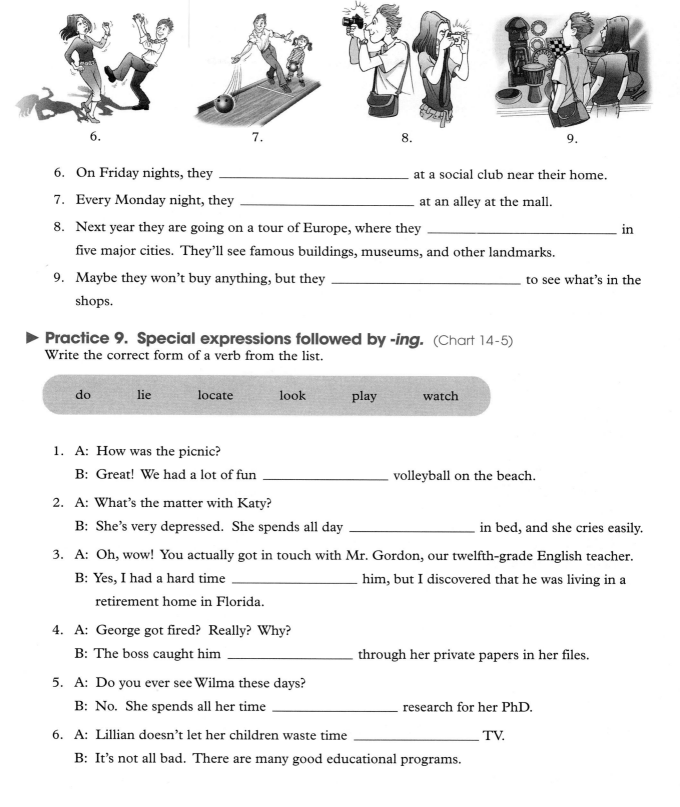

6.   7.   8.   9.

6. On Friday nights, they _____ at a social club near their home.

7. Every Monday night, they _____ at an alley at the mall.

8. Next year they are going on a tour of Europe, where they _____ in five major cities. They'll see famous buildings, museums, and other landmarks.

9. Maybe they won't buy anything, but they _____ to see what's in the shops.

▶ **Practice 9. Special expressions followed by -ing.** (Chart 14-5)
Write the correct form of a verb from the list.

do	lie	locate	look	play	watch

1. A: How was the picnic?

    B: Great! We had a lot of fun _____ volleyball on the beach.

2. A: What's the matter with Katy?

    B: She's very depressed. She spends all day _____ in bed, and she cries easily.

3. A: Oh, wow! You actually got in touch with Mr. Gordon, our twelfth-grade English teacher.

    B: Yes, I had a hard time _____ him, but I discovered that he was living in a retirement home in Florida.

4. A: George got fired? Really? Why?

    B: The boss caught him _____ through her private papers in her files.

5. A: Do you ever see Wilma these days?

    B: No. She spends all her time _____ research for her PhD.

6. A: Lillian doesn't let her children waste time _____ TV.

    B: It's not all bad. There are many good educational programs.

▶ **Practice 10. Verbs followed by infinitives.** (Chart 14-6)
Circle the letter of all the possible completions.

1. I want _____ that movie.
   a. to see   b. seeing   c. him to see

2. They told _____ them as soon as I got home.
   a. to call   b. calling   c. me to call

3. I expect _____ there early.
   a. to be   b. being   c. you to be

4. The police ordered _____ the building.
   a. not to enter   b. not entering   c. the people not to enter

5. We were asked _____ food and clothing for the hurricane victims.
   a. to contribute   b. contributing   c. them to contribute

6. Lisa expected _____ the lecture.
   a. to attend   b. attending   c. us to attend

▶ **Practice 11. Verbs followed by infinitives.** (Chart 14-6)
Complete the sentences with *to work* or *me to work*. Write the correct completion(s). In some cases, both are possible.

1. She hoped ____*to work*____ .   8. They didn't allow _____ .

2. He ordered ____*me to work*____ .   9. You told _____ .

3. We agreed _____ .   10. They would like _____ .

4. They wanted _____ .   11. They expected _____ .

5. She promised _____ .   12. She decided _____ .

6. They refused _____ .   13. They needed _____ .

7. He pretended _____ .   14. They required _____ .

▶ **Practice 12. Verbs followed by infinitives.** (Chart 14-6)
Rewrite each sentence. Use an infinitive phrase to make active sentences. Use the given ideas and the verbs in parentheses.

1. The teacher said to me, "You may leave early." (*permit*)

   The teacher _____ .

2. The secretary said to me, "Please give this note to Sue." (*ask*)

   The secretary _____ .

3. My advisor said to me, "You should take Biology 109." (*advise*)

   My advisor _____ .

4. When I went to traffic court, the judge said to me, "You must pay a fine." (*order*)

   The judge _____ .

5. During the test, the teacher said to Greg, "Keep your eyes on your own paper." (*warn*)

   The teacher _____ .

6. During the test, the teacher said to Greg, "Don't look at your neighbor's paper." (*warn*)

   The teacher _____ .

7. Mr. Lee said to the children, "Be quiet." (*tell*)

Mr. Lee _____.

8. When I was growing up, my parents said to me, "You may stay up late on Saturday night." (*allow*)

My parents _____.

9. The teacher said to the students, "Speak slowly and clearly." (*encourage*)

The teacher _____.

10. The teacher always says to the students, "You are supposed to come to class on time." (*expect*)

The teacher _____.

▶ **Practice 13. Verbs followed by infinitives.** (Chart 14-6)
On a separate piece of paper, rewrite each sentence in two ways. Use an infinitive phrase to make active and passive sentences with the given ideas and the verbs in parentheses. (Omit the *by*-phrase in passive sentences.)

1. The teacher said to the children, "You may go outside and play." (*allow*)
   The teacher allowed the children to go outside and play.
   The children were allowed to go outside and play.

2. The doctor said to my father, "Don't eat high-cholesterol foods." (*warn*)

3. The sergeant said to the soldiers, "March in formation." (*order*)

4. The soccer coach told the girls, "Play hard and win." (*encourage*)

5. Mary said to her roommate, "Don't forget to wake me up at 7:00." (*remind*)

6. The police officer told the drivers in our lane of traffic, "You may go ahead." (*permit*)

7. The letter said, "You must complete this form by November 15th." (*tell*)

▶ **Practice 14. Gerund or infinitive.** (Charts 14-3 and 14-6)
Write the letter of the correct completion.

1. William wants _____ us for dinner tonight.
   a. to join   b. joining

2. We offered _____ ice cream for all the children.
   a. to buy   b. buying

3. I enjoy _____ large dishes of Indian food for my friends.
   a. to cook   b. cooking

4. Avoid _____ Highway 98. There's a lot of construction going on.
   a. to take   b. taking

5. Keep on _____! Sooner or later, you'll be able to finish the puzzle.
   a. to try   b. trying

6. Would you mind ____ up the heat? It's freezing in here.
   a. to turn   b. turning

7. I pretended ____ what Irv was saying, but in reality, I didn't understand a thing.
   a. to understand   b. understand

8. Phil seems ____ in a bad mood. Do you know why?
   a. to be   b. being

9. You should consider ____ this course. It's too hard for you.
   a. to drop   b. dropping

10. Because of the stormy weather, everyone was allowed ____ work early.
    a. to leave   b. leaving

11. Students are not permitted ____ their cell phones in class.
    a. to use   b. using

12. If you quit ____ coffee, you might sleep better.
    a. to drink   b. drinking

▶ **Practice 15. Gerund or infinitive.** (Charts 14-3 and 14-6)
Circle the verb to complete the sentence correctly.

1. John doesn't mind (*to live* / *living*) alone.

2. The traffic sign warns drivers (*to be* / *being*) careful of the slippery road.

3. Travelers are required (*to show* / *showing*) their IDs at the gate.

4. Don't delay (*to make* / *making*) your reservations! Book your travel now!

5. We expect the plane (*to be* / *being*) on time.

6. I certainly appreciate (*to be* / *being*) here! Thank you for inviting me.

7. Please stop (*to hum* / *humming*) that song over and over. It bothers me.

8. My doctor suggests (*to exercise* / *exercising*) for thirty minutes every day.

9. My doctor advises (*to exercise* / *me to exercise*) for thirty minutes every day.

10. My doctor advised me (*to exercise* / *exercising*) for thirty minutes every day.

11. I was advised (*to exercise* / *exercising*) for thirty minutes every day by my doctor.

12. I advised (*to consult* / *my friend to consult*) a lawyer.

13. My friend was advised (*to consult* / *consulting*) a lawyer.

14. She asked me (*to recommend* / *recommending*) a good lawyer.

► **Practice 16. Gerund or infinitive.** (Charts 14-3 and 14-6)

Complete the sentences with the gerund or infinitive form of the verb in **bold**. Use *him* if a pronoun is required.

Part I. Complete the sentences with *stay*.

1. I expect _____.
2. I want _____.
3. I forced _____.
4. I invited _____.
5. I considered _____.

6. I told _____.
7. I was told _____.
8. I refused _____.
9. I encouraged _____.
10. I would like _____.

Part II. Complete the sentences with *travel*.

1. He doesn't mind _____.
2. He enjoys _____.
3. He needed _____.
4. He quit _____.
5. He is allowed _____.

6. He put off _____.
7. He recommends _____.
8. He can't stand _____.
9. He finished _____.
10. He mentioned _____.

Part III. Complete the sentences with *work*.

1. They discussed _____.
2. They intend _____.
3. They were ordered _____.
4. They decided _____.
5. They offered _____.

6. They delayed _____.
7. They required _____.
8. They hope _____.
9. They plan _____.
10. They avoided _____.

► **Practice 17. Gerund or infinitive.** (Chart 14-7)

Complete the sentences with the gerund or infinitive form of the verb.

1. Don't forget (*turn*) _____ off your computers before you leave the office.
2. I'll never forget (*meet*) _____ the president when I was a child.
3. I'll remember (*stop*) _____ at the grocery store if I write myself a note and stick it in the window of my car.
4. Do you remember (*see*) _____ a man running out of the bank with a large bag in his hand?
5. Don't give me any more advice. Please stop (*tell*) _____ me what to do.
6. At the mall, I met my old English teacher. We stopped (*talk*) _____ for a while. That was very pleasant.
7. I had a bad argument with my friend Jerry two years ago. We stopped (*speak*) _____ then and haven't spoken since.
8. We regret (*buy*) _____ this house. It needs too many repairs.
9. The letter said, "I regret (*tell*) _____ you that your application has been denied."

10. I tried very hard *(learn)* _____ Chinese, but I couldn't do it. I am just not good at languages.

11. We don't know how to communicate with that man. We've tried *(talk)* _____ to him in Spanish, we've tried in Greek, we've tried in German, and we've tried in French. So far nothing's worked.

▶ **Practice 18. Gerund or infinitive.** (Chart 14-7)
Circle the letter of the sentence that has the same meaning as the given sentence.

1. Jean and her husband stopped drinking coffee.
   a. They had a cup of coffee together.
   b. They don't drink coffee anymore.

2. I regret to tell you that your aunt is very ill.
   a. I am sorry to inform you that your aunt is very ill.
   b. I am sorry that I informed you that your aunt was very ill.

3. Rita remembers locking the door this morning.
   a. Rita never forgets to lock the door in the morning.
   b. Rita remembers that she locked the door this morning.

4. I forgot to call my grandmother.
   a. I didn't call my grandmother.
   b. I don't remember whether I called my grandmother or not.

5. My back was sore from being at the computer all morning. I stopped to rest.
   a. I kept working.
   b. I took a break.

▶ **Practice 19. Gerund or infinitive.** (Chart 14-7)
Circle the letter of the correct completions. In some sentences, both are correct.

1. It was raining hard, but we continued _____.
   a. to drive   b. driving

2. The veterinarian tried _____ the horse's life, but he failed.
   a. to save   b. saving

3. As soon as the play ended, the audience began _____ wildly.
   a. to applaud   b. applauding

4. I prefer _____ a movie rather than see one in a theater.
   a. to rent   b. renting

5. I prefer _____ movies at home.
   a. to see   b. seeing

6. I hate _____ in the house when the weather is beautiful.
   a. to stay   b. staying

7. I love _____ on the beach.

    a. to walk   b. walking

8. Most people enjoy _____ to music.

    a. to listen   b. listening

9. When you finish _____, call me and I'll come to pick you up.

    a. to shop   b. shopping

10. Please don't cry. I can't stand _____ you cry.

    a. to see   b. seeing

▶ **Practice 20. *It* + infinitive; gerunds and infinitives as subjects.** (Charts 14-8)
Circle the correct word or phrase in parentheses.

1. (*Is / It's*) easy to use a computer.

2. Using a computer (*is / it's*) easy.

3. To speak another language (*is not / it's not*) easy.

4. (*Is it / Is*) difficult to speak another language?

5. (*Go / Going*) dancing is fun.

6. (*It's / Is*) fun to go dancing.

7. Traveling (*is / it's*) sometimes tiring.

8. It's dangerous (*jump / to jump*) out of airplanes in a parachute.

9. (*See / To see*) the Grand Canyon is a thrilling experience.

10. (*Is / Is it*) collecting coins an interesting hobby?

▶ **Practice 21. Review.** (Charts 14-2 → 14-8)
Circle the letter of all the possible completions.

1. _____ to play tennis.

    a. I would like   g. I told Ted

    b. I asked Jack   h. We discussed

    c. I'm thinking about   i. It's a good day

    d. I invited Ann   j. I enjoyed

    e. We had fun   k. We began

    f. I suggested   l. I hope

2. _____ playing tennis early.

    a. We finished   g. I promised Fred

    b. We want   h. We stopped

    c. I want them   i. I was invited

    d. We quit   j. We tried

    e. It's a lovely day   k. We recommended

    f. I'm interested in   l. We considered

▶ **Practice 22. Gerund or infinitive.** (Charts 14-9 and 14-10)
Write the letter of the correct completion.

1. Air travelers have to anticipate _____ in long lines.
   a. to wait   b. waiting

2. The electronics store agreed _____ back the damaged radio.
   a. to take   b. taking

3. Doctor, would you mind _____ me the information in language I can understand?
   a. to give   b. giving

4. I miss _____ you in class every day.
   a. to see   b. seeing

5. Dan failed _____ the firefighter's examination and was quite upset.
   a. to pass   b. passing

6. The bad weather caused us _____ our connecting flight to Rome.
   a. to miss   b. missing

7. We dislike _____ dinner at 9:00 P.M.
   a. to eat   b. eating

8. Most of the students finished _____ their research papers on time.
   a. to write   b. writing

9. My niece hopes _____ with me to Disneyland next April.
   a. to go   b. going

10. This note will remind me _____ the chicken for dinner tomorrow night.
    a. to defrost   b. defrosting

11. Billy denied _____ the whole bag of potato chips that was on the table.
    a. to eat   b. eating

12. In a court of law, you must swear _____ the truth, the whole truth, and nothing but the truth.
    a. to tell   b. telling

13. I'm sorry. I didn't mean _____ you.
    a. to frighten   b. frightening

14. I regret not _____ harder when I was in high school.
    a. to study   b. studying

▶ Practice 23. Review. (Chapter 14)

Write the correct form of a verb from the list.

> apply   end   operate   run   speak   use
> camp   get   read   sleep   turn   watch

1. Our family goes _____ in the summer and fall. We love to cook outdoors and sleep in tents under the stars.

2. The doctor was forced _____ immediately to save the patient's life.

3. I have to drive more carefully. I can't risk _____ another speeding ticket.

4. Think about _____ for that new job. You can do it, I know.

5. The sign at the intersection warns drivers not _____ right when the light is red.

6. When Bess entered the room, she found her two cats _____ on her bed.

7. When you get through _____ the newspaper, could you please give me a little help in the kitchen?

8. I was furious at Bill's rude behavior. I threatened _____ our friendship.

9. Bill regretted _____ rude language and apologized for _____ to me in the way that he did.

10. The customers at the bank just stood _____ helplessly as a masked gunman held everyone at gunpoint.

11. But two police officers caught the gunman _____ out of the bank carrying two large bags of money.

▶ Practice 24. Chapter review.

Correct the errors. All the errors are in the use of gerunds and infinitives and the words that go with them.

1. I don't enjoy to watch TV.

2. I prefer to spend time to play board games and computer games.

3. It's important keep your mind active.

4. There is some evidence that older people can avoid to become senile by exercise their brain.

5. Playing word games it is one good way to stimulate your brain.

6. In addition, is beneficial for everyone to exercise regularly.

7. Doctors advise older people eating fish two or three times a week.

8. Everyone should try eat well and exercise every day.

9. Pedro is interested to learn about other cultures.

10. He wants live in Japan next year.

11. He's excited about attend a university there.

12. Right now he is struggling learning Japanese.

13. He has a hard time to pronounce the words.

14. He keeps on to study and to practice.

15. At night, he lies in bed to listen to Japanese language-teaching programs.

16. Then he dreams to travel to Japan.

Chapter 15
Gerunds and Infinitives, Part 2

▶ **Practice 1. Infinitive of purpose:** *in order to.* (Chart 15-1)
Correct the errors. Not every sentence has an error.

David is in Mexico . . . .

1. for visit
2. for a convention
3. for his cousin's wedding
4. to go sightseeing
5. for learn Spanish
6. to his health
7. for see the Mayan ruins
8. for the cool mountain air

▶ **Practice 2. Infinitive of purpose:** *in order to.* (Chart 15-1)
Circle the letter of the correct completion. In some sentences, both are correct.

1. Emily likes _____ ice skating every weekend.
   a. to go   b. in order to go

2. Darcy opened the door _____ some fresh air in.
   a. to let   b. in order to let

3. Beth practices night and day _____ ready for her piano recital next month.
   a. to be   b. in order to be

4. Sue sent me an email _____ me that the meeting had been canceled.
   a. to inform   b. in order to inform

5. We've decided not _____ a vacation this year.
   a. to take   b. in order to take

6. Did you remember _____ Mr. Johnson?
   a. to call   b. in order to call

7. On nice summer nights, we often walk on the beach _____ the sunsets.
   a. to watch   b. in order to watch

8. The boys were so noisy that I had to ring a loud bell _____ their attention.
   a. to get   b. in order to get

9. Airport workers wear ear protectors _____ their ears from jet noise.
   a. to protect   b. in order to protect

► **Practice 3. Adjectives followed by infinitives.** (Chart 15-2)
Complete the conversations. Write the letter of the phrase from the list.

a. to hear that
b. to bring the paper cups and paper plates
c. to get into one
d. to be alive
e. to introduce our country's president
f. to lose the next game

1. A: Marta had a bad accident, I heard.

   B: Yes, she did. She's lucky _____ .

2. A: Why does Mr. Carlin walk up twelve flights of stairs every day? Is it for the exercise?

   B: No, not at all. He has a phobia about elevators. He's afraid _____ .

3. A: Who is going to cook dinner for our next meeting?

   B: I can't cook, but I'm willing _____ .

4. A: Our dog died.

   B: Oh, that's a shame. I'm very sorry _____ .

5. A: Our three best soccer players are out with injuries.

   B: I know. Without them, you're likely _____ .

6. A: Turn the volume up. I want to hear what the senator is saying.

   B: "Ladies and gentlemen, I am proud _____ ."

► **Practice 4. Using infinitives with *too* and *very*.** (Chart 15-3)
Write *very* or *too* to complete each sentence correctly.

1. The box is _____ very _____ heavy, but I can lift it.

2. John dropped his physics course because it was _____ difficult for him.

3. I think it's _____ late to get tickets to the concert. I heard they were all sold out.

4. Peter has turned 20. Now he's _____ old to take part in the ski races for teenagers.

5. Nancy was _____ ill. Nevertheless, she came to the family reunion.

6. Learning a second language can be _____ difficult, but most students in the class are doing well.

7. Professor Andrews is always _____ interesting, but I'm _____ tired to go to the lecture tonight.

8. Phil is _____ young to understand. He'll understand when he's older.

9. I'm _____ sleepy to watch the rest of the TV movie. Let me know how it turns out in the end.

10. A: I like your pin. It looks antique.

    B: It is. It's _____ old. It belonged to my great-grandmother.

▶ **Practice 5. Using infinitives with _too_ and _enough._** (Chart 15-3)
Write **very**, **too**, or **enough** to complete each sentence correctly.

1. The classroom is _____very_____ small, but it's big _____enough_____ to hold fifteen students.

2. It's _____ dark to see in here. Please turn on the lights.

3. There's not _____ light in here. Can you turn on another light?

4. These new windows are made of specially treated glass. The glass is _____ strong. It's strong _____ to resist the strong winds of hurricanes.

5. We'd like to go out in our sailboat today because the weather is _____ nice. However, there isn't _____ wind to sail.

6. A trip to Europe is _____ expensive for our family this year. We don't have _____ money to travel this year.

7. You're _____ young to drive a car, Emily. You're only twelve years old! There will be time _____ to drive when you're older.

8. Dinner was _____ good. This restaurant is good _____ to come back to.

9. It's _____ hot today, but I'm going to take my daily walk anyway.

10. It's hot _____ to fry an egg on the sidewalk!

▶ **Practice 6. Passive infinitives and gerunds.** (Chart 15-4)
Complete the sentences with the passive form of the verbs in parentheses.

1. I hope (_accepted_) _____ at State College.

2. I would like (_given_) _____ a scholarship.

3. Leo wants (_picked_) _____ for the soccer team.

4. Cats enjoy (_petted_) _____.

5. Babies need (_held_) _____.

6. I really appreciate (_invited_) _____ to join this group.

7. Al is shy. He avoids (_noticed_) _____.

8. Harold mentioned (_invited_) _____ to a dinner at his boss's house.

▶ **Practice 7. Passive infinitives and gerunds.** (Chart 15-4)
Choose the infinitive or the passive infinitive. Write the letter of the correct completion.

1. The mail is supposed _____ before noon.
   a. to deliver   b. to be delivered

2. The mail carrier is supposed _____ the mail before noon.
   a. to deliver   b. to be delivered

3. Janice is going to fill out an application. She wants _____ for the job.
   a. to consider   b. to be considered

4. I expect _____ at the airport by my uncle.
   a. to meet   b. to be met

5. Mr. Steinberg offered _____ us to the train station.
   a. to drive   b. to be driven

6. The children appear _____ about the trip.
   a. to excite   b. to be excited

7. My co-worker and I agreed _____ the work equally.
   a. to divide   b. to be divided

8. Our boss appears _____ with this arrangement.
   a. to please   b. to be pleased

▶ **Practice 8. Passive infinitives and gerunds.** (Chart 15-4)
Choose the gerund or the passive gerund. Write the letter of the correct completion.

1. Shhh! Don't ask questions! The professor doesn't appreciate _____ when he's speaking.
   a. interrupting   b. being interrupted

2. Avoid _____ Highway 77. There are a lot of delays because of construction.
   a. taking   b. being taken

3. The mountain climbers are in danger of _____ by an avalanche.
   a. killing   b. being killed

4. Does Dr. Johnson mind _____ at home if his patients need his help?
   a. calling   b. being called

5. I'm interested in _____ my conversational skills.
   a. improving   b. being improved

6. When Alex got home from school, he didn't mention _____ by his teacher.
   a. scolding   b. being scolded

7. Sally's low test scores kept her from _____ to the university.
   a. admitting   b. being admitted

8. Mr. Miller gave no indication of _____ his mind.
   a. changing   b. being changed

▶ **Practice 9. Passive infinitives and gerunds.** (Chart 15-4)
Complete the sentences with the correct form of the verbs in parentheses.

1. We turn off the phone during dinner. We don't want (*call*) _____
   at that time.

2. Not many people enjoy (*call*) _____ by salespeople.

3. Each candidate hopes (*elect*) _____ by a large majority of the people.

4. It's not easy (*elect*) _____.

5. Our mayor has an excellent chance (*re-elect*) _____.

6. Sometimes teenagers complain about not (*understand*) _____ by
   their parents.

7. Sometimes teenagers would like just (*leave*) _____ alone.

8. Don't all of us want (*love*) _____ and (*need*) _____ by other people?

▶ **Practice 10. Using gerunds or passive infinitives following *need*.** (Chart 15-5)
Circle the letters of all the sentences that can follow the given sentence.

1. A lot of things in our house don't work.
    a. We need to repair them.
    b. They need to repair.
    c. They need to be repaired.
    d. They need repairing.

2. The refrigerator is so old that it hardly works anymore.
    a. We need to replace the refrigerator.
    b. It needs to replace.
    c. It needs to be replaced.
    d. It needs replacing.

3. The sink has been leaking for a month.
    a. A plumber needs to fix the sink.
    b. The sink needs to fix.
    c. The sink needs to be fixed.
    d. The sink needs fixing.

4. The color of the walls has faded.
    a. We need to paint the walls.
    b. The walls need to paint.
    c. The walls need to be painted.
    d. The walls need painting.

5. We don't have a good repair person.
    a. We need to find a good repair person.
    b. A good repair person needs to find.
    c. A good repair person needs to be found.
    d. We need a repair person to find.

6. Please tell your repair person to call me.
    a. I need to call your repair person.
    b. I need to be called by your repair person.
    c. Your repair person needs to call me.
    d. Your repair person needs calling.

▶ **Practice 11. Using verbs of perception.** (Chart 15-6)
Complete the sentences with a verb from the list. Use each word only once. Use the simple form or the *-ing* form, whichever seems better to you. Sometimes both are OK.

arrive	do	pass	reach	talk
cry	leave	practice	rock	win

1. Whenever I can, I like to watch the basketball team _____ for the upcoming game.

2. It's interesting to sit in the airport and watch all the people _____ by.

3. I heard an upset baby _____.

4. Did you see Charles _____ the office? He ran out in a really big hurry!

5. It was a thrill to see my brother _____ the chess tournament last year.

6. I was amazed to see the firefighters _____ so soon after my call.

7. I can't stand to be on a boat. When I feel the boat _____, I get seasick.

8. When I watch my yoga instructor _____ the exercises, it seems easy, but when I try them, it is hard.

9. We listened to the newscaster _____ about the oncoming tornadoes.

10. A security guard at the bank observed a suspicious-looking man _____ into his pocket for something. The guard thought it was a gun, but it turned out to be the man's asthma inhaler.

▶ **Practice 12. Using the simple form after *let* and *help*.** (Chart 15-7)
Write the letter of the correct completion. More than one completion may be correct. If so, write both.

1. The school guard stopped all the traffic to let the children _____ the street.
   a. cross   b. to cross   c. crossing

2. My friend Ole is very relaxed. He never lets anything _____ him.
   a. to bother   b. bother   c. bothering

3. My daughter helped me _____ an application online.
   a. filling out   b. filled out   c. fill out

4. Will you please help me _____ the kitchen? Otherwise, I'll be here all night!
   a. clean up   b. to clean up   c. cleaning up

5. Elsa used to have very short hair, but now it is longer. She is letting it _____.
   a. growing   b. to grow   c. grow

6. We don't let our dog _____ around outside. We always take him for walks on a leash.
   a. run   b. to run   c. running

7. Is it true that if you eat fish every day, it will help you _____ smarter?
   a. to become   b. becoming   c. become

8. Did someone help you _____ this research paper?
   a. write   b. wrote   c. writing

▶ **Practice 13. Using causative verbs: *make, have, get*.** (Chart 15-8)
Complete the sentences with the correct form of the verbs in parentheses.

1. The general made the soldiers (*stand*) _____ at attention.

2. Don't get rid of those shoes just because they are old. Have them (*fix*) _____ at the shoe repair shop.

3. Exercise makes your heart (*beat*) _____ faster.

4. What can we do to get Marissa (*stop*) _____ smoking?

5. Jean finally got her son (*clean*) _____ his room.

6. Paula's new haircut makes her (*look*) _____ ten years younger.

7. I'm sorry, sir. Your prescription is not renewable. Have your physician
   (*call*) _____ us here at the pharmacy, and then we can refill
   it for you.

8. Please take this document to the copy store and have 15 copies
   (*make*) _____. There are 150 pages, so you'd better have
   spiral bindings (*put*) _____ on too.

▶ **Practice 14. Using causative verbs: *make, have, get.*** (Chart 15-8)
Circle the letter of the correct completions. More than one completion may be correct.

1. You can ____ the bookstore order some books for you.
   a. make   b. have   c. get

2. You can order your books from the online bookstore and ____ them sent to you.
   a. make   b. have   c. get

3. If you're nice to James, maybe you can ____ him to drive you to the airport.
   a. make   b. have   c. get

4. I'll ____ the taxi driver take me to the airport.
   a. make   b. have   c. get

5. The comedian is so funny. I can't help laughing even though I'm sad. That comedian can ____ anyone laugh.
   a. make   b. have   c. get

6. The students tried to ____ the professor to postpone the exam, but he didn't.
   a. make   b. have   c. get

7. I'm going to ____ my car washed on Saturday.
   a. make   b. have   c. get

8. Ms. Andrews isn't there? ____ her call me, please.
   a. Make   b. Have   c. Get

9. A magician can ____ a rabbit appear and disappear.
   a. make   b. have   c. get

▶ **Practice 15. Verb form review.** (Chapters 14 and 15)
Circle the letter of the correct completion.

1. I enjoy ____ to the park on summer evenings.
   a. to go   b. going   c. being gone   d. go

2. Don't forget ____ home as soon as you arrive at your destination.
   a. to call   b. calling   c. call   d. to be called

3. When we kept getting unwanted calls, I called the phone company and had my phone number ____ .
   a. change   b. changed   c. to change   d. changing

4. Jean should seriously consider ____ an actress. She is a very talented performer.
   a. to become   b. become   c. becoming   d. will become

5. ____ television to the exclusion of all other activities is not a healthy habit for a growing child.
   a. Watch   b. Being watched   c. Watching   d. To be watched

6. After their children had grown up, Mr. and Mrs. Sills decided ____ to a condominium in the city. They've never been sorry.
   a. moved   b. moving   c. move   d. to move

7. Are you interested in ____ the movie at University Theater?
   a. see   b. to see   c. being seen   d. seeing

8. The store manager caught the cashier _____ money from the cash register and promptly called the police. They discovered that it had been going on for a long time.
   a. to steal   b. stealing   c. stole   d. being stolen

9. The municipal authorities advised us _____ all drinking water during the emergency.
   a. to boil   b. to be boiled   c. boiling   d. boil

10. If we leave now for our trip, we can drive half the distance before we stop _____ lunch.
    a. having   b. to have   c. have   d. for having

11. It was difficult _____ the dialogue in the movie. The acoustics in the theater were very bad.
    a. to hear   b. hearing   c. heard   d. to heard

12. Our school basketball team won the championship game by _____ two points in the last five seconds. It was the most exciting game I have ever attended.
    a. being scored   b. to score   c. scoring   d. score

13. The flight attendants made all the passengers _____ their seat belts during the turbulence.
    a. to buckle   b. buckling   c. to buckled   d. buckle

14. At our class reunion, we had a lot of fun _____ at pictures of ourselves from twenty years ago.
    a. looking   b. look   c. looked   d. to look

15. It has become necessary _____ water in the metropolitan area because of the severe drought.
    a. rationing   b. ration   c. have rationed   d. to ration

▶ **Practice 16. Verb form review.** (Chapters 14 and 15)
Complete the sentences with the correct form of the verb in parentheses. Some sentences are passive.

1. Bill decided (*buy*) _____ a new car rather than a used one.

2. We delayed (*open*) _____ the doors of the testing center until exactly 9:00.

3. I really dislike (*ask*) _____ to answer questions in class when I haven't prepared my lesson.

4. I certainly didn't anticipate (*have*) _____ to wait in line for three hours for tickets to the baseball game!

5. When I was younger, I used (*wear*) _____ mini-skirts and bright colors. Now I am accustomed to (*dress*) _____ more conservatively.

6. Skydivers must have nerves of steel. I can't imagine (*jump*) _____ out of a plane and (*fall*) _____ to the earth. What if the parachute didn't open?

7. We are looking forward to (*take*) _____ on a tour of Athens by our Greek friends.

8. I told the mail carrier that we would be away for two weeks on vacation. I asked her (*stop*) _____ (*deliver*) _____ our mail until the 21st. She told me (*fill*) _____ out a form at the post office so that the post office would hold our mail until we returned.

9. The elderly man next door is just sitting in his rocking chair (*gaze*) _____ out the window. I wish there were something I could do (*cheer*) _____ him up.

10. I resent (*have*) _____ to work on this project with Fred. I know I'll end up with most of the work falling on my shoulders.

▶ **Practice 17. Review.** (Chapters 14 and 15)
Circle the letter of the correct form of the verb to complete each sentence.

1. Alice didn't expect _____ to Bill's party.
   a. to ask   b. to be asked   c. asking

2. Matthew left the office without _____ anyone.
   a. tell   b. telling   c. told

3. It's useless. Give up. Enough's enough. Don't keep _____ your head against a brick wall.
   a. beat   b. beating   c. to beat

4. I hope _____ a scholarship for the coming semester.
   a. to award   b. to be awarded   c. being awarded

5. We are very pleased _____ your invitation.
   a. to accept   b. to be accepted   c. accept

6. It was exciting _____ to faraway places last year.
   a. travel   b. to travel   c. to traveled

7. Conscientious parents don't let their children _____ too much television.
   a. watch   b. to watch   c. watching

8. Did you see that deer _____ across the road?
   a. run   b. ran   c. to run

9. Mr. Carson was very lucky _____ to represent the company in Paris.
   a. to be chosen   b. choosing   c. to chose

10. Last Saturday, we went _____.
    a. to shop   b. shopping   c. to shopping

11. _____ in the mountains is Tom's favorite activity.
    a. Hike   b. Hiking   c. Go to hike

12. The physical activity makes him _____ good.
    a. feel   b. to feel   c. feeling

13. Martha opened the window _____ in some fresh air.
    a. let   b. letting   c. to let

14. Scott wastes a lot of time _____ out with his friends at the mall.
    a. hanging   b. to hang   c. hang

15. Did you remember _____ the front door?
    a. lock   b. to lock   c. locking

16. I don't remember ever _____ that story before.
    a. hearing   b. heard   c. to hear

17. You should stop _____ if you get sleepy.
    a. drive   b. driving   c. to drive

18. I have trouble _____ asleep at night.
    a. fall   b. to fall   c. falling

19. After driving for three hours, we stopped _____ something to eat.
    a. to get   b. getting   c. got

20. The refrigerator needs _____ again.
    a. fixing   b. to fix   c. fixed

21. That pan is really hot. It's too hot _____ up without an oven mitt.
    a. pick   b. picking   c. to pick

▶ **Practice 18. Verb form review.** (Chapters 14 and 15)
Correct the errors.

1. You shouldn't let children playing with matches.

2. Bobby was lying in bed to cry.

3. You can get there more quickly by take River Road instead of the interstate highway.

4. Isabel expected being admitted to the university, but she wasn't.

5. Our lawyer advised us not signing the contract until she had a chance to study it very carefully.

6. John was responsible for to notify everyone about the meeting.

7. Apparently, he failed to calling several people.

8. I couldn't understand what the passage said, so I asked my friend translated it for me.

9. You can find out the meaning of the word by look it up in a dictionary.

10. No, that's not what I meant to say. How can I make you understanding?

11. Serena wore a large hat for protect her face from the sun.

12. We like to go to fish on weekends.

13. Maybe you can get Charlie taking you to the airport.

14. My doctor advised me not eating food with a high fat content.

15. Doctors always advise eat less and exercising more.

16. Allen smelled something to burn. When he ran into the
    kitchen, he saw fire coming out of the oven.

Chapter 16
Coordinating Conjunctions

▶ **Practice 1. Parallel structure.** (Chart 16-1)
Write the letter of the correct completion.

1. In the winter, Iceland is cold and _____.
   a. ice   b. dark   c. a country

2. Dan opened the door and _____ the room.
   a. enter   b. entering   c. entered

3. This dish is made of meat, potatoes, and _____.
   a. spicy   b. salty   c. vegetables

4. Jerry was driving and _____ on the phone at the same time.
   a. talks   b. talking   c. talked

5. Mimi learned how to sing and _____ at the Academy of the Arts.
   a. danced   b. dancing   c. dance

6. I have written and _____ her, but I have received no response.
   a. call   b. calling   c. called

7. Somebody called and _____ up.
   a. hung   b. hang   c. hanging

8. Don't call and _____ up. Leave a short message.
   a. hung   b. hang   c. hanging

▶ **Practice 2. Parallel structure.** (Chart 16-1)
Circle the conjunction that joins the parallel words. Then <u>underline</u> the words that are parallel and circle the letter of the part of speech that describes them.

1. These apples are <u>fresh</u> (and) <u>sweet</u>.
   (a.) adjective   d. adverb
   b. noun   e. gerund
   c. verb   f. infinitive

2. These apples and pears are fresh.
   a. adjective   d. adverb
   b. noun   e. gerund
   c. verb   f. infinitive

3. I washed and dried the apples.
   a. adjective   d. adverb
   b. noun   e. gerund
   c. verb   f. infinitive

4. I am washing and drying the apples.
    a. adjective   d. adverb
    b. noun   e. gerund
    c. verb   f. infinitive

5. We ate the fruit happily and quickly.
    a. adjective   d. adverb
    b. noun   e. gerund
    c. verb   f. infinitive

6. Those imported apples are delicious but expensive.
    a. adjective   d. adverb
    b. noun   e. gerund
    c. verb   f. infinitive

7. Apples, pears, and bananas are kinds of fruit.
    a. adjective   d. adverb
    b. noun   e. gerund
    c. verb   f. infinitive

8. I like an apple or a banana with my cereal.
    a. adjective   d. adverb
    b. noun   e. gerund
    c. verb   f. infinitive

9. Those apples are red, ripe, and juicy.
    a. adjective   d. adverb
    b. noun   e. gerund
    c. verb   f. infinitive

▶ **Practice 3. Parallel structure.** (Chart 16-1)
Write the letter of the word or phrase that best completes the sentence.

    a. carefully   e. reliable health care
    b. excellence in   f. responsible
    c. in agriculture   g. seeking practical solutions
    d. provide quality education   h. finds a way to get the important jobs done

1. Mr. Li has had wide experience. He has worked in business, in the news media, and _____.

2. People want safe homes, good schools, and _____.

3. As a taxpayer, I want my money used wisely and _____.

4. Mrs. Adams is respected for researching issues and _____.

5. Ms. Hunter has established a record of effective and _____ leadership in government.

6. She has worked hard to control excess government spending, protect our environment, and

    _____.

7. Carol is a hard-working personnel manager who welcomes challenges and _____.

8. I will continue to fight for adequate funding of and _____ education.

▶ **Practice 4. Parallel structure: using commas.** (Chart 16-2)
Add commas as necessary.

1. Jack was calm and quiet.

2. Jack was calm quiet and serene.

3. The football players practiced kicking and throwing the ball and they ran laps.

4. The football players practiced kicking throwing and running.

5. The children collected rocks and insects, and flew kites.

6. The teacher told the children to sit down be quiet and open their reading books.

7. The teacher told the children to sit down and be quiet.

8. Did you know that the pupil of your eye expands and contracts slightly with each heartbeat?

pupil

9. Our server carried two cups of coffee three glasses of water one glass of orange juice and three orders of eggs on her tray.

10. My parents were strict but fair with their children.

▶ **Practice 5. Parallel structure.** (Charts 16-1 and 16-2)
<u>Underline</u> the words that are supposed to be parallel. Write "C" if the parallel structure is correct. Write "I" if the parallel structure is incorrect, and make any necessary corrections.

1. __I__ I admire him for his <u>intelligence</u>, cheerful <u>disposition</u>, and ~~he is honest~~. *honesty*

2. __C__ Abraham Lincoln was a <u>lawyer</u> and a <u>politician</u>.

3. _____ The boat sailed across the lake smoothly and quiet.

4. _____ Barb studies each problem carefully and works out a solution.

5. _____ Aluminum is plentiful and relatively inexpensive.

6. _____ Many visitors to Los Angeles enjoy visiting Disneyland and to tour movie studios.

7. _____ Children are usually interested in but a little frightened by snakes.

8. _____ So far this term, the students in the writing class have learned how to write thesis statements, organize their material, and summarizing their conclusions.

9. _____ When I looked more closely, I saw that it was not coffee but chocolate on my necktie.

10. _____ Physics explains why water freezes and how the sun produces heat.

11. _____ All plants need light, a suitable climate, and they require an ample supply of water and minerals from the soil.

12. _____ With their keen sight, fine hearing, and refined sense of smell, wolves hunt day or night in quest of elk, deer, moose, or caribou.

► **Practice 6. Paired conjunctions:** *both . . . and; not only . . . but also; either . . . or; neither . . . nor.* (Chart 16-3)

Complete the sentences with the correct present tense form of the verb in parentheses.

1. Neither the students nor the teacher (*know*) _____*knows*_____ the answer.

2. Neither the teacher nor the students (*know*) _____*know*_____ the answer.

3. Not only the students but also the teacher (*know*) _____ the answer.

4. Not only the teacher but also the students (*know*) _____ the answer.

5. Both the teacher and the students (*know*) _____ the answer.

6. Neither Alan nor Carol (*want*) _____ to go skiing this weekend.

7. Both John and Ted (*like*) _____ to go cross-country skiing.

8. Either Jack or Alice (*have*) _____ the information you need.

9. Neither my parents nor my brother (*agree*) _____ with my decision.

10. Both intelligence and skill (*be*) _____ essential to good teaching.

11. Neither my classmates nor my teacher (*realize*) _____ that I have no idea what's going on in class.

12. Not only my husband but also my children (*be*) _____ in favor of my decision to return to school and finish my graduate degree.

► **Practice 7. Paired conjunctions:** *both . . . and; not only . . . but also; either . . . or; neither . . . nor.* (Chart 16-3)

Write sentences with the given words and the paired conjunctions. Use capital letters and punctuation where necessary.

1. Mary drinks coffee. Her parents drink coffee.

   a. both . . . and _____.

   b. neither . . . nor _____.

2. John will do the work. Henry will do the work.

   a. either . . . or _____.

   b. neither . . . nor _____.

3. Our school recycles trash. The restaurants in town recycle trash.

   a. not only . . . but also _____.

   b. both . . . and _____.

► **Practice 8. Paired conjunctions:** *both . . . and; not only . . . but also; either . . . or; neither . . . nor.* (Chart 16-3)

Part I. Use *both . . . and*.

1. You know her mother. Do you know her father too?

   Yes, I know _____*both her mother and her father*_____.

2. The nurses usually arrive early. Does the doctor arrive early too?

   Yes, _____ early.

3. Bananas originated in Asia. Did mangos originate in Asia too?

Yes, _____ in Asia.

4. Whales are mammals. Are dolphins mammals too?

Yes, _____ mammals.

Part II. Use **not only . . . but also**.

5. Ethiopia exports coffee. Does it export oil too?

Ethiopia _____.

6. Air Greenland flies to Greenland. What about Icelandair?

_____ to Greenland.

7. You bought a lime-green jacket. What about pants? Did you buy lime-green pants too?

Yes, I bought _____ to go with it.

8. Al attended Harvard University. Did he attend Harvard Law School too?

Yes, Al _____.

Part III. Use **either . . . or**.

9. Someone knows the answer. Is it Ricky? Paula? One of them knows.

_____ the answer.

10. You're going to Mexico on your vacation. Are you going to Costa Rica too?

We're going _____, not to both.

11. Who will take Taka to the airport: Jim or Taka's parents?

_____ to the airport.

12. Helen's buying salmon. Is she buying tuna too?

No. She's buying _____, whichever looks fresher.

Part IV. Use **neither . . . nor**.

13. Fred doesn't eat red meat. Do his children eat red meat?

No, _____ eat red meat.

14. She doesn't have health insurance. Do her children have health insurance?

No, _____ health insurance.

15. Luis doesn't have a family. Does he have friends?

No, _____.

16. How's the weather there? Is it hot? Is it cold?

It's perfect! It's _____.

▶ **Practice 9. Separating independent clauses with periods; connecting them with *and* and *but*.** (Chart 16-4)

Punctuate the sentences by adding commas or periods. Do not add any words. Add capitalization as necessary.

1. The rain stopped the birds sang.

2. The rain stopped and the birds sang.

3. The rain stopped the birds sang and the clouds disappeared.

4. A young boy ran out on the street his mother ran after him.

5. A young boy ran out on the street and his mother ran after him.

6. A young boy ran out on the street his mother ran after him and caught him by his shirt collar.

7. The café serves delicious pastries and coffee and it is always crowded.

8. The café serves delicious pastries and coffee it is always crowded.

9. The café serves delicious pastries, coffee, and ice cream but it is never crowded.

▶ **Practice 10. Separating independent clauses with periods; connecting them with *and* and *but*.** (Chart 16-4)

Correct the errors in punctuation and capitalization.

(1) My brother is visiting me for a couple of days we spent yesterday together in the city and we had a really good time.

(2) first I took him to the waterfront we went to the aquarium we saw fearsome sharks some wonderfully funny marine mammals and all kinds of tropical fish after the aquarium, we went downtown to a big mall and went shopping.

(3) I had trouble thinking of a place to take him for lunch because he's a strict vegetarian but I remembered a restaurant that has vegan food we went there and we had a wonderful lunch of fresh vegetables and whole grains I'm not a vegetarian but I must say that I really enjoyed the meal.

(4) In the afternoon it started raining we decided to go to a movie it was pretty good but had too much violence for me I felt tense when we left the theater I prefer comedies or dramas my brother loved the movie.

(5) We ended the day with a delicious home-cooked meal and some good conversation in my living room it was an excellent day I like spending time with my brother.

▶ **Practice 11. Chapter review.** (Chapter 16)

Correct the errors. Add the necessary punctuation.

1. Either John will call Mary or Bob.

2. Not only Sue saw the mouse but also the cat.

3. Both my mother talked to the teacher and my father.

4. Either Mr. Anderson or Ms. Wiggins are going to teach our class today.

5. I enjoy not only reading novels but also magazines I enjoy.

6. Smallpox is a dangerous disease. Malaria too. Both are dangerous.

7. She wants to buy a compact car, she is saving her money.

8. According to the news report, it will snow tonight the roads may be dangerous in the morning.

9. While we were in New York, we attended an opera, while we were in New York, we ate at marvelous restaurants, we visited some old friends.

▶ **Practice 12. Chapter review.**
Complete the crossword puzzle. Use the clues under the puzzle. All the words come from Chapter 16.

Across

3. I drink tea, _____ I don't drink coffee.
4. Carl is not _____ a chemist but also a biologist.
6. Thankfully, _____ Mary or Joe will help us.
7. He has neither friends _____ money.

Down

1. _____ Jane nor Al speaks Spanish.
2. _____ Sue and Sam are doctors.
5. Salt _____ pepper are on the table.

Chapter 17
Adverb Clauses

▶ **Practice 1. Adverb clauses.** (Chart 17-1)
Underline the adverb clause in each sentence.

1. Sue dropped a carton of eggs <u>as she was leaving the store</u>.
2. Tomorrow, we'll all take a run in the park before we have breakfast.
3. Since Douglas fell off his bicycle last week, he has had to use crutches to walk.
4. Because I already had my boarding pass, I didn't have to stand in line at the airline counter.
5. Productivity in a factory increases if the workplace is made pleasant.
6. After Ceylon had been independent for 24 years, its name was changed to Sri Lanka.
7. Ms. Johnson regularly returns her email messages as soon as she receives them.
8. Tarik will be able to work more efficiently once he becomes familiar with the new computer program.

▶ **Practice 2. Periods and commas.** (Chart 17-1)
Add periods and commas as necessary. Do not change, add, or omit any words. Capitalize as necessary.

1. The lake was calm. Tom went fishing.
2. Because the lake was calm Tom went fishing.
3. Tom went fishing because the lake was calm he caught two fish.
4. When Tom went fishing the lake was calm he caught two fish.
5. The lake was calm so Tom went fishing he caught two fish.
6. Because the lake was calm and quiet Tom went fishing.
7. The lake was calm quiet and clear when Tom went fishing.
8. Because Mr. Hood has dedicated his life to helping the poor he is admired in his community.
9. Mr. Hood is admired because he has dedicated his life to helping the poor he is well known for his work on behalf of homeless people.
10. Microscopes automobile dashboards and cameras are awkward for left-handed people to use they are designed for right-handed people when "lefties" use these items they have to use their right hand to do the things that they would normally do with their left hand.

► **Practice 3. Verb tenses in adverb clauses of time.** (Charts 17-1 and 17-2)
Circle the letter of the correct answer.

1. After Ismael _____ his degree, he plans to seek employment in an engineering firm.
   a. will finish   b. finishes   c. is going to finish   d. is finishing

2. By the time Colette leaves work today, she _____ the budget report.
   a. will finish   b. finishes   c. will have finished   d. had finished

3. When my aunt _____ at the airport tomorrow, I'll be at work, so I can't pick her up.
   a. will arrive   b. arrived   c. will have arrived   d. arrives

4. Natasha heard a small "meow" and looked down to discover a kitten at her feet. When she saw it, she _____.
   a. is smiling   b. had smiled   c. smiled   d. smiles

5. Ahmed has trouble keeping a job. By the time Ahmed was thirty, he _____ eight different jobs.
   a. has   b. was having   c. had had   d. had been having

6. Maria waits until her husband, Al, _____ to work before she calls her friends on the phone.
   a. will go   b. went   c. will have gone   d. goes

7. I went to an opera at Lincoln Center the last time I _____ to New York City.
   a. go   b. went   c. had gone   d. have gone

8. When the police arrived, the building was empty. The thieves _____ and escaped through an unlocked window.
   a. will have   b. have entered   c. had entered   d. were entering

9. It seems that whenever I try to take some quiet time for myself, the phone _____.
   a. has been ringing   b. rings   c. is ringing   d. has rung

10. I'll invite the Thompsons to the potluck dinner the next time I _____ them.
    a. see   b. will see   c. will have seen   d. have seen

11. I _____ hard to help support my family ever since I was a child.
    a. worked   b. work   c. am working   d. have worked

12. A small rabbit ran across the path in front of me as I _____ through the woods.
    a. was walking   b. had walked   c. am walking   d. had been walking

► **Practice 4. Verb tense review.** (Chart 17-2)
Write "1" before the event that happened first. Write "2" before the event that happened second. Write "S" for *same* if the events happened at the same time.

1. As soon as it stopped snowing, the children ran out to go sledding in the fresh snow.

   _1_ It stopped snowing.

   _2_ The children ran out to go sledding.

2. I'll call you as soon as we arrive at the motel.

   _____ I'll call you.

   _____ We arrive at the hotel.

3. We turned on the heat when it got cold.

   _____ It got cold.

   _____ We turned on the heat.

4. We will turn on the heat when it gets cold.

_____ We will turn on the heat.

_____ It will get cold.

5. By the time Sharon gets home from Africa, she will have been away for two years.

_____ Sharon gets home.

_____ She will have been away.

6. By the time Marc graduated from medical school, he had been studying for 20 years.

_____ He had been studying.

_____ Marc graduated from medical school.

7. We were crying while we were watching the movie.

_____ We were crying.

_____ We were watching the movie.

8. When I have some news, I'll tell you.

_____ I have some news.

_____ I'll tell you.

▶ **Practice 5. Using adverb clauses to show cause and effect.** (Chart 17-3)
Complete the sentences in Column A with a clause from Column B.

Column A

1. I left a message on Jane's voice mail because _____.
2. Since everybody in my office dresses informally, _____.
3. Now that it's summer, _____.
4. I was late for work because _____.
5. Because the temperature dropped below 0 degrees C (32 degrees F), _____.
6. Sue hopes to find a good job now that _____ .
7. I'm not going to the party since _____.
8. We had to eat dinner by candlelight because _____.
9. Since our favorite restaurant was closed, _____.
10. I prefer a small car because _____.

Column B

a. the days are longer
b. we went to another one
c. I wasn't invited
d. she didn't answer her phone
e. the electricity went off
f. there was a big traffic jam
g. it uses less gasoline
h. the water in the lake froze
i. I usually wear jeans to work
j. she has received her master's degree in business

▶ **Practice 6. Using adverb clauses to show cause and effect.** (Chart 17-3)
Combine the sentences. Write one clause in each blank.

1. My registration was canceled. I didn't pay the registration fee on time.

_____ because _____.

2. I'm late. There was a lot of traffic.

_____ because _____.

3. Harry lost 35 pounds. He was on a strict weight-loss diet.

Because _____, _____.

4. We can't have lunch at Mario's tomorrow. It is closed on Sundays.

Since _____, _____.

5. Jack drives to work. He has a car.

Now that _____, _____.

6. Natalie should find another job. She is very unhappy in this job.

_____ since _____.

7. David knows the way. He will lead us.

_____ because _____.

8. Frank has graduated from law school. He is looking for a job in a law office.

_____ now that _____.

▶ **Practice 7. *Even though* vs. *because*.** (Charts 17-3 and 17-4)
Circle *even though* or *because*.

1. I put on my raincoat (*even though* / *because*) it was a bright, sunny day.

2. I put on my raincoat (*even though* / *because*) it was raining.

3. (*Even though* / *Because*) Sue is a good student, she received a scholarship.

4. (*Even though* / *Because*) Ann is a good student, she didn't receive a scholarship.

5. (*Even though* / *Because*) I was so tired, I didn't want to walk all the way home. I took a taxi.

6. (*Even though* / *Because*) I was dead tired, I walked all the way home.

7. This letter was delivered (*even though* / *because*) it didn't have enough postage.

8. That letter was returned to the sender (*even though* / *because*) it didn't have enough postage.

▶ **Practice 8. *Even though* vs. *because*.** (Charts 17-3 and 17-4)
Complete the sentences with *even though* or *because*.

1. I'm going horseback riding with Judy this afternoon _____ I'm afraid of horses.

2. I'm going horseback riding with Judy this afternoon _____ I enjoy it.

3. _____ the economy is not good right now, people are not buying new cars and other expensive items.

4. _____ the economy is not good right now, the supermarket is still a profitable business. People always have to eat.

5. Members of the Polar Bear Club are swimmers who go swimming in the ocean _____ the temperature may be freezing.

6. Members of the Polar Bear Club are swimmers who swim in the ocean every day in summer and winter _____ they love to swim in the ocean.

7. Janet got a grade of 98 percent on her history test _____ she studied hard.

8. Mike got a grade of 98 percent on his history test _____ he didn't study at all. I wonder how that happened.

► **Practice 9. Showing direct contrast: *while.*** (Chart 17-5)
Circle the letter of the phrase that shows direct contrast.

1. Larry and Barry are twins, but they are very different. Larry never studies, while Barry _____.
   a. rarely studies
   b. sleeps all day
   c. is very studious

2. My roommate and I disagree about the room temperature. While she likes it warm, I _____.
   a. prefer cold temperatures
   b. have trouble when it is cool
   c. don't like my roommate

3. Athletes need to be strong, but they may need different physical characteristics for different sports. For example, weight-lifters have well-developed chest muscles, while _____.
   a. basketball players' muscles are strong
   b. basketball players should be tall
   c. basketball players' chest muscles are very large

4. Portland, Maine, is on the East Coast of the United States, while Portland, Oregon, _____.
   a. is on the East Coast too
   b. lies on the West Coast
   c. is another medium-sized city

5. Crocodiles and alligators look a lot alike, but they have certain differences. While a crocodile has a very long, narrow, V-shaped snout, the alligator's snout is _____.
   a. wider and U-shaped
   b. long, narrow, and V-shaped
   c. large and green

6. The Earth is similar to Venus in some ways, but their atmospheres are different. While the Earth's atmosphere contains mostly nitrogen and oxygen, _____.
   a. Venus has mainly nitrogen and oxygen
   b. Venus' air is very cold
   c. Venus' atmosphere consists mostly of the gas carbon dioxide

7. Polar bears live near the North Pole, while _____.
   a. penguins live there too
   b. penguins live at the South Pole
   c. they live in the South Pole

8. Potatoes and tomatoes originated in the Americas, while _____.
   a. mangos and bananas come from Asia
   b. corn and chocolate come from the Americas
   c. turkeys first lived in North America

► **Practice 10. If-clauses.** (Chart 17-6)

Underline the entire *if*-clause. Correct any errors in verb forms. Some sentences have no errors.

1. We won't go to the beach if it ~~will rain~~ tomorrow.

rains

2. <u>If my car doesn't start tomorrow morning</u>, I'll take the bus to work. (*no change*)

3. If I have any free time during my work day, I'll call you.

4. I'll send you an email if I will have some free time tomorrow.

5. If we don't leave within the next ten minutes, we are late for the theater.

6. If we will leave within the next ten minutes, we will make it to the theater on time.

7. The population of the world will be 9.1 billion in 2050 if it will continue to grow at the present

   rate.

► **Practice 11. Shortened if-clauses.** (Chart 17-7)

First, complete the sentences in two ways:
   a. Use **so** or **not**.
   b. Use a helping verb or main verb **be**.
Then, give the full meaning of the shortened *if*-clause.

1. Does Tom live near you?
   a. If _____*so*_____, ask him to pick you up at 5:30.
   b. If he ____*does*____, ask him to pick you up at 5:30.
   Meaning: ____*If Tom lives near you*____

2. Are you a resident of Springfield?
   a. If _____, you can get a library card for the Springfield Library.
   b. If you _____, you can get a library card for the Springfield Library.
   Meaning: _____

3. Do you have enough money to go out to dinner?
   a. If _____, I'll pay for you.
   b. If you _____, I'll pay for you.
   Meaning: _____

4. Are you going to do the laundry?
   a. If _____, I have some things that need washing too.
   b. If you _____, I have some things that need washing too.
   Meaning: _____

5. I think I left the water running in the sink.
   a. If _____, we'd better go home and turn it off.
   b. If I _____, we'd better go home and turn it off.
   Meaning: _____

▶ **Practice 12. Using *whether or not* and *even if.*** (Chart 17-8)
Complete the sentences using the given information.

1. Juan is going to go to the horse races no matter what. He doesn't care if his wife approves. In other words, Juan is going to go to the horse races even if his wife _____*doesn't approve*_____ . He's going to go whether his wife _____*approves*_____ or not.

2. Fatima is determined to buy an expensive car. It doesn't matter to her if she can't afford it. In other words, Fatima is going to buy an expensive car whether she _____ it or not. She's going to buy one even if she _____ it.

3. William wears his raincoat every day. He wears it when it's raining. He wears it when it's not raining. In other words, William wears his raincoat whether it _____ or not. He wears it even if it _____ .

4. Some students don't understand what the teacher is saying, but still they smile and nod. In other words, even if they _____ what the teacher is saying, they smile and nod. They smile and nod whether they _____ what the teacher is saying or not.

5. Everybody has to pay taxes. It doesn't matter whether you want to or not. In other words, even if you _____ , you have to pay them. You have to pay your taxes _____ or not.

▶ **Practice 13. Adverb clauses of condition: using *unless.*** (Chart 17-10)
The sentences in *italics* are well-known proverbs or sayings. Write sentences with the same meaning as the sentences in *italics*. Use *unless*.

1. *If you can't stand the heat, get out of the kitchen.*
   (This means that if you can't take the pressure, then you should remove yourself from the situation.)
   Get out of the kitchen _____*unless you can stand the heat*_____ .

2. *If it isn't broken, don't fix it.* (This is often said as *If it ain't broke, don't fix it.*)
   (This means that any attempt to improve something that already works is pointless and may even hurt it.)
   Don't fix it _____ .

3. *If you can't beat 'em, join 'em.*
   (This means if you can't beat your opponents, you can join them.)
   You might not be successful _____ .

► **Practice 14. Adverb clauses of condition: using *only if.*** (Chart 17-11)
Complete the sentences with the information in the given sentence.

1. Jack never calls his uncle unless he wants something.

   Jack calls his uncle only if _____.

2. When Helen runs out of clean clothes, she does her laundry. Otherwise, she never does laundry.

   Helen does laundry only if _____.

3. José doesn't like to turn on the heat in his house unless the temperature outside goes below 50 degrees F (10 degrees C).

   José turns on the heat only if _____.

4. Zack hates to fly. He usually travels by car or train except when it is absolutely necessary to get somewhere quickly.

   Zack flies only if _____.

5. Most applicants cannot get into Halley College. You probably won't get in. Only the top students will get in.

   Only if you are a top student _____.

6. I could never afford a big house like that! Well, maybe if I win the lottery. That would be the only way.

   Only if I win the lottery _____.

► **Practice 15. Review: adverb clauses of condition.** (Charts 17-8 → 17-11)
Circle the correct words in parentheses to logically complete each sentence.

1. I'll pass the course only if I (*pass / don't pass*) the final examination.
2. I'm (*going to go / not going to go*) to the park unless the weather is nice.
3. I'm going to the park unless it (*rains / doesn't rain*).
4. I'm sorry that you won't join us on Saturday. But please call us (*in case / even if*) you change your mind.
5. Bob doesn't like to work. He'll get a job (*unless / only if*) he has to.
6. I (*always eat / never eat*) breakfast unless I get up late and don't have enough time.
7. I always finish my homework (*even if / only if*) I'm sleepy and want to go to bed.
8. Ali is at his desk at 8:00 A.M. sharp (*whether / unless*) his boss is there or not.
9. You (*will / won't*) learn to play the guitar well unless you practice every day.
10. Even if the president calls, (*wake / don't wake*) me up. I don't want to talk to anyone. I need to sleep.
11. Burt is going to come to the game with us today (*if / unless*) his boss gives him the afternoon off.
12. Only if people succeed in reducing greenhouse gases (*we can / can we*) avoid the effects of global warming.

▶ **Practice 16. Adverb clauses.** (Chapter 17)
Complete the sentences with the correct phrase from the list. Write the letter of the phrase.

a. her friend goes with her
b. I don't eat meat
c. I don't have an 8:00 A.M. class anymore
d. I eat meat

e. I'm working on the weekends now
f. none of her friends will go with her
g. you have a real emergency
h. you promise to keep it a secret

1. A: Won't you tell me about Emma and Tom? Oh, please tell me!

   B: Well, OK, I'll tell you, but only if ____ .

2. A: Hello, 911? Police? I want to report a barking dog.

   B: This is 911. You've dialed the wrong number. Call this number only in case ____ .

3. A: Isn't Sara coming to the party?

   B: I don't think so. She's too shy to come alone. She doesn't go anyplace unless ____ .

4. A: Your grandmother has traveled to 32 countries all by herself?

   B: Yes, she has! She loves to travel to exotic places even if ____ .

5. A: Do you want to go to Johnson's Steak House or Vernon's Vegetable Stand for lunch?

   B: Definitely, Vernon's Vegetable Stand since ____ .

6. A: They say that people who don't eat meat live longer than people who do.

   B: Well, I think that I will live a certain number of years whether or not ____ .

7. A: You haven't come to our book club for months! How come?

   B: Oh, I can't come on Saturdays anymore because ____ .

8. A: Hi, Kevin. . . . Oh, did I wake you up? It's 7:30 already! You need to get up.

   B: I sleep later now, Andy, since ____ .

▶ **Practice 17. Chapter review.**
Circle the letter of the adverb or adverb phrase that best completes each sentence.

1. Alice will tutor you in math ____ you promise to show up promptly every day.
   a. unless   b. only if   c. whereas   d. even though

2. Oscar won't pass his math course ____ he gets a tutor.
   a. in case   b. unless   c. only if   d. because

3. Most people you meet will be polite to you ____ you are polite to them.
   a. in case   b. even though   c. unless   d. if

4. I'm glad that my mother made me take piano lessons when I was a child ____ I hated it at the time. Now, I enjoy playing the piano every day.
   a. even though   b. because   c. unless   d. if

5. Chicken eggs will not hatch ____ they are kept at the proper temperature.
   a. because   b. unless   c. only if   d. even though

6. You'd better take your raincoat with you _____ the weather changes. It could rain before you get home again.
   a. now that   b. even if   c. in case   d. only if

7. Ms. Jackson was assigned the fifth-grade science class _____ she has the best science qualifications of all the teachers in that elementary school.
   a. although   b. whereas   c. if   d. since

8. My sister can fall asleep under any conditions, but I can't get to sleep _____ the light is off and the room is perfectly quiet.
   a. if   b. unless   c. in case   d. now that

9. In a democratic government, a leader is directly responsible to the people, _____ in a dictatorship, a leader has no direct responsibility to the people.
   a. because   b. even though   c. while   d. unless

10. Parents love and support their children _____ the children misbehave or do foolish things.
    a. even if   b. since   c. if   d. only if

Chapter 18

Reduction of Adverb Clauses to Modifying Adverbial Phrases

▶ **Practice 1. Introduction.** (Chart 18-1)
Each sentence contains either an adverb clause or an adverb phrase. <u>Underline</u> the adverb clause or phrase in each sentence.

1. <u>While they were riding in the car for six hours,</u> the children became restless.

2. <u>While riding in the car for six hours,</u> the children became restless.

3. Before taking our long car trip across the country, we had drawn our route on a large road map.

4. While watching the exciting basketball game on TV, the boys forgot all about dinner.

5. While they were watching the exciting basketball game on TV, the boys forgot all about dinner.

6. Before leaving for the airport, we checked to make sure we had all our travel necessities with us.

7. We heard a lot of thunder while we were walking on the beach this afternoon.

8. We heard a lot of thunder while walking on the beach this afternoon.

9. While I was trying to get a taxi, I was almost run over by several taxis that

    passed me by.

10. Before getting into a taxi, I was almost run over by several that passed me by.

▶ **Practice 2. Modifying adverbial phrases.** (Chart 18-2)
Check the grammatically correct sentences.

1. ____ While watching an exciting program, the TV suddenly went off.
2. ____ While starting up, my computer suddenly crashed.
3. ____ While watching an exciting program, I fell asleep.
4. ____ Before going to bed, I always open the bedroom windows.
5. ____ Before going to bed, the bedroom windows are always open.
6. ____ After opening the bedroom windows, I crawl into bed for the night.
7. ____ Since graduating from college, nobody has offered me a job yet.
8. ____ Since graduating from college, I haven't found a job yet.
9. ____ After sitting on her eggs for four weeks, we saw the mother duck welcome her baby ducklings.
10. ____ After sitting on her eggs for four weeks, the mother duck welcomed her baby ducklings.

► **Practice 3. Changing time clauses to modifying adverbial phrases.**
   (Chart 18-2)
Change the adverb clause to a modifying phrase.

1. Since ~~he opened~~ *opening* his new business, Bob has been working sixteen hours a day.

2. I shut off the lights before I left the room.

3. After I had met the movie star in person, I understood why she was so popular.

4. After I searched through all my pockets, I found my keys.

5. While he was herding his goats in the mountains, an Ethiopian named Kaldi discovered the coffee plant more than 1,200 years ago.

6. Before they marched into battle, ancient Ethiopian soldiers ate a mixture of coffee beans and fat for extra energy.

7. While she was flying across the Pacific Ocean in 1937, the famous pilot Amelia Earhart disappeared.

8. After they imported rabbits to Australia, the settlers found that these animals became pests.

► **Practice 4. Adverb clauses and modifying phrases.** (Charts 18-1 → 18-3)
Complete the sentences with the correct form of the verb in parentheses.

1. a. Before (*leave*) _____leaving_____ on his trip, Tom renewed his passport.
   b. Before Tom (*leave*) _____left_____ on his trip, he renewed his passport.

2. a. After Thomas Edison (*invent*) _____invented / had invented_____ the light bulb, he went on to create many other useful inventions.
   b. After (*invent*) _____inventing / having invented_____ the light bulb, Thomas Edison went on to create many other useful inventions.

3. a. While (*work*) _____ with uranium ore, Marie Curie discovered two new elements, radium and polonium.
   b. While she (*work*) _____ with uranium ore, Marie Curie discovered two new elements, radium and polonium.

4. a. Before an astronaut (*fly*) _____ on a space mission, she will have undergone thousands of hours of training.
   b. Before (*fly*) _____ on a space mission, an astronaut will have undergone thousands of hours of training.

5. a. After they (*study*) _____ the stars, the ancient Mayans in Central America developed a very accurate solar calendar.
   b. After (*study*) _____ the stars, the ancient Mayans in Central America developed a very accurate solar calendar.

6. a. Since (*learn*) _____ that cigarettes cause cancer, many people have stopped smoking.

    b. Since they (*learn*) _____ that cigarettes cause cancer, many people have stopped smoking.

7. a. When (*take*) _____ any medication, you should be sure to follow the directions on the label.

    b. When you (*take*) _____ any medication, you should be sure to follow the directions on the label.

8. a. While I (*drive*) _____ to my uncle's house, I took a wrong turn and ended up back where I had started.

    b. While (*drive*) _____ to my uncle's house, I took a wrong turn and ended up back where I had started.

▶ **Practice 5. Expressing the idea of "during the same time" in modifying adverbial phrases.** (Chart 18-3)

<u>Underline</u> the subject of the adverb clause and the subject of the main clause. Change the adverb clauses to modifying phrases if possible.

1. While <u>Sam</u> was driving to work in the rain, his <u>car</u> got a flat tire.

    ___*(no change)*_____

2. While <u>Sam</u> was driving to work, <u>he</u> had a flat tire.

    ___*While driving to work, Sam had a flat tire.*_____

3. Before Nick left on his trip, his son gave him a big hug and a kiss.

    _____

4. Before Nick left on his trip, he gave his itinerary to his secretary.

    _____

5. After Tom had worked hard in the garden all afternoon, he took a shower and then went to the movies with his friends.

    _____

6. After Sunita had made a delicious chicken curry for her friends, they wanted the recipe.

    _____

7. Before a friend tries to do something hard, an American may say "Break a leg!" to wish him or her good luck.

    _____

8. Emily always cleans off her desk before she leaves the office at the end of each day.

    _____

► **Practice 6. Expressing the idea of "during the same time" and cause/effect in modifying adverbial phrases.** (Charts 18-3 and 18-4)

<u>Underline</u> the modifying adverbial phrase in each sentence. Then circle the letter of the meaning of each modifying phrase. In some sentences, both meanings may be given.

1. Riding his bicycle to school, Enrique fell off and scraped his knee.
   a. while   b. because

2. Being seven feet tall, the basketball player couldn't sit in a regular airplane seat.
   a. while   b. because

3. Driving to work this morning, I remembered that I had already missed the special 8:00 A.M. breakfast meeting.
   a. while   b. because

4. Running five miles on a very hot day, James felt exhausted.
   a. while   b. because

5. Having run for 26 miles in the marathon, the runners were exhausted at the end of the race.
   a. while   b. because

6. Drinking a tall glass of soothing iced tea, Ann felt her tired muscles relax.
   a. while   b. because

7. Clapping loudly at the end of the game, the fans showed their appreciation of the team.
   a. while   b. because

8. Speaking with her guidance counselor, Carol felt that she was being understood.
   a. while   b. because

9. Knowing that I was going to miss the plane because of heavy traffic, I phoned the airline to get a seat on a later plane.
   a. while   b. because

10. Having missed my plane, I had to wait four hours to take the next one.
    a. while   b. because

11. Waiting for my plane to depart, I watched thousands of people walking through the airport.
    a. while   b. because

► **Practice 7. Expressing the idea of "during the same time" and cause/effect in modifying adverbial phrases.** (Charts 18-3 and 18-4)

Complete the sentences in Column A with a clause from Column B.

Column A

1. Talking on the phone with my friend, _____.
2. While watching an old movie on TV _____.
3. Drinking a big glass of water in four seconds, _____.
4. Because I like old movies, _____.
5. Since receiving a big job promotion, _____.
6. Having finished my long report, _____.
7. Unable to reach my friend by phone, _____.
8. Being a shy person, _____.
9. Having lived in Rome for two years, _____.
10. Wanting to get home quickly, _____.

Column B

a. I handed it in to my supervisor this morning
b. I watch a lot of them on TV late at night
c. I decided to email her
d. I have more responsibility
e. I can speak Italian
f. I don't like to go to parties alone
g. I ran all the way
h. I heard the click of the phone disconnecting
i. I fell asleep
j. I quenched my thirst

► **Practice 8. Modifying phrases and clauses.** (Charts 18-2 →18-4)

Circle all the possible completions for each sentence. More than one may be correct.

1. Before _____ you, I had not known such a wonderful person existed!
   a. met   b. meeting   c. I met

2. After _____ what the candidate had to say, I am considering voting for him.
   a. I heard   b. having heard   c. hearing

3. Since _____ married, Fred seems very happy and content.
   a. he got   b. getting   c. got

4. _____ through outer space at a speed of 25,000 miles per hour (40,000 kilometers), the astronauts were able to see the Earth.
   a. Speeding   b. While speeding   c. Sped

5. _____ president of his new country, George Washington had been a general in its army.
   a. Before becoming b. While becoming   c. Before he became

6. _____ rap music before, our grandparents wondered why it was so popular.
   a. Had never heard b. Because they had never heard   c. Never having heard

7. _____ the English faculty, Professor Wilson has become the most popular teacher at our university.
   a. Since joining   b. While joining   c. Since he joined

▶ **Practice 9. Modifying phrases with *upon*.** (Chart 18-5)
Rewrite the sentences with the given words.

1. When Sarah received her acceptance letter for medical school, she shouted for joy.

    a. Upon _____.

    b. On _____.

2. On hearing the sad news, Kathleen began to cry.

    a. Upon _____.

    b. When _____.

3. Upon looking at the accident victim, the paramedics decided to transport him to the hospital.

    a. On _____.

    b. When _____.

▶ **Practice 10. Modifying phrases with *upon*.** (Chart 18-5)
Complete the sentences using the ideas in the given list.

    a. She learned the problem was not at all serious.
    b. She was told she got it.
    c. She discovered a burnt-out wire.
    ✓d. She arrived at the airport.
    e. She reached the other side of the lake.

1. It had been a long, uncomfortable trip. Upon _____*arriving at the airport*_____, Sue

    quickly unfastened her seat belt and stood in the aisle waiting her turn to disembark.

2. Kim rented a small fishing boat last weekend, but she ended up doing more rowing than

    fishing. The motor died halfway across the lake, so she had to row to shore. It was a long

    distance away. Upon _____, she was exhausted.

3. At first, we thought the fire had been caused by lightning. However, upon

    _____, the fire chief determined it had been

    caused by faulty electrical wiring.

4. Amy felt terrible. She was sure she had some terrible disease, so she went to the doctor for

    some tests. Upon _____, she was extremely

    relieved.

5. Janet wanted that scholarship with all her heart and soul. Upon _____

    _____, she jumped straight up in the air and let out a scream of

    happiness.

► **Practice 11. Modifying phrases.** (Charts 18-1 → 18-5)
Write the letter of a clause from the list that logically follows the modifying phrase.

a. the desperate woman grasped a floating log after the boat turned over
b. the taxi driver caused a multiple-car accident
c. carefully proofread all your answers
d. the students repeated the experiment
e. the athletes waved to the cheering crowd
f. the little girl raised her hand
g. the manager learned of their dissatisfaction with their jobs
h. the passengers angrily walked back to the ticket counter
i. Margo hasn't been able to play tennis
j. the worker in charge of Section B of the assembly line told the assistant manager about a production problem

1. Trying to understand the physics problem, _____.

2. Fighting for her life, _____.

3. Wanting to ask a question, _____.

4. After having injured her ankle, _____.

5. Not wanting to disturb the manager, _____.

6. Upon hearing the announcement that their plane was delayed, _____.

7. Talking with the employees after work, _____.

8. Attempting to get onto the freeway, _____.

9. Stepping onto the platform to receive their medals, _____.

10. Before turning in your exam paper, _____.

Chapter 19
Connectives That Express Cause and Effect, Contrast, and Condition

▶ **Practice 1. Using *because of* and *due to*.** (Chart 19-1)
Circle the letters of the words that can complete each sentence. More than one answer is possible.

1. The plane was delayed because _____.
   a. bad weather
   b. the weather was bad
   c. there was heavy air traffic
   d. heavy air traffic
   e. mechanical difficulty
   f. the mechanics had to make a repair

2. The plane was delayed because of _____.
   a. bad weather
   b. the weather was bad
   c. there was heavy air traffic
   d. heavy air traffic
   e. mechanical difficulty
   f. the mechanics had to make a repair

3. The thief was caught because _____.
   a. the police responded quickly
   b. the quick police response
   c. he left fingerprints
   d. the fingerprints on the door
   e. there was a security video
   f. a security video

4. The thief was caught due to _____.
   a. the police responded quickly
   b. the quick police response
   c. he left fingerprints
   d. the fingerprints on the door
   e. there was a security video
   f. a security video

▶ **Practice 2. Using *because of* and *due to*.** (Chart 19-1)
Circle the words or phrases that can complete the sentences correctly. In some sentences, more than one completion is correct.

1. We delayed our trip (*because / because of / due to*) Dad was sick with the flu.

2. Sue's eyes were red (*due to / because of / because*) she had been crying.

3. The water in most rivers is unsafe to drink (*because / due to / because of*) pollution.

4. The water in most rivers is unsafe to drink (*because / due to / because of*) it is polluted.

5. Some people think Harry succeeded in business (*due to / because of / because*) his charming personality rather than his business skills.

6. You can't enter this secured area (*because of / because / due to*) you don't have an official permit.

7. My lecture notes were incomplete (*due to / because of / because*) the instructor talked too fast.

8. It's unsafe to travel in that country (*because / due to / because of*) the ongoing civil war.

▶ **Practice 3. Using *because of* and *due to*.** (Chart 19-1)
Use the ideas in parentheses to complete the sentences.

1. (*There was heavy traffic.*) We were late due to _____*heavy traffic*_____.

2. (*There was heavy traffic.*) We were late because _____.

3. (*Grandpa is getting old.*) Grandpa doesn't like to drive at night anymore because

   _____.

4. (*Our history professor is quite old.*) Our history professor is going to retire because of

   _____.

5. (*Sarah is afraid of heights.*) She will not walk across a bridge because

   _____.

6. (*Sarah is afraid of heights.*) She will not walk across a bridge because of

   _____.

7. (*There was a cancellation.*) Due to _____, you can

   have an appointment with the doctor this afternoon.

8. (*There was a cancellation today.*) Because _____, you

   can have an appointment with the doctor this afternoon.

▶ **Practice 4. Cause and effect: using *therefore, consequently*, and *so*.**
(Chart 19-2)
Punctuate the sentences in Column B. Add capital letters if necessary.

Column A	Column B
1. *adverb clause:*	Because she had a headache she took some aspirin.
2. *adverb clause:*	She took some aspirin because she had a headache.
3. *prepositional phrase:*	Because of her headache she took some aspirin.
4. *prepositional phrase:*	She took some aspirin because of her headache.
5. *transition:*	She had a headache therefore she took some aspirin.
6. *transition:*	She had a headache she therefore took some aspirin.
7. *transition:*	She had a headache she took some aspirin therefore.
8. *conjunction:*	She had a headache so she took some aspirin.

▶ **Practice 5. Cause and effect: using *therefore, consequently*, and *so*.**
(Chart 19-2)
Each sentence in *italics* is followed by sentences that refer to it. Circle the letter of the word that
logically completes each sentence. Notice the punctuation and capitalization.

SENTENCE 1. *Water boils when its temperature reaches 212 degrees Fahrenheit* (100 degrees Celsius).

1. The water in the pot had reached 212 degrees Fahrenheit. _____, it started to boil.
   ⓐ Therefore   b. So   c. Because

2. The water in the pot started to boil _____ it had reached 212 degrees Fahrenheit.
   a. so   b. because   c. therefore

3. The water in the pot had reached 212 degrees Fahrenheit, _____ it started to boil.
   a. because   b. therefore   c. so

SENTENCE 2. *The main highway is closed.*

1. The main highway is closed. _____ , we are going to take another road.
   a. Therefore   b. Because   c. so

2. We are going to take another road _____ the main highway is closed.
   a. so   b. because   c. therefore

3. The main highway is closed. We are going to take another road, _____ .
   a. therefore   b. Therefore   c. so

4. The main highway is closed, _____ we are going to take another road.
   a. So   b. so   c. therefore

▶ **Practice 6. Cause and effect: using *therefore, consequently,* and *so.***
(Chart 19-2)

Combine the two sentences in *italics* in four different ways. Notice the punctuation and capitalization.

1. *The store didn't have orange juice. I bought lemonade instead.*

   a. _____I bought lemonade_____ because the store _____didn't have any orange juice_____ .

   b. Because _____ , _____ .

   c. _____ . Therefore, _____

   _____ .

   d. _____ , so _____ .

2. *Mel has excellent grades. He will go to a top university.*

   a. _____ . Therefore, _____ .

   b. _____ . He, therefore, _____ .

   c. _____ . _____ , therefore.

   d. _____ , so _____ .

3. *There had been no rain for several months. The crops died.*

   a. Because _____ , _____ .

   b. _____ . Consequently, _____ .

   c. _____ . _____ , therefore,

   _____ .

   d. _____ , so _____ .

► **Practice 7. Showing cause and effect.** (Charts 17-3, 19-1, and 19-2)

Part I. Complete the sentences with ***because of***, ***because***, or ***therefore***. Add any necessary punctuation and capitalization.

1. _____*Because*_____ it rained **,** we stayed home.

2. It rained. _____*Therefore*_____ **,** we stayed home.

3. We stayed home _____*because of*_____ the bad weather.

4. The weather was bad. _____ we stayed home.

5. The typhoon was moving directly toward a small coastal town. _____ all residents were advised to move inland until it passed.

6. The residents moved inland _____ the typhoon.

7. _____ the typhoon was moving directly toward the town all residents were advised to move inland.

8. Giraffes, which are found in the African plains, are the tallest of all animals. Although their bodies are not extremely large, they have very long necks. _____ their long necks, they are tall enough to eat the leaves from the tops of the trees.

Part II. Complete the sentence with ***due to***, ***since***, or ***consequently***. Add any necessary punctuation and capitalization.

9. _____ his poor eyesight John has to sit in the front row in class.

10. _____ John has poor eyesight he has to sit in the front row.

11. John has poor eyesight _____ he has to sit in the front row.

12. Sarah is afraid of heights _____ she will not walk across a bridge.

13. Sarah will not walk across a bridge _____ her fear of heights.

14. Mark is overweight _____ his doctor has advised him to exercise regularly.

15. _____ a diamond is extremely hard, it can be used to cut glass.

► **Practice 8. Periods and commas.** (Chart 19-3)
Punctuate the sentences properly, using periods and commas. Add capital letters if necessary.

1. Edward missed the final exam. ~~t~~^Therefore **,** he failed the course.

2. Edward failed the course because he missed the final exam. (*no change*)

3. Edward missed the final exam **.** ~~h~~^He simply forgot to go to it.

4. Because we forgot to make a reservation we couldn't get a table at our favorite restaurant last night.

5. The waitress kept dropping trays full of dishes therefore she was fired.

6. The waiter kept forgetting customers' orders so he was fired.

7. Ron is an unpleasant dinner companion because of his terrible table manners.

8. The needle has been around since prehistoric times the button was invented about 2,000 years ago the zipper wasn't invented until 1890.

9. It is possible for wildlife observers to identify individual zebras because the patterns of stripes on each zebra are unique no two zebras are alike.

10. When students in the United States are learning to type, they often practice this sentence: *The quick brown fox jumps over the lazy dog* because it contains all the letters of the English alphabet.

▶ **Practice 9. Summary of patterns and punctuation.** (Chart 19-3)
Combine the two sentences in *italics*. Use the words in parentheses in the new sentences.

SENTENCE 1. *Kim ate some bad food. She got sick.*

a. (*because*) _____

b. (*because of*) _____

c. (*so*) _____

d. (*due to*) _____

SENTENCE 2. *Adam was exhausted. He had driven for thirteen hours.*

a. (*therefore*) _____

b. (*since*) _____

c. (*due to the fact that*) _____

d. (*so*) _____

▶ **Practice 10. *Such . . . that* and *so . . . that*.** (Chart 19-4)
Write *such* or *so* to complete the sentences.

1. It was _____such_____ a hot day that we canceled our tennis game.

2. The test was _____so_____ easy that everyone got a high score.

3. The movie was _____ bad that we left early.

4. It was _____ a bad movie that we left early.

5. Professor James is _____ a demanding teacher that many students refuse to take his class.

6. The restaurant patron at the table near us was _____ angry that we became very frightened and left our meals unfinished.

7. The intricate metal lacework on the Eiffel Tower in Paris was _____ complicated that the structure took more than two and a half years to complete.

8. Charles and his brother are _____ hard-working carpenters that I'm sure they'll make a success of their new business.

9. The children had _____ much fun at the carnival that they begged to go again.

10. I feel like I have _____ little energy that I wonder if I'm getting sick.

▶ **Practice 11. *Such . . . that* and *so . . . that.*** (Chart 19-4)
Combine the two sentences. Use *so . . . that* or *such . . . that*.

1. We took a walk. It was a nice day.

    It was _____*such a nice day that we took a walk*_____.

2. The weather was hot. You could fry an egg on the sidewalk.

    The weather _____.

3. I couldn't understand her. She talked too fast.

    She talked _____.

4. It was an expensive car. We couldn't afford to buy it.

    It was _____.

5. There were few people at the meeting. It was canceled.

    There were _____.

6. Ted couldn't fall asleep last night. He was worried about the exam.

    Ted was _____.

7. The tornado struck with great force. It lifted automobiles off the ground.

    The tornado _____.

8. I can't figure out what this sentence says. Joe's handwriting is illegible.

    Joe's handwriting _____.

9. David has too many girlfriends. He can't remember all of their names.

    David has _____.

10. Too many people came to the meeting. There were not enough seats for everyone.

    There were _____.

▶ **Practice 12. Expressing purpose.** (Chart 19-5)
Check the sentences that express purpose.

1. _____ Ali changed jobs in order to be closer to his family.

2. _____ Ali changed jobs, so he has a lot of new information to learn.

3. _____ Ali changed jobs so he could be involved in more interesting work.

4. _____ Ali changed jobs so that he could be closer to his family.

5. _____ The highway will be closed tomorrow so that road crews can make repairs to the road.

6. _____ The highway will be closed tomorrow, so you will need to take a detour.

7. _____ The highway will be closed tomorrow so the road can be repaired.

8. _____ The highway will be closed tomorrow in order for road crews to make repairs.

9. _____ The highway will be closed tomorrow, so we can expect long delays.

10. _____ The highway will be closed tomorrow, so let's do our errands today.

► **Practice 13. Expressing purpose: using *so that*.** (Chart 19-5)
Complete the sentences in Column A with a clause from Column B.

Column A

1. Please open the windows so that ____.
2. Sam put on his boots so that ____.
3. I spoke softly on the phone so that ____.
4. Li bought a very small car so that ____.
5. Fred stayed up all night so that ____.
6. You could lower the price on the house you are trying to sell so that ____.
7. The city has put up a traffic light at the busy intersection so that ____.
8. We are painting the kitchen yellow so that ____.
9. Sid wore a suit and tie for his interview so that ____.
10. Mr. Kim studies advanced Russian so that ____.

Column B

a. my roommate wouldn't wake up
b. he can be a translator
c. it can sell more quickly
d. we can have some fresh air
e. it will be safer for drivers and pedestrians
f. he will be able to save money on gasoline
g. it will look bright and cheerful
h. he would look serious and businesslike
i. he could go hiking in the mountains
j. he could finish writing his long report by morning

► **Practice 14. Using modals with *so that*.** (Chart 19-5)
Decide the meaning of the *so that* clause. Write "1" if the modal verb expresses the idea of *to be able to*. Write "2" if the modal verb expresses the idea of *to make sure*.

1 = to be able to   2 = to make sure

1. ____ The hotel manager asked a guest to turn down her music so that other guests could sleep.
2. ____ Ellen looks for airline tickets online so that she can compare prices.
3. ____ Yoshi arrived at the theater early so that he could get a good seat.
4. ____ Yoshi arrived at the theater early so that he would get a good seat.
5. ____ I'll send your package express mail so that you'll get it the day after tomorrow.
6. ____ I left your dinner in the oven so that it would stay warm.
7. ____ Karin changes her bank password regularly so that no one can access her account.
8. ____ John, you overslept, but I'll drive you to work so that you won't be late.

► **Practice 15. Expressing purpose: using *so that*.** (Chart 19-5)
Write a sentence with the same meaning. Use *so that*.

1. Rachel wanted to watch the news. She turned on the TV.

   Rachel turned on the TV so that she could watch the news.

2. Alex wrote down the time and date of his appointment. He didn't want to forget to go.

   Alex wrote down the time and date of his appointment so that he wouldn't forget to go.

3. Nancy is taking extra courses every semester. She wants to graduate early.

   _____

4. Sue didn't want to disturb her roommate. She lowered the volume on the TV set.

   _____

5. Ed took some change from his pocket. He wanted to buy a newspaper.

   _____

6. I wanted to listen to the news while I was making dinner. I turned on the TV.

   _____

7. I turned off my phone. I didn't want to be interrupted while I was working.

   _____

8. It's a good idea for you to learn keyboarding skills. You'll be able to use your computer more efficiently. _____

   _____

9. Lynn wanted to make sure that she didn't forget to take her book back to the library. She tied a string around her finger. _____

   _____

10. The Parks Department has placed wastebaskets in convenient places in the park. The department wants to make sure people don't litter.

   _____

   _____

▶ **Practice 16. Showing contrast (unexpected result).** (Chart 19-6)
Make logical completions by completing the sentences with *is* or *isn't*.

1. It's the middle of the summer, but the weather _____ very cold.
2. It's the middle of the summer; nevertheless, the weather _____ very cold.
3. The weather _____ warm today even though it's the middle of summer.
4. Although it's the middle of the summer, the weather _____ very cold today.
5. Even though it's the middle of summer, the weather _____ very cold today.
6. It's the middle of summer in spite of the fact that the weather _____ very warm today.
7. Despite the fact that it is the middle of summer, the weather _____ very cold today.
8. It's the middle of summer. However, the weather _____ warm today.
9. It's the middle of summer, yet the weather _____ very warm today.
10. Despite the cold weather, it _____ the middle of summer.

▶ **Practice 17. *Despite, in spite of* vs. *even though, although*.** (Chart 19-6)
Circle the word or phrase to complete the sentence correctly.

1. a. (*Even though* / *Despite*) her doctor has prescribed frequent exercise for her, Carol never does any exercise at all.

   b. (*Even though* / *Despite*) her doctor's orders, Carol has not done any exercise at all.

   c. (*Even though* / *Despite*) the orders her doctor gave her, Carol still hasn't done any exercise.

   d. (*Even though* / *Despite*) the dangers of not exercising, Carol still doesn't exercise.

   e. (*Even though* / *Despite*) she has been warned about the dangers of not exercising by her doctor, Carol still hasn't begun to exercise.

2. a. (*Although* / *In spite of*) an approaching storm, the two climbers continued their trek up the mountain.

   b. (*Although* / *In spite of*) a storm was approaching, the two climbers continued their trek.

   c. (*Although* / *In spite of*) there was an approaching storm, the two climbers continued up the mountain.

   d. (*Although* / *In spite of*) the storm that was approaching the mountain area, the two climbers continued their trek.

   e. (*Although* / *In spite of*) the fact that a storm was approaching the mountain area, the two climbers continued their trek.

3. a. (*Although* / *Despite*) his many hours of practice, George failed his driving test for the third time.

   b. (*Although* / *Despite*) he had practiced for many hours, George failed his driving test for the third time.

   c. (*Although* / *Despite*) practicing for many hours, George failed his driving test again.

   d. (*Although* / *Despite*) his mother and father spent hours with him in the car trying to teach him how to drive, George failed his driving test repeatedly.

   e. (*Although* / *Despite*) his mother and father's efforts to teach him how to drive, George failed his driving test.

4. a. (*Even though* / *In spite of*) repeated crop failures due to drought, the villagers are refusing to leave their traditional homeland for resettlement in other areas.

   b. (*Even though* / *In spite of*) their crops have failed repeatedly due to drought, the villagers are refusing to leave their traditional homeland for resettlement in other areas.

   c. The villagers refuse to leave (*even though* / *in spite of*) the drought.

   d. The villagers refuse to leave (*even though* / *in spite of*) the drought seriously threatens their food supply.

   e. The villagers refuse to leave (*even though* / *in spite of*) the threat to their food supply because of the continued drought.

   f. The villagers refuse to leave (*even though* / *in spite of*) the threat to their food supply is serious because of the continued drought.

   g. The villagers refuse to leave (*even though* / *in spite of*) their food supply is threatened.

   h. The villagers refuse to leave (*even though* / *in spite of*) their threatened food supply.

▶ **Practice 18. Showing contrast.** (Chart 19-6).
Complete the sentences with the letter of the correct phrase from the list.

    a. an inability to communicate well in any language besides English
    b. he had the necessary qualifications
    c. he is afraid of heights
    d. he is normally quite shy and sometimes inarticulate
    e. his fear of heights
    f. his parents were worried about his intelligence because he didn't speak until he was four years old
    g. it has been shown to be safe
    h. they have been shown to cause birth defects and sometimes death
    i. its many benefits
    j. his competence and experience

1. In spite of _____, Carl enjoyed his helicopter trip over the Grand Canyon in Arizona.

2. Although _____, Mark rode in a cable car to the top of Sugar Loaf mountain in Rio de Janeiro for the magnificent view.

3. Because of his age, John was not hired even though _____.

4. Although _____, many people avoid using a microwave oven for fear of its radiation.

5. Jack usually has little trouble making new friends in other countries despite _____.

6. In spite of _____, the use of chemotherapy to treat cancer has many severe side effects.

7. Though _____, Bob managed to give an excellent presentation at the board meeting.

8. Jerry continued to be denied a promotion despite _____.

9. Dangerous pesticides are still used in many countries even though _____.

10. Despite the fact that Einstein turned out to be a genius, _____.

▶ **Practice 19. Showing contrast.** (Chart 19-6).
Combine the two sentences in *italics*. Add any other necessary punctuation.

1. *It was night. We could see the road very clearly.*

    a. Even though _____ .

    b. Although _____ .

    c. _____ , but _____ .

2. *Helen has a fear of heights. She enjoys skydiving.*

    a. Despite the fact that _____ , _____ .

    b. Despite _____ , _____ .

    c. _____ ; nevertheless _____ .

3. *Millie has the flu. She is working at her computer.*

    a. Though _____ , _____ .

    b. _____ , but _____ anyway.

    c. _____ , but _____ still _____

    _____ .

► **Practice 20. Showing direct contrast.** (Chart 19-7)
Connect the given ideas using the words in parentheses. Add punctuation and capital letters as necessary.

1. (*while*) red is bright and lively gray is a dull color

   _____ *Red is bright and lively, while gray is a dull color.* _____ OR

   _____ *While red is bright and lively, gray is a dull color.* _____

2. (*on the other hand*) Jane is insecure and unsure of herself her sister is full of self-confidence

   _____

3. (*while*) a rock is heavy a feather is light

   _____

4. (*however*) some children are unruly others are quiet and obedient

   _____

5. (*on the other hand*) language and literature classes are easy and enjoyable for Alex math and science courses are difficult for him

   _____

6. (*however*) strikes can bring improvements in wages and working conditions strikes can also cause loss of jobs and bankruptcy

   _____

► **Practice 21. Expressing condition: using *otherwise*.** (Chart 19-8.)
Write sentences with the same meaning by using *otherwise*. Use a modal or phrasal modal in your sentence.

1. If I don't call my mother, she'll start worrying about me.

   _____ *I am going to have to (should / had better / must) call my mother. Otherwise, she'll* _____

   _____ *start worrying about me.* _____

2. If the bus doesn't come soon, we'll be late to work.

   _____

3. Unless you've made a reservation, you won't get seated at the restaurant.

   _____

4. If Beth doesn't stop complaining, she will lose the few friends she has.

   _____

5. You can't get on the plane unless you have a government-issued ID.

   _____

6. Louis can replace his driver's license only if he applies for it in person.

   _____

7. Only if you are a registered voter can you vote in the general election.

   _____

8. If you don't clean up the kitchen tonight, you'll have to clean it up early tomorrow.

   _____

▶ **Practice 22. Expressing cause and effect.** (Chart 19-9)
Complete the sentences in Column A with a phrase from Column B.

Column A

1. We see lightning first and then hear the thunder because _____.
2. Plants need light to live. These plants didn't have light; therefore, _____.
3. Halley's Comet appears in the sky every 76 years, so _____.
4. Children in Scandinavia go to school in darkness in the winter since _____.
5. Objects fall to the ground because of _____.
6. Now that _____, newspapers are not as necessary as they used to be.
7. People get their news faster than they used to due to _____.
8. Because _____, people can heat the air in a balloon and make it fly.

Column B

a. faster means of communication
b. gravity
c. hot air rises to the top
d. it will next be seen in 2061
e. light travels faster than sound
f. people can get their news instantly by computer or on TV
g. there is almost no daylight then
h. they died

▶ **Practice 23. Expressing contrast.** (Chart 19-9)
Circle the word(s) to complete the sentences.

1. Colombia exports a lot of emeralds, while South Africa (*exports* / *doesn't export*) gold.
2. Even though Colombia exports some precious stones, it (*exports* / *doesn't export*) diamonds.
3. Although Japan (*uses* / *doesn't use*) a lot of oil, oil isn't found in Japan.
4. Despite the declining population of Japan, Tokyo's population (*is* / *isn't*) getting larger.
5. Most people believe that the pineapple is native to Hawaii, a state in the middle of the Pacific Ocean; however, pineapples (*originated* / *didn't originate*) in South America.
6. China (*is* / *isn't*) the largest producer of pineapples today. Nevertheless, Hawaii still produces a lot of pineapples.

▶ **Practice 24. Expressing condition.** (Chart 19-9)
Write the correct form of the verb **pass** in each sentence.

1. Keith will graduate if he _____*passes*_____ all of his courses.
2. Sam won't graduate if he _____*doesn't pass*_____ all of his courses.

3. Ed won't graduate unless he _____ all of his courses.

4. Sue will graduate only if she _____ all of her courses.

5. Jessica will graduate even if she _____ all of her courses.

6. Alex won't graduate even if he _____ all of his courses.

7. Jennifer will graduate unless she _____ all of her courses.

▶ **Practice 25. Summary of connectives: cause and effect, contrast, condition.**
(Chart 19-9)

Complete the sentences logically using the ideas in the list. Write each verb in its correct tense.

    a. take care of the garden (or not)
    b. the flowers bloom (or not)
    c. my care

Punctuate and capitalize correctly.

1. Because I took good care of the garden, _____*the flowers bloomed*_____.

2. The flowers bloomed because _____*I took good care of the garden*_____.

3. The flowers bloomed because of _____*my care*_____.

4. The flowers didn't bloom in spite of _____.

5. Although I took good care of the garden _____.

6. I did not take good care of the garden therefore _____.

7. I didn't take good care of the garden however _____.

8. I took good care of the garden nevertheless _____.

9. I did not take good care of the garden so _____.

10. Even though I did not take good care of the garden _____.

11. Since I did not take good care of the garden _____.

12. I didn't take good care of the garden, but _____ anyway.

13. If I take good care of the garden _____.

14. Unless I take good care of the garden _____.

15. I must take good care of the garden otherwise _____.

16. I did not take good care of the garden consequently _____.

17. I did not take good care of the garden nonetheless _____.

18. I have to take good care of the garden so that _____.

19. Only if I take good care of the garden _____.

20. I took good care of the garden yet _____.

21. You'd better take good care of the garden or else _____.

22. The flowers will probably bloom whether _____.

Chapter 20
Conditional Sentences and Wishes

▶ **Practice 1. Introduction to conditional sentences.** (Chart 20-1)

Read the sentences under the *italicized* sentence. Circle *yes* if the sentence describes the situation. Circle *no* if the sentence doesn't describe the situation.

1. *If Sally didn't have the flu, she would be at work today.*
   a. Sally has the flu.   yes   no
   b. Sally is at work today.   yes   no

2. *If Albert didn't take his allergy medication, he would sneeze and cough all day.*
   a. Albert takes his allergy medication.   yes   no
   b. Albert sneezes and coughs all day.   yes   no

3. *If our first flight had been on time, we would not have missed our connecting flight.*
   a. The first flight was on time.   yes   no
   b. We missed our connecting flight.   yes   no

4. *If we had a reliable car, we would drive from the East Coast to the West Coast.*
   a. We have a reliable car.   yes   no
   b. We are going to drive from the East Coast to the West Coast   yes   no
   c. We would like to drive from the East Coast to the West Coast.   yes   no

5. *Tim would have married Tina if she had accepted his proposal of marriage.*
   a. Tina accepted Tim's marriage proposal.   yes   no
   b. Tina and Tim got married.   yes   no
   c. Tim wanted to marry Tina.   yes   no
   d. Tina wanted to marry Tom.   yes   no

▶ **Practice 2. Overview of basic verb forms in conditional sentences.**
(Chart 20-1)

Complete each sentence according to its description. Write the letter of the correct completion.

Group 1.
1. Present true: If it snows, _c_ .
2. Present untrue: If it snowed, _a_ .
3. Past untrue: If it had snowed, _b_ .

   a. I would walk to work
   b. I would have walked to work
   c. I will walk to work

Group 2.

1. Present true: If you come early, ____.
2. Present untrue: If you came early, ____.
3. Past untrue: If you had come early, ____.

   a. we wouldn't be late
   b. we wouldn't have been late
   c. we won't be late

Group 3.

1. Present untrue: If Professor Smith were absent, ____.
2. Present true: If Professor Smith is absent, ____.
3. Past untrue: If Professor Smith had been absent, ____.

   a. class would have been canceled
   b. class will be canceled
   c. class would be canceled

Group 4.

1. Present true: If John quits his job, ____.
2. Past untrue: If John had quit his job, ____.
3. Present untrue: If John quit his job, ____.

   a. his wife will be upset
   b. his wife would be upset
   c. his wife would have been upset

▶ **Practice 3. True in the present or future.** (Chart 20-2)
Read the given sentence and the two sentences that follow. Complete the sentences with the verbs in the list.

be, be	forget, look	heat, boil
eat, get	have, call	pet, purr

1. Water boils at 100 degrees C. (212 degrees F.)

    (General truth) If you _____ water to 100 degrees C., it

    _____ .

    (Future) If you _____ the water in that pot to 100 degrees C., it

    _____ .

2. Sometimes I forget my own schedule.

    (Habitual activity) If I _____ my schedule, I _____ at

    my appointment calendar.

    (Future) If I _____ my schedule tomorrow, I _____

    at my appointment calendar.

3. Sometimes the cat purrs.

    (Habitual situation) If you _____ the cat gently, she

    _____ .

    (Future) If you _____ the cat gently right now, she

    _____ .

4. I might have some news tomorrow.

    (Future) If I _____ any news tomorrow, I _____ you.

    (Habitual situation) If I _____ any news, I _____

    you.

5. You eat too much junk food.

(Future) If you _____ too much junk food , you

_____ fat.

(Predictable fact) If you _____ too much junk food, you

_____ fat.

6. It might be cloudy tonight.

(Predictable fact) If it _____ cloudy, the stars _____

visible.

(Future) If it _____ cloudy tonight, the stars _____

visible.

▶ **Practice 4. Untrue (contrary to fact) in the present or future.** (Chart 20-3)
What is the true situation? Circle the letter of the sentence that describes the true situation.

1. If I had a million dollars, I would travel around the world.
   a. I have a million dollars.   b. I don't have a million dollars.

2. If I didn't have a bad cold, I'd go swimming with you.
   a. I have a bad cold.   b. I don't have a bad cold.

3. If Jenny were here, she could help us.
   a. Jenny is here.   b. Jenny isn't here.

4. If Henry weren't in charge here, nothing would ever get done.
   a. Henry is in charge here.   b. Henry isn't in charge here.

5. If I spoke Chinese, I could converse with your grandmother.
   a. I speak Chinese.   b. I don't speak Chinese.

6. If I knew the answer, I would tell you.
   a. I know the answer.   b. I don't know the answer.

▶ **Practice 5. Untrue (contrary to fact) in the present or future.** (Chart 20-3)
Read the given sentence(s) and the sentence that follows. Complete the second sentence with the
verbs in the list.

be, be	have, go	have, travel
be, can have	have, like	like, cook

1. There aren't any trees on our street, and consequently, there is no shade.

   If there _____ trees on our street, there _____ shade.

2. We don't have enough money to travel abroad.

   If we _____ enough money, we _____ abroad.

3. The students don't have a good history teacher. They don't like history because of her.

   If the students _____ a better history teacher, they

   _____ history.

4. Sam doesn't like fish, so his mother doesn't cook it for him.

If Sam _____ fish, his mother _____ fish for him.

5. The weather is bad. We can't have our usual weekend picnic today.

If the weather _____ bad, we _____ our usual weekend picnic today.

6. I have so much work to do. I will not go out with you tonight.

If I _____ so much work, I _____ out with you tonight.

▶ **Practice 6. True vs. untrue in the present or future.** (Charts 20-2 and 20-3)
Complete the sentences in Column A with a clause in Column B.

Column A

1. If the temperature goes below freezing, _____.
2. If the temperature were below freezing right now, _____.
3. If the baby is hungry, _____.
4. If the baby were hungry, _____.
5. If this fish were not fresh, _____.
6. If fish is not fresh, _____.
7. If a car runs out of gas, _____.
8. If this car had more power, _____.
9. If you threw a rock into the water, _____.
10. If you throw a life ring into the water, _____.

Column B

a. it stops
b. he cries
c. it smells bad
d. we would be very cold
e. it would go faster
f. it floats
g. it would sink
h. we will be very cold
i. it would smell bad
j. he would cry

▶ **Practice 7. Untrue (contrary to fact) in the past.** (Chart 20-4)
Circle the letter of the sentence that describes the true situation.

1. If you had been here last night, you would have had a wonderful time. But _____.
   a. you were here   b. you weren't here

2. If I hadn't been rude, Jenna wouldn't have gotten angry. But _____.
   a. I was rude   b. I wasn't rude

3. If Anna hadn't been late, we could have seen the beginning of the movie. But _____.
   a. Anna was late   b. Anna wasn't late

4. If Henry hadn't fallen asleep, he wouldn't have crashed into the tree. But _____.
   a. he fell asleep   b. he didn't fall asleep

5. If Max had studied, he might have passed the test. But _____.
   a. he studied   b. he didn't study

6. If I had known the password, I would have told you. But _____.
   a. I knew the password   b. I didn't know the password

► **Practice 8. Untrue (contrary to fact) in the past.** (Chart 20-4)
Using the information in the first sentence, complete the conditional sentences with the correct form of the *italicized verbs*.

1. Adam met his future wife, Alice, on a flight to Tokyo.

    take, meet

    If Adam (*not*) _____ that flight to Tokyo, he (*not*) _____ Alice.

2. I forgot my credit card, so I couldn't pay for my groceries.

    forget, can pay

    If I (*not*) _____ my credit card, I _____ for my groceries.

3. I didn't know Jane was in the hospital, so I didn't visit her.

    know, visit

    If I _____ that Jane was in the hospital, I _____ her.

4. Alex didn't pay the electric bill. The electric company cut off his power.

    pay, cut off

    If Alex _____ the bill, the electric company (*not*) _____ his electricity.

5. The weather was bad. The outdoor concert was canceled.

    be, be

    If the weather _____ good, the outdoor concert (*not*) _____ canceled.

6. Alexander Fleming accidentally discovered the medical usefulness of a certain kind of mold. Scientists developed penicillin from that mold.

    discover, develop

    If Fleming (*not*) _____ that mold, scientists (*not*) _____ penicillin.

► **Practice 9. Conditional sentences: present, future, or past.** (Charts 20-2 → 20-4)
Write the letter of the correct phrase to complete each conversation.

a.	I can join you	d.	I had joined one
b.	I could have joined you	e.	I join one
c.	I could join you	f.	I joined one

1. A: Hi, Kim! Will you have lunch with us?

    B: I'm sorry, I can't. If ____, I would, but I have another appointment.

2. A: Hi, Sid! Say, will you have lunch with us tomorrow?

    B: Maybe. I might have to work through lunch, but if ____, I will.

3. A: Hey, Mary! What happened? Why didn't you have lunch with us?

    B: Oh, if ____, I would have, but I had an emergency at my office.

4. A: Mr. Simmons, you should exercise more.

   B: I'll try, Dr. Scott. Maybe I'll join a gym. If _____, I'll get more exercise.

5. A: Ms. Mora, you need to exercise. Why don't you join a gym?

   B: Oh, Doctor, if _____, it would be a waste of money. I would never use it.

6. A: Mrs. Smith, you said you were going to join a gym. You didn't!

   B: Right, I didn't. If _____, it would have been a waste of money. I would never have used it.

▶ **Practice 10. Conditional sentences: present, future, or past.** (Charts 20-2 → 20-4)
Write the correct form of the verbs in parentheses.

1. There's too much traffic these days. It's too bad we don't have wings. If we
   (*have*) _____ wings, we (*can, fly*) _____ over all this traffic
   instead of being stuck in it.

2. If we (*can, fly*) _____ over all this traffic, we (*arrive*) _____
   at our destination very quickly.

3. Maybe we'll get there before noon. If we (*get*) _____ there before noon, I
   (*have*) _____ a chance to talk with Olga before lunch.

4. I might have a chance to talk with Olga before we have lunch. If I (*have*) _____
   a chance to talk with Olga before we have lunch, I (*tell*) _____ her about
   the job opening in our department.

5. I didn't have a chance to talk to John yesterday. If I (*have*) _____ a chance to
   talk to him, I (*tell*) _____ him about the job opening.

6. You didn't tell John about the job opening at the meeting yesterday. But, even if you
   (*tell*) _____ him about the job opening, I'm sure that he
   (*be, not*) _____ interested at all. He's very happy with the job he has.

▶ **Practice 11. Conditional sentences.** (Charts 20-2 → 20-4)
Write a conditional sentence about each given sentence.

1. I was sick yesterday, so I didn't go to class.

   If _____*I hadn't been sick yesterday, I would have gone to class*_____.

2. Because Alan never eats breakfast, he always overeats at lunch.

   If _____.

3. Kostas was late to his own wedding because his watch was slow.

   If _____.

4. I don't ride the bus to work every morning because it's always so crowded.

   If _____.

5. Sara didn't know that Highway 57 was closed, so she didn't take an alternative route.

   If _____.

6. Camille couldn't finish unloading the truck because no one was there to help her.

   If _____.

► **Practice 12. Progressive verb forms in conditional sentences.**
(Chart 20-5)

Write a conditional sentence about each given sentence. Use *if*.

1. The wind is blowing so hard. We can't go sailing.

   If the wind weren't blowing so hard, we could go sailing.

2. The wind was blowing so hard. We couldn't go sailing.

   _____

3. The water is running. I can't hear you.

   _____

4. The water was running. I couldn't hear the phone.

   _____

5. The baby is hungry. That's why she's crying.

   _____

6. Dick was sleeping soundly so he didn't hear his alarm clock.

   _____

7. I was watching an exciting mystery on TV, so I didn't answer the phone.

   _____

8. I'm trying to concentrate, so I can't talk to you now.

   _____

► **Practice 13. Using "mixed time" in conditional sentences.** (Chart 20-6)

Circle the letters of the sentences that describe the situation.

1. If I hadn't stayed up late last night, I wouldn't be tired this morning.
   a. I went to bed late.
   b. I went to bed early.
   c. I am tired this morning.
   d. I am not tired this morning.

2. If Bob had saved some money, he could buy a house now.
   a. Bob saved some money.
   b. Bob didn't save any money.
   c. Bob can buy a house.
   d. Bob can't buy a house.

3. If I hadn't apologized to Ben, he would still be angry at me.
   a. I apologized to Ben.
   b. I didn't apologize to Ben.
   c. Ben is still angry at me.
   d. Ben is not angry at me anymore.

4. If I had taken Grandpa's advice, I wouldn't be in this mess now!
   a. I took Grandpa's advice.
   b. I didn't take Grandpa's advice.
   c. I am in a mess now.
   d. I am not in a mess now.

5. If Laura hadn't been wearing her seat belt, she would have been severely injured.
   a. Laura was wearing her seat belt.
   b. Laura wasn't wearing her seat belt.
   c. Laura was severely injured.
   d. Laura was not severely injured.

6. If new houses had not been built near the campgrounds, the area would still be wilderness.
   a. New houses have been built near the campgrounds.
   b. New houses have not been built near the campgrounds.
   c. The area is still wilderness.
   d. The area is not wilderness anymore.

▶ **Practice 14. Using progressive forms and "mixed time" in conditional sentences.** (Charts 20-5 and 20-6)

Write a conditional sentence about each given sentence.

1. It is raining, so we won't finish the game.

   If _____*it weren't raining, we would finish the game*_____.

2. I didn't eat lunch, and now I'm hungry.

   If _____.

3. Bob left his wallet at home this morning, and now he doesn't have money for lunch.

   If _____.

4. Bruce is always daydreaming, and so he never gets his work done.

   If _____.

5. My muscles hurt today because I played basketball for three hours last night.

   If _____.

6. I couldn't hear what you said because the band was playing so loud.

   If _____.

7. Because Diane asked the technician a lot of questions, she understands how to use her computer now.

   If _____.

8. Olga and Ivan weren't paying attention, so they didn't see the exit sign on the highway.

   If _____.

9. I really don't know what the test results mean because the doctor didn't explain them to me.

   If _____.

10. We were sleeping last night, so we didn't hear the thunder and lightning.

    If _____.

► **Practice 15. Omitting *if.*** (Chart 20-7)
Write sentences with the same meaning by omitting *if*.

1. If I were you, I wouldn't go there.

   _____*Were I*_____ you, I wouldn't go there.

2. If you should need my help, please call.

   _____*Should you need*_____ my help, please call.

3. If I had known about her accident, I would have gone to the hospital immediately.

   _____ about her accident, I would have gone to the hospital

   immediately.

4. If I had been offered a job at the law office, I would have gladly accepted.

   _____ a job at the law office, I would have gladly accepted.

5. If anyone should call, would you please take a message?

   _____, would you please take a message?

6. Directions on the pizza box: "If this pizza needs reheating, place it in a hot oven for five minutes."

   _____, place it in a hot oven for five minutes.

7. Directions on a medicine bottle: "If you feel any dizziness, nausea, or muscle pain, discontinue

   taking this medicine and call your doctor immediately."

   _____ any dizziness, nausea, or muscle pain, discontinue taking this

   medicine and call your doctor immediately.

8. If you were really a lawyer, I would take your advice.

   _____, I would take your advice.

► **Practice 16. Omitting *if.*** (Chart 20-7)
Circle the letter of the one sentence that has the same meaning as the given sentence.

1. Had I seen the hole in the sidewalk, I wouldn't have tripped and fallen down.
   a. I had to see the hole in the sidewalk.
   b. I saw the hole in the sidewalk.
   c. I didn't see the hole in the sidewalk.
   d. I didn't fall down.

2. Should you have further questions, please don't hesitate to contact us again.
   a. You should ask more questions.
   b. You might have more questions.
   c. You will certainly have more questions.
   d. Don't bother calling us again.

3. Had the building been properly built, it would have withstood the hurricane.
   a. The building was properly built.
   b. The building survived the hurricane.
   c. The building wasn't properly built.
   d. The building was built after the hurricane.

4. Were you rich, you could fly across the ocean to visit your family every week.
   a. Are you rich?
   b. You are not rich.
   c. You visit your family every week.
   d. You used to be rich, but you are not anymore.

▶ **Practice 17. Implied conditions.** (Chart 20-8)
Complete the sentences with *if*-clauses.

1. Sara's dad would have picked her up, but I forgot to tell him that she needed a ride.

   Sara's dad would have picked her up if _I hadn't forgotten to tell him that she needed a ride_.

2. I couldn't have finished the project without your help.

   I couldn't have finished the project if _____.

3. I opened the door slowly. Otherwise, I could have hit someone.

   If _____, I could have hit someone.

4. Doug would have gone on vacation with me, but he couldn't get time off from work.

   Doug would have gone with me if _____.

5. CAROL: Why didn't Oscar tell his boss about the problem?

   ALICE: He would have gotten into a lot of trouble.

   Oscar would have gotten into a lot of trouble if _____

   _____.

▶ **Practice 18. Review: conditional sentences.** (Charts 20-1 → 20-8)
Write the letter of the correct completion for each sentence.

1. If I could speak Spanish, I _____ next year studying in Spain.
   a. will spend   c. had spent
   b. would have spent   d. would spend

2. It would have been a much more serious accident _____ fast at the time.
   a. had she been driving   c. she had driven
   b. was she driving   d. if she drove

3. A: Can I borrow your car for this evening?
   B: Sure, but Nora's using it right now. If she _____ it back in time, you're welcome to borrow it.
   a. brought   c. brings
   b. would bring   d. will bring

4. I didn't get home until well after midnight last night. Otherwise, I _____ your call.
   a. returned   c. would return
   b. had returned   d. would have returned

5. If energy _____ inexpensive and unlimited, many things in the world would be different.
   a. is   c. were
   b. will be   d. would be

6. We _____ the game if we'd had a few more minutes.
    a. will win   c. had won
    b. won   d. could have won

7. I _____ William with me if I had known you and he didn't get along with each other.
    a. hadn't brought   c. wouldn't have brought
    b. didn't bring   d. won't bring

8. Dr. Mason was out of town, so a guest lecturer gave the talk. It was boring and I almost fell asleep. If Dr. Mason _____, I would have paid attention and not fallen asleep.
    a. lectured   c. was lecturing
    b. had been lecturing   d. would lecture

9. If you _____ to my advice in the first place, you wouldn't be in this mess right now.
    a. listen   c. will listen
    b. had listened   d. listened

10. _____ interested in that subject, I would try to learn more about it.
    a. Were I   c. I was
    b. Should I   d. If I am

11. If I _____ the problems you had as a child, I might not have succeeded in life as well as you have.
    a. have   c. had had
    b. would have   d. should have

12. I _____ your mother to dinner if I had known she was visiting you.
    a. invite   c. had invited
    b. invited   d. would have invited

13. _____ more help, I can call my neighbor.
    a. Needed   c. I have needed
    b. Should I need   d. I should need

14. _____ then what I know today, I would have saved myself a lot of time and trouble over the years.
    a. If I know   c. If I would know
    b. Did I know   d. Had I known

15. Do you think there would be less conflict in the world if all people _____ the same language?
    a. speak   c. spoke
    b. will speak   d. had spoken

16. If you can tell me why I wasn't included, _____ this incident again.
    a. I don't mention   c. I never mention
    b. I will never mention   d. will I never mention

17. I didn't know you were asleep. Otherwise, I _____ so much noise when I came in.
    a. didn't make   c. won't make
    b. wouldn't have made   d. don't make

18. Unless you _____ all of my questions, I can't do anything to help you.
    a. answered   c. would answer
    b. answer   d. are answering

19. Had you told me that this was going to happen, I _____ it.
    - a. never would have believed
    - c. hadn't believed
    - b. don't believe
    - d. can't believe

20. If Jake _____ to go on the trip, would you have gone alone?
    - a. doesn't agree
    - c. hadn't agreed
    - b. didn't agree
    - d. wouldn't agree

▶ **Practice 19. Verb forms following *wish*.** (Chart 20-9)
Circle the letter of the sentence that describes the true situation.

1. I wish that you were my true friend.
   - a. You are my true friend.
   - b. You are not my true friend.

2. I wish I had known the truth.
   - a. I knew the truth.
   - b. I didn't know the truth.

3. I wish you hadn't lied to me.
   - a. You lied to me.
   - b. You didn't lie to me.

4. I wish we were going on vacation.
   - a. We are going on vacation.
   - b. We are not going on vacation.

5. I wish I had a motorcycle.
   - a. I have a motorcycle.
   - b. I don't have a motorcycle.

6. I wish John could have met my father.
   - a. John was able to meet my father.
   - b. John was not able to meet my father.

▶ **Practice 20. Verb forms following *wish*.** (Chart 20-9)
Make wishes. Complete the sentences with a verb.

1. The sun isn't shining.

   I wish the sun _____were shining_____ right now.

2. You didn't go to the concert with us last night.

   I wish you _____ with us to the concert last night.

3. Spiro didn't drive to this party.

   I wish Spiro _____ to the party. I'd ask him for a ride home.

4. I can't swim.

   I wish I _____ so I would feel safe in a boat.

5. Our team didn't win.

   I wish our team _____ the game last night.

6. Bill didn't get the promotion.

   I wish Bill _____ the promotion. He feels bad.

7. I quit my job.

   I wish I _____ my job until I'd found another one.

8. It isn't winter.

   I wish it _____ winter so that I could go skiing.

9. Al probably won't sing for us because he's so shy. I wish Al _____ a

   couple of songs. He has a good voice.

► **Practice 21. Verb forms following *wish*.** (Chart 20-9)
Write the correct form of the verbs in parentheses.

1. Heinrich doesn't like his job as a house painter. He wishes he (*go*) _____ to art
   school when he was younger. He wishes he (*can, paint*) _____ canvasses
   instead of houses for a living.

2. I don't like living here. I wish I (*move, not*) _____ to this big city. I
   can't seem to make any friends, and everything is so crowded. I wish I (*take*) _____
   _____ the job I was offered before I moved here.

3. I know I shouldn't eat junk food every day, but I wish you (*stop*) _____
   nagging me about it.

4. I wish you (*invite, not*) _____ the neighbors over for dinner
   when you talked to them earlier this afternoon. I don't feel like cooking a big dinner.

5. A: Did you get your car back from the garage?
   B: Yes, and it still isn't fixed. I wish I (*pay, not*) _____ them in full
      when I picked up the car. I should have waited to be sure that everything was all right.

6. A: I wish you (*hurry*) _____! We're going to be late.
   B: I wish you (*relax*) _____. We've got plenty of time.

7. A: How do you like the new president of our neighborhood association?
   B: Not much. I wish she (*elect, not*) _____. I never should
      have voted for her.
   A: Oh, really? Then you probably wish I (*vote, not*) _____ for
      her either. If you recall, she won by only one vote. You and I could have changed the
      outcome of the election if we'd known then what we know now.

8. A: My thirteen-year-old daughter wishes she (*be, not*) _____ so tall and
      that her hair (*be*) _____ black and straight.
   B: Really? My daughter wishes she (*be*) _____ taller and that her hair
      (*be*) _____ blond and curly.

9. A: I can't go to the game with you this afternoon.
   B: Really? That's too bad. But I wish you (*tell*) _____ me sooner so that
      I could have invited someone else to go with me.

10. A: How long have you been sick?
    B: For over a week.
    A: I wish you (*go*) _____ to see a doctor later today. You should find out
       what's wrong with you.
    B: Maybe I'll go tomorrow.

► **Practice 22. Using *would* to make wishes about the future.** (Chart 20-10)
Complete the sentences. Make wishes about the future by writing *would* and a verb from the list.

cook	end	get	hang up	leave	snow

1. A: So, Mom, how do you like my haircut?

   B: You had a haircut? Your hair is still long. I wish you _____ a real haircut.

2. A: Aren't you going on your annual ski trip this year?

   B: No, not unless it snows. There hasn't been any snow this year. I wish it _____ so we could go skiing.

3. A: Helen! How long are our guests going to stay? It's almost midnight.

   B: I don't know. I wish they _____, but Henry just keeps on talking. Everyone is falling asleep.

4. A: I love you, Pat, but I wish you were neater.

   B: Neater? What do you mean? I pick up everything, I clean up everything . . .

   A: Well, I mean I wish you _____ your clothes instead of leaving them on a chair.

5. A: What's the matter? Don't you like the movie?

   B: Not at all! I wish it _____. We have to stay, though because the kids are enjoying it so much.

6. A: Meatballs again?

   B: Don't you like meatballs?

   A: You know I do, but sometimes I wish you _____ something else.

► **Practice 23. Conditionals.** (Chapter 20)
Complete the sentences. Write the correct form of the verb in parentheses.

TOM: What's wrong, Bob? You look awful!

BOB: Well, you (*look*) _____ bad too if you (*have*) _____ a day

　　　　　　　　　　　　　　　　　　1　　　　　　　　　　　　　　　　2
like mine yesterday. My car slid into a tree because the roads were icy.

TOM: Oh? What happened?

BOB: Well, I suppose if I (*drive, not*) _____ so fast, I

　　　　　　　　　　　　　　　　　　　　　　　　　3
(*slide, not*) _____ into the tree.

　　　　　　　　　4

TOM: Gosh, Bob, speeding again? Don't you know that if a driver (*step*)
_____ on the gas on ice, the car will spin around in a circle?

　　5

BOB: I know that now, but I didn't know that yesterday! If I (*know*) _____ that yesterday, I (*not, crash*) _____. And besides, I didn't have my driver's license with me, so I'll have to pay an extra fine for that when I go to court next month.

TOM: You were driving without your license?

BOB: Yeah. It slipped out of my pocket.

TOM: You sure have bad luck! Maybe if you (*take, not*) _____ that bus, you (*lose, not*) _____ your wallet. If you (*lose, not*) _____ your wallet, you (*have*) _____ your driver's license with you when you hit a tree. If you (*have*) _____ your license with you, you (*have to pay, not*) _____ a steep fine when you go to court next week. And of course, if you (*drive, not*) _____ too fast, you (*run into, not*) _____ a tree, and you (*be, not*) _____ in this mess now. If I (*be*) _____ you, I (*take*) _____ it easy and just (*stay*) _____ home where you'll be no danger to yourself or to anyone else.

BOB: Enough about me! How about you?

TOM: Well, things are really looking up for me. I'm planning to take off for Florida soon. I'm sick of all this cold, rainy weather. I (*stay*) _____ here for vacation if the weather (*be, not*) _____ so bad. But I need some sun!

BOB: I wish I (*can, go*) _____ with you. How are you planning on getting there?

TOM: If I have enough money, I (*fly*) _____. Otherwise, I (*take*) _____ the bus. I wish I (*can, drive*) _____ my own car there because it (*be*) _____ nice to have it to drive around in once I get there, but it's such a long trip. I wish I (*have*) _____ someone to go with me and share the driving.

BOB: Hey, what about me? Why don't I go with you? I can share the driving. I'm a great driver!

TOM: Didn't you just get through telling me that you'd wrapped your car around a tree?

Appendix
Supplementary Grammar Units

▶ **Practice 1. Subjects, verbs, and objects.** (Chart A-1)
Underline and identify the subject (**s**), verb (**v**), and object of the verb (**o**) in each sentence.

         s   **v**   **o**
1. Airplanes have wings.

2. The teacher explained the problem.

3. Children enjoy games.

4. Jack wore a blue suit.

5. Some animals eat plants. Some animals eat other animals.

6. According to an experienced waitress, you can carry full cups of coffee without spilling them just by never looking at them.

▶ **Practice 2. Transitive vs. intransitive verbs.** (Chart A-1)
Underline and identify the verb in each sentence. Write **VT** if it is transitive. Write **VI** if it is intransitive.

           VI
1. Alice arrived at six o'clock.
          VT
2. We drank some tea.

3. I agree with you.

4. I waited for Sam at the airport for two hours.

5. They're staying at a resort hotel in San Antonio, Texas.

6. Mr. Chan is studying English.

7. The wind is blowing hard today.

8. I walked to the theater, but Janice rode her bicycle.

9. Crocodiles hatch from eggs.

10. Rivers flow toward the sea.

► **Practice 3. Adjectives and adverbs.** (Charts A-2 and A-3)
Underline and identify the adjectives (**ADJ**) and adverbs (**ADV**) in these sentences.

                            ADJ   **ADV**

1. Jack opened the <u>heavy</u> door <u>slowly</u>.

2. Chinese jewelers carved beautiful ornaments from jade.

3. The old man carves wooden figures skillfully.

4. A busy executive usually has short conversations on the telephone.

5. The young woman had a very good time at the picnic yesterday.

► **Practice 4. Adjectives and adverbs.** (Charts A-2 and A-3)
Complete each sentence with the correct adjective or adverb.

1. *quick, quickly*   We ate _____*quickly*_____ and ran to the theater.

2. *quick, quickly*   We had a _____*quick*_____ dinner and ran to the theater.

3. *polite, politely*   I've always found Fred to be a _____ person.

4. *polite, politely*   He responded to my question _____ .

5. *regular, regularly*   Mr. Thomas comes to the store _____ for cheese and bread.

6. *regular, regularly*   He is a _____ customer.

7. *usual, usually*   The teacher arrived at the _____ time.

8. *usual, usually*   She _____ comes to class five minutes before it begins.

9. *good, well*   Jennifer Cooper paints _____ .

10. *good, well*   She is a _____ artist.

11. *gentle, gently*   A _____ breeze touched my face.

12. *gentle, gently*   A breeze _____ touched my face.

13. *bad, badly*   The audience booed the actors' _____ performance.

14. *bad, badly*   The audience booed and whistled because the actors performed _____ throughout the show.

▶ **Practice 5. Midsentence adverbs.** (Chart A-3)
Put the adverb in parentheses in its usual midsentence position.

   1. (*always*)   Sue ∧ takes a walk in the morning.
                     always

   2. (*always*)   Tim is a hard worker.

   3. (*always*)   Beth has worked hard.

   4. (*always*)   Jack works hard.

   5. (*always*)   Do you work hard?

   6. (*usually*)   Taxis are available at the airport.

   7. (*rarely*)   Yusef takes a taxi to his office.

   8. (*often*)   I have thought about quitting my job and sailing to Alaska.

   9. (*probably*)   Yuko needs some help.

  10. (*ever*)   Have you attended the show at the Museum of Space?

  11. (*seldom*)   Al goes out to eat at a restaurant.

  12. (*hardly ever*)   The students are late.

  13. (*usually*)   Do you finish your homework before dinner?

  14. (*generally*)   In India, the monsoon season begins in April.

  15. (*usually*)   During the monsoon season, Mr. Singh's hometown receives around

                     610 centimeters (240 inches) of rain, which is an unusually large amount.

▶ **Practice 6. Identifying prepositions.** (Chart A-4)
<u>Underline</u> the prepositions.

   1. Jim came to class <u>without</u> his books.
   2. We stayed at home during the storm.
   3. Sonya walked across the bridge over the Cedar River.
   4. When Alex walked through the door, his little sister ran toward him and put her arms around his neck.
   5. The two of us need to talk to Tom too.
   6. Animals live in all parts of the world. Animals walk or crawl on land, fly in the air, and swim in the water.
   7. Scientists divide living things into two main groups: the animal kingdom and the plant kingdom.
   8. Asia extends from the Pacific Ocean in the east to Africa and Europe in the west.

► **Practice 7. Sentence elements.** (Charts A-1 → A-4)
Underline and identify the subject (**S**), verb (**V**), object (**O**), and prepositional phrases (**PP**) in the following sentences.

              S   **V**   **O**   **PP**
1. Jack put the letter in the mailbox.

2. The children walked to school.

3. Mary did her homework at the library.

4. Chinese printers created the first paper money in the world.

5. Dark clouds appeared on the horizon.

6. Mary filled the shelves of the cabinet with boxes of old books.

► **Practice 8. Linking verbs.** (Chart A-6)
Some of the *italicized* words in the following are used as linking verbs. Identify which ones are linking verbs by <u>underlining</u> them. Also underline the adjective that follows the linking verb.

1. Olga *looked* at the fruit. *(no underline)*

2. It *looked* fresh.

3. Dan *noticed* a scratch on the door of his car.

4. Morris *tasted* the candy.

5. It *tasted* good.

6. The crowd *grew* quiet as the official began her speech.

7. Felix *grows* tomatoes in his garden.

8. Sally *grew* up in Florida.

9. I can *smell* the chicken in the oven.

10. It *smells* delicious.

11. Barbara *got* a package in the mail.

12. Al *got* sleepy after dinner.

13. During the storm, the sea *became* rough.

14. Nicole *became* a doctor after many years of study.

15. Diana *sounded* her horn to warn the driver of the other car.

16. Helen *sounded* happy when I talked to her.

17. The weather *turns* hot in July.

18. When Bob entered the room, I *turned* around to look at him.

19. I *turned* a page in the book.

20. It *appears* certain that Mary Hanson will win the election.

21. Dick's story *seems* strange. Do you believe it?

▶ **Practice 9. Linking verbs; adjectives and adverbs.** (Charts A-2 → A-6)
Complete each sentence with the correct adjective or adverb.

1. *clean, cleanly*   The floor looks ____*clean*____ .

2. *slow, slowly*   The bear climbed ____*slowly*____ up the tree.

3. *safe, safely*   The plane landed _____ on the runway.

4. *anxious, anxiously*   When the wind started to blow, I grew _____ .

5. *complete, completely*   This list of names appears _____ . No more names need to be added.

6. *wild, wildly*   The crowd yelled _____ when we scored a goal.

7. *honest, honestly*   The clerk looked _____ , but she wasn't. I discovered when I got home that she had cheated me.

8. *thoughtful, thoughtfully*   Jane looked at her book _____ before she answered the teacher's question.

9. *good, well*   Most of the students did _____ on their tests.

10. *fair, fairly*   The contract offer sounded _____ to me, so I accepted the job.

11. *terrible, terribly*   Jim felt _____ about forgetting his son's birthday.

12. *good, well*   A rose smells _____ .

13. *light, lightly*   As dawn approached, the sky became _____ .

14. *confident, confidently*   Beth spoke _____ when she delivered her speech.

15. *famous, famously*   The actor became _____ throughout much of the world.

16. *fine, finely*   I don't think this milk is spoiled. It tastes _____ to me.

► **Practice 10. Review: basic question forms.** (Chart B-1)
From the <u>underlined</u> sentences, make questions for the given answers. Fill in the blank spaces with the appropriate words. If no word is needed, write Ø.

1.   _Bob can live there_.

	Question word	Auxiliary verb	Subject	Main verb	Rest of question	→	Answer
1a.	Ø	Can	Bob	live	there ?	→	Yes.
1b.	Where	can	Bob	live	Ø ?	→	There.
1c.	Who	can	Ø	live	there ?	→	Bob.

2.   _Ron is living there_.

	Question word	Auxiliary verb	Subject	Main verb	Rest of question	→	Answer
2a.	Ø	___	___	___	there ?	→	Yes.
2b.	Where	___	___	___	Ø ?	→	There.
2c.	Who	___	___	___	there ?	→	Ron.

3.   _Sue lives there_.

	Question word	Auxiliary verb	Subject	Main verb	Rest of question	→	Answer
3a.	Ø	___	___	___	there ?	→	Yes.
3b.	Where	___	___	___	Ø ?	→	There.
3c.	Who	___	___	___	there ?	→	Sue.

4.   _Ann will live there_.

	Question word	Auxiliary verb	Subject	Main verb	Rest of question	→	Answer
4a.	Ø	___	___	___	there ?	→	Yes.
4b.	Where	___	___	___	Ø ?	→	There.
4c.	Who	___	___	___	there ?	→	Ann.

5.   _Jack lived there_.

	Question word	Auxiliary verb	Subject	Main verb	Rest of question	→	Answer
5a.	___	___	___	___	there ?	→	Yes.
5b.	___	___	___	___	Ø ?	→	There.
5c.	___	___	___	___	there ?	→	Jack.

6.   _Mary has lived there_.

	Question word	Auxiliary verb	Subject	Main verb	Rest of question	→	Answer
6a.	___	___	___	___	___ ?	→	Yes.
6b.	___	___	___	___	___ ?	→	There.
6c.	___	___	___	___	___ ?	→	Mary.

► **Practice 11. Yes / no and information questions.** (Charts B-1 and B-2)
Make questions to fit the conversations. Notice in the examples that there is a short answer and then in parentheses a long answer. Your questions should produce those answers.

1. A: _____When are you going to the zoo?_____
   B: Tomorrow. (*I'm going to the zoo tomorrow.*)

2. A: _____Are you going downtown later today?_____
   B: Yes. (*I'm going downtown later today.*)

3. A: _____
   B: Yes. (*I live in an apartment.*)

4. A: _____
   B: In a condominium. (*Sue lives in a condominium.*)

5. A: _____
   B: Jack. (*Jack lives in that house.*)

6. A: _____
   B: Yes. (*I can speak French.*)

7. A: _____
   B: Ron. (*Ron can speak Arabic.*)

8. A: _____
   B: Two weeks ago. (*Olga arrived two weeks ago.*)

9. A: _____
   B: Ali. (*Ali arrived late.*)

10. A: _____
    B: The window. (*Ann is opening the window.*)

11. A: _____
    B: Opening the window. (*Ann is opening the window.*)

12. A: _____
    B: Her book. (*Mary opened her book.*)

13. A: _____
    B: Tom. (*Tom opened the door.*)

14. A: _____
    B: Yes. (*The mail has arrived.*)

15. A: _____
    B: Yes. (*I have a bicycle.*)

16. A: _____
    B: A pen. (*Alex has a pen in his hand.*)

17. A: _____

    B: Yes. (*I like ice cream.*)

18. A: _____

    B: Yes. (*I would like an ice cream cone.*)

19. A: _____

    B: A candy bar. (*Joe would like a candy bar.*)

20. A: _____

    B: Ann. (*Ann would like a soft drink.*)

▶ **Practice 12. Information questions.** (Charts B-1 and B-2)
Make questions from these sentences. The *italicized* words in parentheses should be the answers to your questions.

1. I take my coffee (*black*). → *How do you take your coffee?*

2. I have (*an English-Spanish*) dictionary.

3. He (*runs a grocery store*) for a living.

4. Margaret was talking to (*her uncle*).

5. (*Only ten*) people showed up for the meeting.

6. (*Because of heavy fog*), none of the planes could take off.

7. She was thinking about (*her experiences as a rural doctor*).

8. I was driving (*sixty-five miles per hour*) when the police officer stopped me.

9. I like (*hot and spicy Mexican*) food best.

10. (*The*) apartment (*at the end of the hall on the second floor*) is mine.

11. Oscar is (*friendly, generous, and kindhearted*).

12. Oscar is (*tall and thin and has short black hair*).

13. (*Ann's*) dictionary fell to the floor.

14. Abby isn't here (*because she has a doctor's appointment*).

15. All of the students in the class will be informed of their final grades (*on Friday*).

16. I feel (*awful*).

17. Of those three books, I preferred (*the one by Tolstoy*).

18. I like (*rock*) music.

19. The plane is expected to be (*an hour*) late.

20. The driver of the stalled car lit a flare (*in order to warn oncoming cars*).

21. I want (*the felt-tip*) pen, (*not the ballpoint*).

22. The weather is (*hot and humid*) in July.

23. I like my steak (*medium rare*).

24. I did (*very well*) on the test.

25. There are (*31,536,000*) seconds in a year.

▶ **Practice 13. Information questions.** (Charts B-1 and B-2)
Make questions from the following sentences. The words in parentheses should be the answers to your questions.

1. I need (*five dollars*). → *How much money do you need?*

2. Roberto was born (*in Panama*).

3. I go out to eat (*at least once a week*).

4. I'm waiting for (*Maria*).

5. (*My sister*) answered the phone.

6. I called (*Benjamin*).

7. (*Benjamin*) called.

8. She bought (*twelve gallons of*) gas.

9. *Deceitful* means (*"dishonest"*).

10. An abyss is (*a bottomless hole*).

11. He went (*this*) way, (*not that way*).

12. These are (*Jim's*) books and papers.

13. They have (*four*) children.

14. He has been here (*for two hours*).

15. It is (*two hundred miles*) to Madrid.

16. The doctor can see you (*at three on Friday*).

17. Her roommate is (*Jane Peters*).

18. Her roommates are (*Jane Peters and Sue Lee*).

19. My parents have been living there (*for three years*).

20. This is (*Alice's*) book.

21. (*Fred and Jack*) are coming over for dinner.

22. Ann's dress is (*blue*).

23. Ann's eyes are (*brown*).

24. (*Bob*) can't go on the picnic.

25. Bob can't go (*because he is sick*).

26. I didn't answer the phone (*because I didn't hear it ring*).

27. I like (*classical*) music.

28. I don't understand (*the chart on page 50*).

29. Janet is (*studying*) right now.

30. You spell *sitting* (*with two "t's"—S-I-T-T-I-N-G*).

31. Tom (*is about medium height and has red hair and freckles*).

32. Tom is (*very serious and hard-working*).

33. Ron (*works as a civil engineer for the railroad company*).

34. Mexico is (*eight hundred miles*) from here.

35. I take my coffee (*black with sugar*).

36. Of Stockholm and Moscow, (*Stockholm*) is farther north.

37. (*Fine.*) I'm getting along (*just fine*).

▶ **Practice 14. Negative questions.** (Chart B-4)
In these dialogues, make negative questions from the words in parentheses, and determine the expected response.

1. A: Your infected finger looks terrible. (*you, see, not*) ___Haven't you seen___ a doctor yet?

   B: ___No___. But I'm going to. I don't want the infection to get any worse.

2. A: You look pale. What's the matter? (*you, feel*) _____ well?

   B: _____. I think I might be coming down with something.

3. A: Did you see Mark at the meeting?

   B: No, I didn't.

   A: Really? (*he, be, not*) _____ there?

   B: _____.

   A: That's funny. I've never known him to miss a meeting before.

4. A: Why didn't you come to the meeting yesterday afternoon?

   B: What meeting? I didn't know there was a meeting.

   A: (*Mary, tell, not*) _____ you about it?

   B: _____. No one said a word to me about it.

5. A: I have a package for Janet. (*Janet and you, work, not*) _____
      _____ in the same building?

   B: _____. I'd be happy to take the package to her tomorrow when I go to work.

6. A: Frank didn't report all of his income on his tax forms.

   B: (*that, be, not*) _____ against the law?

   A: _____. And that's why he's in a lot of legal trouble. He might even go to jail.

7. A: Did you give Linda my message when you went to class this morning?

   B: No. I didn't see her.

   A: Oh? (*she, be*) _____ in class?

   B: _____. She didn't come today.

8. A: Do you see that woman over there, the one in the blue dress? (*she, be*) _____ Mrs. Robbins?

    B: _____ .

    A: I thought so. I wonder what she is doing here.

▶ Practice 15. Tag questions. (Chart B-5)
Add tag questions to the following.

1. You live in an apartment, __*don't you*__ ?

2. You've never been in Italy, __*have you*__ ?

3. Sally turned in her report, _____ ?

4. There are more countries north of the equator than south of it, _____ ?

5. You've never met Jack Freeman, _____ ?

6. You have a ticket to the game, _____ ?

7. You'll be there, _____ ?

8. Tom knows Alice Reed, _____ ?

9. We should call Rita, _____ ?

10. Ostriches can't swim, _____ ?

11. These books aren't yours, _____ ?

12. That's Bob's, _____ ?

13. Your neighbors died in the accident, _____ ?

14. I'm right, _____ ?

15. This grammar is easy, _____ ?

▶ Practice 16. Contractions. (Chart C)
Write the contraction of the pronoun and verb if appropriate. Write Ø if the pronoun and verb cannot be contracted.

1. He is (__*He's*__) in my class.

2. He was (__*Ø*__) in my class.

3. He has (__*He's*__) been here since July.

4. He has (__*Ø*__) a Volvo.*

---

*NOTE: **has, have,** and **had** are NOT contracted when they are used as main verbs. They are contracted only when they are used as helping verbs.

5. She had (_____) been there for a long time before we arrived.

6. She had (_____) a bad cold.

7. She would (_____) like to go to the zoo.

8. I did (_____) well on the test.

9. We will (_____) be there early.

10. They are (_____) in their seats over there.*

11. It is (_____) going to be hot tomorrow.

12. It has (_____) been a long time since I've seen him.

13. A bear is a large animal. It has (_____) four legs and brown hair.

14. We were (_____) on time.

15. We are (_____) always on time.

16. She has (_____) a good job.

17. She has (_____) been working there for a long time.

18. She had (_____) opened the window before class began.

19. She would (_____) have helped us if we had (_____) asked her.

20. He could (_____) have helped us if he had (_____) been there.

▶ **Practice 17. Using *not* and *no*.** (Chart D-1)
Change each sentence into the negative in two ways: use ***not ... any*** in one sentence and ***no*** in the other.

1. I have some problems. → *I don't have any problems. I have no problems.*

2. There was some food on the shelf.

3. I received some letters from home.

4. I need some help.

5. We have some time to waste.

6. You should have given the beggar some money.

7. I trust someone. → *I don't trust anyone. I trust no one.***

8. I saw someone.

9. There was someone in his room.

10. She can find somebody who knows about it.

---

*__They're, their,__ and __there__ all have the same pronunciation.
**Also spelled with a hyphen in British English: *no-one*

► **Practice 18. Avoiding double negatives.** (Chart D-2)
Correct the errors in these sentences, all of which contain double negatives.

1. We don't have no time to waste.

    → *We have no time to waste.* OR *We don't have any time to waste.*

2. I didn't have no problems.

3. I can't do nothing about it.

4. You can't hardly ever understand her when she speaks.

5. I don't know neither Ann nor her husband.

6. Don't never drink water from that river without boiling it first.

7. Because I had to sit in the back row of the auditorium, I couldn't barely hear the speaker.

► **Practice 19. Beginning a sentence with a negative word.** (Chart D-3)
Change each sentence so that it begins with a negative word.

1. I had hardly stepped out of bed when the phone rang.

    → *Hardly had I stepped out of bed when the phone rang.*

2. I will never say that again.

3. I have scarcely ever enjoyed myself more than I did yesterday.

4. She rarely makes a mistake.

5. I will never trust him again because he lied to me.

6. It is hardly ever possible to get an appointment to see him.

7. I seldom skip breakfast.

8. I have never known a more generous person than Samantha.

► **Practice 20. Preposition combinations.** (Chart E)
Choose <u>all</u> the correct completions for each sentence.

1. Max is known for his (*(honesty)* / *(fairness)* / *famous*).

2. Several students were absent from (*yesterday* / *school* / *class*).

3. Has Maya recovered from (*her illness* / *her husband's death* / *the chair*)?

4. The criminal escaped from (*jail* / *the key* / *prison*).

5. Do you believe in (*ghosts* / *UFOs* / *scary*)?

6. Anthony is engaged to (*my cousin* / *a friend* / *marriage*).

7. Chris excels in (*mathematics* / *sports* / *his cousins*).

8. I'm very fond of (*you* / *exciting* / *your children*).

9. Henry doesn't approve of (*smoking* / *cigarettes* / *rain*).

10. I subscribe to (*magazines* / *a newspaper* / *websites*).

► **Practice 21. Preposition combinations.** (Chart E)
Choose the correct prepositions in parentheses.

1. Water consists (*of* / *with*) oxygen and hydrogen.

2. I am uncomfortable because that man is staring (*to* / *at*) me.

3. Ella hid the candy (*from* / *back*) the children.

4. I arrived (*in* / *to*) this country two weeks ago.

5. We arrived (*to* / *at*) the airport ten minutes late.

6. I am envious (*in* / *of*) people who can speak three or four languages fluently.

7. The students responded (*at* / *to*) the teacher's questions.

8. The farmers are hoping (*on* / *for*) rain.

9. I'm depending (*on* / *in*) you to finish this work for me.

10. Tim wore sunglasses to protect his eyes (*for* / *from*) the sun.

► **Practice 22. Preposition combinations.** (Chart E)
Complete the sentences with appropriate prepositions.

SITUATION 1: Mr. and Mrs. Jones just celebrated their 50th wedding anniversary.

1. They have been married ____*to*____ each other for 50 years.

2. They have always been faithful _____ each other.

3. They are proud _____ their marriage.

4. They are polite _____ one another.

5. They are patient _____ each other.

6. They are devoted _____ one another.

7. They have been committed _____ their marriage.

SITUATION 2: Jacob and Emily have been together for five months. They don't have a healthy relationship, and it probably won't last long.

1. They are often annoyed _____ each other's behavior.

2. They argue _____ each other every day.

3. They are bored _____ their relationship.

4. They are tired _____ one another.

5. Jacob is jealous _____ Emily's friends.

6. Emily is sometimes frightened _____ Jacob's moods.

► **Practice 23. Preposition combinations.** (Chart E)
Complete each sentence in Column A with the correct phrase from Column B.

Column A

1. My boots are made _c_ .

2. We hope you succeed ____ .

3. She forgave him ____ .

4. I'm going to take care ____ .

5. The firefighters rescued many people ____ .

6. I pray ____ .

7. Trucks are prohibited ____ .

Column B

a. from the burning building

b. for telling a lie

✓c. of leather

d. from entering the tunnel

e. in winning the scholarship

f. of the children tonight

g. for peace

► **Practice 24. Preposition combinations.** (Chart E)
Complete the sentences with appropriate prepositions.

1. Andrea contributed her ideas ____to____ the discussion.

2. Ms. Ballas substituted ____ our regular teacher.

3. I can't distinguish one twin ____ the other.

4. Children rely ____ their parents for food and shelter.

5. I'm worried ____ this problem.

6. I don't care ____ spaghetti. I'd rather eat something else.

7. Charles doesn't seem to care ____ his bad grades.

8. I'm afraid I don't agree ____ you.

9. We decided ____ eight o'clock as the time we should meet.

10. I am not familiar ____ that author's works.

11. Do you promise to come? I'm counting ____

    you to be here.

12. The little girl is afraid ____ an imaginary bear

    that lives in her closet.

► **Practice 25. Preposition combinations.** (Chart E)
Complete the sentences with appropriate prepositions.

1. We will fight ____*for*____ our rights.

2. Who did you vote _____ in the last election?

3. Jason was late because he wasn't aware _____ the time.

4. I am grateful _____ you _____ your assistance.

5. Elena is not content _____ the progress she is making.

6. Paul's comments were not relevant _____ the topic under discussion.

7. Have you decided _____ a date for your wedding yet?

8. Patricia applied _____ admission _____ the university.

9. Daniel dreamed _____ some of his childhood friends last night.

10. Mr. Miyagi dreams _____ owning his own business someday.

11. The accused woman was innocent _____ the crime with which she was charged.

12. Ms. Sanders is friendly _____ everyone.

13. The secretary provided me _____ a great deal of information.

14. Ivan compared the wedding customs in his country _____ those in the United States.

► **Practice 26. The subjunctive in noun clauses.** (Chart F)
Complete the sentences with appropriate verbs. There is often more than one possible completion.

1. Mr. Adams insists that we ____*be*____ careful in our writing.

2. They requested that we not _____ after midnight.

3. She demanded that I _____ her the truth.

4. I recommended that Rita _____ to the head of the department.

5. I suggest that everyone _____ a letter to the governor.

6. It is essential that I _____ you tomorrow.

7. It is important that he _____ the director of the English program.

8. It is necessary that everyone _____ here on time.

► **Practice 27. The subjunctive in noun clauses.** (Chart F)
Complete each sentence with the correct form of the verb in parentheses. Some of the verbs are passive.

1. Her advisor recommended that she (*take*) ____take____ five courses.

2. Roberto insisted that the new baby (*name*) __be named__ after his grandfather.

3. The doctor recommended that she (*stay*) _____ in bed for a few days.

4. The students requested that the test (*postpone*) _____ , but the instructor decided against a postponement.

5. It is essential that no one (*admit*) _____ to the room without proper identification.

6. It is critical that pollution (*control*) _____ and eventually (*eliminate*) _____ .

7. It was such a beautiful day that one of the students suggested we (*have*) _____ class outside.

8. The movie director insisted that everything about his productions (*be*) _____ authentic.

9. It is vital that no one else (*know*) _____ about the secret government operation.

10. Mrs. Wah asked that we (*be*) _____ sure to lock the door behind us.

11. I requested that I (*permit*) _____ to change my class.

12. It is important that you (*be, not*) _____ late.

13. It is imperative that he (*return*) _____ home immediately.

14. The governor proposed that a new highway (*build*) _____ .

15. Fumiko specifically asked that I (*tell, not*) _____ anyone else about it.

16. She said it was important that no one else (*tell*) _____ about it.

► **Practice 28. Troublesome verbs.** (Chart G)
Choose the correct verb in parentheses.

1. The student ((raised)/ rose) his hand in class.

2. Hot air (raises / rises).

3. Natasha (set / sat) in a chair because she was tired.

4. I (set / sat) your dictionary on the table a few minutes ago.

5. Hens (lay / lie) eggs.

6. Sara is (laying / lying) on the grass in the park right now.

7. Jan (laid / lay) the comb on top of the dresser a few minutes ago.

8. If you are tired, you should (lay / lie) down and take a nap.

9. San Francisco (lays / lies) to the north of Los Angeles.

10. Mr. Faust (raises / rises) many different kinds of flowers in his garden.

11. The student (raised / rose) from her seat and walked to the front of the auditorium to receive her diploma.

12. Hiroki is a very methodical person. Every night before going to bed, he (lays / lies) his clothes for the next day on his chair.

13. Where are my keys? I (lay / laid) them here on the desk five minutes ago.

14. Fahad (set / sat) the table for dinner.

15. Fahad (set / sat) at the table for dinner.

16. The fulfillment of all your dreams (lies / lays) within you — if you just believe in yourself.

Special Workbook Section
Phrasal Verbs

PHRASAL VERBS (TWO-WORD AND THREE-WORD VERBS)

    The term *phrasal verb* refers to a verb and particle which together have a special meaning. For example, ***put*** + ***off*** means "postpone." Sometimes a phrasal verb consists of three parts. For example, ***put*** + ***up*** + ***with*** means "tolerate." Phrasal verbs are also called *two-word verbs* or *three-word verbs*.

SEPARABLE PHRASAL VERBS	A phrasal verb may be either *separable* or *nonseparable*. With a separable phrasal verb, a noun may come either between the verb and the preposition or after the preposition, as in (a) and (b).
(a) ***I handed*** my paper ***in*** yesterday.	
(b) ***I handed in*** my paper yesterday.	
(c) ***I handed*** it ***in*** yesterday.	A pronoun comes between the verb and the preposition if the phrasal verb is separable, as in (c).
(*INCORRECT:* I handed *in* it yesterday.)	

NONSEPARABLE PHRASAL VERBS	With a nonseparable phrasal verb, a noun or pronoun must follow the preposition, as in (d) and (e).
(d) ***I ran into*** an old friend yesterday.	
(e) ***I ran into*** her yesterday.	
(*INCORRECT:* I ran an old friend *into.*)	
(*INCORRECT:* I ran her *into* yesterday.)	

    Phrasal verbs are especially common in informal English. Following is a list of common phrasal verbs and their usual meanings. This list contains only those phrasal verbs used in the exercises in the text. The phrasal verbs marked with an asterisk (*) are nonseparable.

A   ask out . . . . *ask someone to go on a date*

B   bring about, bring on . . . . *cause*
        bring up . . . . *(1) rear children; (2) mention or introduce a topic*

C   call back . . . . *return a telephone call*
        call in . . . . *ask to come to an official place for a specific purpose*
        call off . . . . *cancel*
        *call on . . . . *ask to speak in class*
        call up . . . . *call on the telephone*
        *catch up (with). . . . . *reach the same position or level*
        *check in, check into . . . . *register at a hotel*
        check into . . . . *investigate*
        check out . . . . *(1) borrow a book from the library; (2) investigate*
        check out (of) . . . . *leave a hotel*
        cheer up . . . . *make (someone) feel happier*
        clean up . . . . *make clean and orderly*
        *come across . . . . *meet / find by chance*
        cross out . . . . *draw a line through*
        cut out . . . . *stop an annoying activity*

D   do over . . . . *do again*
        *drop by, drop in (on) . . . . *visit informally*
        drop off . . . . *leave something / someone at a place*
        *drop out (of) . . . . *stop going to school, to a class, to a club, etc.*

F	figure out	. . . .	*find the answer by reasoning*
	fill out	. . . .	*write the answers to a questionnaire or complete an official form*
	find out	. . . .	*discover information*
G	*get along (with)	. . . .	*have a good relationship with*
	get back (from)	. . . .	*(1) return from a place; (2) receive again*
	*get in, get into	. . . .	*(1) enter a car; (2) arrive*
	*get off	. . . .	*leave an airplane, a bus, a train, a subway, a bicycle*
	*get on	. . . .	*enter an airplane, a bus, a train, a subway, a bicycle*
	*get out of.	. . . .	*(1) leave a car; (2) avoid work or an unpleasant activity*
	get over	. . . .	*recover from an illness*
	get through (with)	. . . .	*finish*
	*get up (from).	. . . .	*arise from a bed, a chair*
	give back.	. . . .	*return an item to someone*
	give up.	. . . .	*stop trying, quit*
	*go over.	. . . .	*review or check carefully*
	*grow up	. . . .	*become an adult*
H	hand in.	. . . .	*submit an assignment*
	hang up	. . . .	*(1) conclude a telephone conversation; (2) put clothes on a hanger or a hook*
	have on	. . . .	*wear*
K	keep out (of)	. . . .	*not enter*
	*keep up (with)	. . . .	*stay at the same position or level*
	kick out (of)	. . . .	*force (someone) to leave*
L	*look after.	. . . .	*take care of*
	*look into	. . . .	*investigate*
	*look out (for).	. . . .	*be careful*
	look over.	. . . .	*review or check carefully*
	look up.	. . . .	*look for information in a reference book, on the internet, etc.*
M	make up	. . . .	*(1) invent; (2) do past-due work*
N	name after, name for.	. . . .	*give a baby the name of someone else*
P	*pass away, pass on	. . . .	*die*
	pass out	. . . .	*distribute*
	*pass out	. . . .	*lose consciousness*
	pick out	. . . .	*select*
	pick up.	. . . .	*(1) go to get someone (e.g., in a car); (2) take in one's hand*
	point out.	. . . .	*call attention to*
	put away	. . . .	*remove to a proper place*
	put back	. . . .	*return to the original place*
	put off	. . . .	*postpone*
	put on	. . . .	*put clothes on one's body*
	put out.	. . . .	*extinguish a cigarette, cigar, fire*
	*put up with	. . . .	*tolerate*
R	*run into, *run across.	. . . .	*meet by chance*
	*run out (of)	. . . .	*finish a supply of something*
S	*show up	. . . .	*appear, come*
	shut off.	. . . .	*stop a machine, light, faucet*

T *take after . . . . resemble
take off. . . . . (1) remove clothing; (2) leave on a trip
take out . . . . (1) take someone on a date; (2) remove
take over . . . . take control
take up . . . . begin a new activity or topic
tear down . . . . demolish; reduce to nothing
tear up . . . . tear into many little pieces
think over . . . . consider carefully
throw away, throw out . . . . discard, get rid of
throw up . . . . vomit; regurgitate food
try on . . . . put on clothing to see if it fits
turn down . . . . decrease volume or intensity
turn in . . . . (1) submit an assignment; (2) go to bed
turn off. . . . . stop a machine, light, faucet
turn on. . . . . start a machine, light, faucet
turn out . . . . extinguish a light
turn up . . . . increase volume or intensity

▶ Practice 1. Phrasal verbs.

Complete each sentence with the appropriate preposition(s). The meaning of the phrasal verb is in parentheses.

1. Lara looked . . .

   a. ____after____ her father when he was sick. (*took care of*)

   b. _____ her children's homework. (*reviewed*)

   c. _____ some information on the internet. (*looked for information*)

   d. _____ an unusual situation at work. (*investigated*)

2. The tourists checked . . .

   a. _____ travel DVDs from the library before their trip. (*borrowed*)

   b. _____ their hotel. (*registered at*)

   c. _____ a famous archeological site. (*investigated*)

   d. _____ _____ their hotel rooms. (*left*)

3. Mrs. Jenkins got . . .

   a. _____ a serious illness. (*recovered from*)

   b. _____ _____ her planning for her daughter's wedding. (*finished*)

   c. _____ _____ doing an unimportant project at work. (*avoided*)

   d. _____ _____ her summer vacation early. (*returned*)

   e. _____ the subway at an unfamiliar stop. (*left*)

4. The school principal called . . .

    a. _____ the school assembly. (*canceled*)

    b. _____ some parents. (*telephoned*)

    c. _____ a few students to answer questions while visiting a class. (*asked them to speak*)

    d. _____ a teacher who was sick. (*returned a phone call*)

    e. _____ a student for discipline. (*asked the student to come to his/her office*)

▶ Practice 2. Phrasal verbs.

Complete each sentence with the correct form of a phrasal verb from the list. One phrasal verb is used twice.

get along with	pass out (2)	put up with	take after	turn in
pass away	pick out	show up	think over	

1. The flight attendants gave one snack to passengers during the flight. They _passed_ _out_ small bags of peanuts.

2. You choose the vegetables for dinner. _____ _____ whatever you like.

3. You look like your mother, but your brother _____ _____ your father.

4. I have three good job offers to consider. I need some time to _____ them _____ .

5. Nathan tolerates his roommate's messy habits. I wonder how he _____ _____ _____ them.

6. Mary's elderly mother died last week. She _____ _____ after a long illness.

7. Julianna was two hours late for the dinner party. When she finally appeared, her friends told her it was rude to _____ _____ so late.

8. The Smiths are a friendly couple and people really like them. They seem to _____ _____ _____ everyone.

9. Good night. It's bedtime. I'm going to _____ _____ now.

10. Helen got hit in the head with a golf ball, but fortunately didn't lose consciousness. The ball was traveling so fast that it was a miracle she didn't _____ _____ .

▶ Practice 3. Phrasal verbs.

Choose the correct completions. More than one completion may be correct.

1. When do we turn in	(our assignment?)	the dinner?	yesterday?
2. Mario made up	a lie.	a story.	a flower.
3. The government took over	the city.	the banks.	the trees.
4. Please put out	your cigarette.	the lights.	the fire.
5. What brought about	the war?	the package?	the crisis?
6. Did you figure out	working?	the problem?	the puzzle?
7. How do I turn on	the lights?	the music?	the printer?
8. Hugo asked out	his classmate.	a question.	a girl.
9. Jill is going to give up	a present.	chocolate.	smoking.
10. At the airport, I came across	a friend.	a classmate.	to fly.
11. Tina dropped out of	high school.	the ball.	college.

▶ Practice 4. Phrasal verbs.

Complete each sentence with an appropriate preposition from the list to form a two-word verb. Some prepositions may be used more than once.

back	into	off	on	out	up

1. A: Guess who I ran _____*into*_____ today as I was walking across campus. Ann Keefe!

   B: You're kidding!

2. A: There will be a test on Chapters 8 and 9 next Friday.

   B: Oh, no! Couldn't you put it _____ until Monday?

3. A: You'd better put _____ your coat before you leave. It's chilly out.

   B: What's the temperature?

4. A: I smell something burning in the kitchen. Can I call you _____ in a minute?

   B: Sure. I hope your dinner hasn't burned.

   A: So do I! Bye.

5. A: I think that if I learn enough vocabulary I won't have any trouble using English.

   B: That's not necessarily so. I'd like to point _____ that language consists of much more than just vocabulary.

6. A: Your children certainly love the outdoors.

   B: Yes, they do. We brought them _____ to appreciate nature.

7. A: What forms do I have to fill out to change my tourist visa to a student visa?

   B: I don't know, but I'll look _____ it first thing tomorrow and try to find _____ . I'll let you know.

8. A: How long were you in the hospital?

   B: About a week. But I've missed almost two weeks of classes.

   A: It's going to be hard for you to make _____ all the work you've missed, isn't it?

   B: Very.

9. A: Could you pick _____ a newspaper on your way home from work tonight? There's a story I want to read.

   B: Sure.

10. A: I like your new shoes.

    B: Thanks. I had to try _____ almost a dozen pairs before I decided to get these.

▶ **Practice 5. Phrasal verbs.**
Complete each sentence with an appropriate preposition from the list to form a two-word verb. Some prepositions may be used more than once.

about	away	in	of	off	on	out	up

1. A: I'm trying to find yesterday's newspaper. Have you seen it?

   B: I'm afraid I threw it ___*away / out*___ . I thought you had finished reading it.

2. A: Where did you grow _____ ?

   B: In Seattle, Washington.

3. A: Don't forget to turn the lights _____ before you go to bed.

   B: I won't.

4. A: I have a car, so I can drive us to the festival.

   B: Good.

   A: What time should I pick you _____?

   B: Any time after five would be fine.

5. A: We couldn't see the show at the outdoor theater last night.

   B: Why not?

   A: It was called _____ on account of rain.

6. A: Thomas looks sad.

   B: I think he misses his girlfriend. Let's try to cheer him _____ .

7. A: What brought _____ your decision to quit your present job?

   B: I was offered a better job.

8. A: Why did you come back early from your trip?

   B: Unfortunately, I ran _____ _____ money.

9. A: Thanks for the ride. I appreciate it.

   B: Where should I drop you _____?

10. A: What time does your plane take _____?

    B: 10:40.

    A: How long does the flight take?

    B: I think we get _____ around 12:30.

► **Practice 6. Phrasal verbs.**
Complete the sentences with appropriate prepositions to form two-word or three-word verbs.

1. A: Look ____*out*____ ! A car is coming!

2. A: May I borrow your dictionary?

   B: Sure. But please be sure to put it _____ on the shelf when you're finished.

3. A: I'm going to be in your neighborhood tomorrow.

   B: Oh? If you have time, why don't you drop _____ to see us?

4. A: How does this tape recorder work?

   B: Push this button to turn it _____ and push that button to shut it

   _____ .

5. A: Did you hear what started the forest fire?

   B: Yes. Some campers built a fire, but when they left their campsite, they didn't

   _____ it _____ completely.

6. A: I need to talk to Karen.

   B: Why don't you call her _____ ? She's probably at home now.

7. A: Uh-oh. I made a mistake on the check I just wrote.

   B: Don't try to correct the mistake. Just tear _____ the check and throw it

   _____ .

8. A: Are you here to apply for a job?

   B: Yes.

   A: Here is an application form. Fill it _____ and then give it _____ to

   me when you are finished.

9. A: Look. There's Mike.

   B: Where?

   A: At the other end of the block, walking toward the administration building. If we run, we

   can catch _____ with him.

10. A: Is your roommate here?

    B: Yes. She decided to come to the party after all. Have you ever met her?

    A: No, but I'd like to.

    B: She's the one standing over there by the far window. She has a blue dress

    _____ . Come on. I'll introduce you.

► **Practice 7. Phrasal verbs.**
Complete each sentence with an appropriate preposition.

1. A: What time did you get _____*up*_____ this morning?

    B: I slept late. I didn't drag myself out of bed until after nine.

2. A: How did you do on your composition?

    B: Not well. It had a lot of spelling mistakes, so I have to do it _____.

3. A: What's the baby's name?

    B: Helen. She was named _____ her paternal grandmother.

4. A: I need to get more exercise.

    B: Why don't you take _____ tennis?

5. A: You can't go in there.

    B: Why not?

    A: Look at that sign. It says, "Keep _____. No trespassing."

6. A: The radio is too loud. Would you mind if I turned it _____ a little?

    B: No.

7. A: I can't hear the radio. Could you turn it _____ a little?

    B: Sure.

8. A: What are you doing Saturday night, Bob?

    B: I'm taking Virginia _____ for dinner and a show.

9. A: Don't you think it's hot in here?

    B: Not especially. If you're hot, why don't you take your sweater _____ ?

10. A: How do you spell *occasionally*?

    B: I'm not sure. You'd better look it _____ in your dictionary.

11. A: I'm tired. I wish I could get _____ of going to the meeting tonight.

    B: Why do you have to go?

► **Practice 8. Phrasal verbs.**
Complete each sentence with an appropriate preposition.

1. A: I need my dictionary, but I lent it to José.

   B: Why don't you get it _____ *back* _____ from him?

2. A: Cindy is only three. She likes to play with the older kids, but when they're running and

   playing, she can't keep _____ with them.

   B: She doesn't seem to mind, does she?

3. A: I made a mistake in my composition. What should I do?

   B: Since it's an in-class composition, just cross it _____ .

4. A: What happened when the pilot of the plane passed out during the flight?

   B: The co-pilot took _____ .

5. I took a plane from Atlanta to Miami. I got _____ the plane in Atlanta. I got

   _____ the plane in Miami.

6. It was a snowy winter day, but I still had to drive to work. First I got _____ the

   car to start the engine. Then I got _____ of the car to scrape the snow and ice

   from the windows.

7. Last year I took a train trip. I got _____ the train in Chicago. I got

   _____ the train in Des Moines.

8. Phyllis takes the bus to work. She gets _____ the bus at Lindbergh Boulevard and

   gets _____ the bus about two blocks from her office on Tower Street.

9. A: Do you like living in the dorm?

   B: It's OK. I've learned to put _____ _____ all the noise.

10. A: What brought _____ your decision to quit your job?

    B: I couldn't get _____ _____ my boss.

11. A: Did you go _____ your paper carefully before you handed it _____ ?

    B: Yes. I looked it _____ carefully.

Index

Answer Key

CHAPTER 1: OVERVIEW OF VERB TENSES

PRACTICE 1, p. 1
1. eat
2. ate . . . visited . . . wrote
3. am talking . . . am answering
4. was looking
5. have asked
6. have been talking
7. will be
8. will be sitting
9. had eaten
10. will have eaten

PRACTICE 2, p. 2
1. 7th, 14th, 21st, 28th
2. 7th
3. 3rd
4. 2nd, 3rd, 4th
5. 10th, 11th, 12th
6. 14th and 15th
7. 7th
8. 24th

PRACTICE 3, p. 2
1. rains
2. visited
3. will win
4. is watching
5. will be flying
6. was thinking
7. will be working
8. went . . . were sleeping
9. fell . . . will help
10. are swimming

PRACTICE 4, p. 3
1. have
2. had
3. has been
4. was
5. will have been
6. have lived
7. had
8. have
9. had
10. had

PRACTICE 5, p. 3
1. have
2. has been
3. will have been
4. had
5. have
6. had
7. have been waiting
8. has
9. had

PRACTICE 6, p. 4
1. a
2. b
3. a
4. b
5. a
6. a
7. b
8. a
9. a

PRACTICE 7, p. 5
1. eats
2. ate
3. will eat / 'll eat
4. am eating / 'm eating
5. was eating
6. will be eating
7. have already eaten
8. had already eaten
9. will have already eaten
10. has been eating
11. had been eating
12. will have been eating dinner

PRACTICE 8, p. 7
1. at this time
2. in the past
3. daily habit
4. past and present
5. past only
6. in the past
7. at this time
8. in the future
9. daily habit
10. in the past

PRACTICE 9, p. 7
1. b. soon c. next week
2. a. right now
3. b. now c. right now
4. b. all day c. since Monday
5. a. now b. this week
6. b. next month c. this weekend
7. a. since 9:00 b. all day c. for two hours
8. a. last week c. yesterday
9. a. at midnight b. when we came
10. a. tomorrow c. in the morning
11. a. soon c. in a few days

PRACTICE 10, p. 8
1. a
2. a
3. b
4. a, b
5. a, b, c
6. a
7. a
8. a, c

PRACTICE 11, p. 8
1.   arriving
2. copying
3.   cutting
4. enjoying
5. filling
6. happening
7.   hoping
8.   leaving
9.   making
10.   rubbing
11. staying
12.   stopping
13.   taking
14.   winning
15. working

PRACTICE 12, p. 9

1. bothered	
2.	copied
3. enjoyed	
4. fastened	
5. feared	
6.	occurred
7.	patted
8. played	
9. rained	
10.	referred
11.	replied
12. returned	
13.	scared
14.	tried
15. walked	

PRACTICE 13, p. 10

1. preferring   preferred
2. studying   studied
3. working   worked
4. offering   offered
5. kissing   kissed
6. playing   played
7. fainting   fainted
8. allowing   allowed
9. stopping   stopped
10. tying   tied
11. dying   died
12. folding   folded
13. trying   tried
14. deciding   decided
15. hopping   hopped

PRACTICE 14, p. 10

1. do you spell
2. spell
3. has
4. are you
5. am
6. lived
7. moved
8. did you grow
9. did you come
10. arrived
11. have been
12. do you like
13. am staying
14. am looking
15. have been looking
16. find
17. Have you found
18. had been looking
19. are you moving
20. give
21. will be moving
22. will have moved
23. will be

CHAPTER 2: PRESENT AND PAST; SIMPLE AND PROGRESSIVE

PRACTICE 1, p. 12

1. sets
2. is setting
3. are practicing
4. practice
5. listen
6. am listening / 'm listening
7. talk
8. are talking
9. are eating / 're eating
10. eat

PRACTICE 2, p. 12

1. fall
2. are falling
3. grows
4. are growing
5. shines
6. is shining . . . are singing
7. sings
8. reads
9. am calling

PRACTICE 3, p. 13

1. own
2. am trying / 'm trying
3. belongs
4. is sleeping
5. means
6. shrinks
7. is biting / 's biting
8. is bleeding / 's bleeding
9. am failing / 'm failing

PRACTICE 4, p. 13

1. a		6. a	
2. b		7. b	
3. a		8. a	
4. b		9. a	
5. a		10. a	

PRACTICE 5, p. 14

1. a		4. a	
2. b		5. b	
3. b		6. a	

PRACTICE 6, p. 15

Part I. changed . . . launched . . . was . . . weighed . . . took . . . ushered . . . was . . . marked

Part II.
1. T
2. F
3. T
4. F
5. T

PRACTICE 7, p. 15

Part I.
1. worked
2. listened
3. studied
4. rained

Part II.
5. broke
6. swam
7. hit

PRACTICE 8, p. 16

Group 1.
1. cost
2. shut
3. cut
4. quit

Group 2.
5. forgot
6. chose
7. took
8. gave

PRACTICE 9, p. 16

Group 3.
1. began
2. sang
3. ran
4. drank

Group 4.
5. bought
6. taught
7. won
8. lost
9. left
10. upset

PRACTICE 10, p. 17

Group 5.
1. knew
2. flew
3. did
4. saw

Group 6.
5. ran
6. came
7. became

Group 7.
8. was
9. went

Group 8.
10. dreamed / dreamt
11. learned / learnt
12. burned / burnt
13. spilled / spilt

PRACTICE 11, p. 18

1. sold   sold
2. bought   bought
3. began   begun
4. had   had
5. caught   caught
6. quit   quit
7. found   found
8. made   made
9. took   taken
10. broke   broken
11. came   come
12. lost   lost
13. slept   slept
14. built   built
15. fought   fought

PRACTICE 12, p. 19

Simple Form	Simple Past	Past Participle
1.	understood	understood
2. spend		spent
3.	let	let
4. see	saw	
5.	taught	taught
6. speak		spoken
7. go	went	
8.	paid	paid
9. forget	forgot	
10. write		written
11.	fell	fallen
12. feel		felt
13. leave	left	
14. upset		upset
15. fly	flew	

PRACTICE 13, p. 19

1. broke
2. stole
3. knew
4. heard
5. came
6. shook
7. hid
8. found
9. fought
10. ran
11. shot
12. caught

PRACTICE 14, p. 20

1. bit
2. held
3. meant
4. blew
5. quit
6. felt
7. stung
8. swam
9. paid
10. caught

PRACTICE 15, p. 21

1. spent
2. led
3. bet
4. wept
5. upset
6. split
7. sank
8. flew
9. spun
10. rang
11. chose
12. froze

PRACTICE 16, p. 21

1. called
2. were watching
3. was humming
4. met
5. saw
6. was cleaning
7. was driving . . . got
8. was blowing . . . were bending
9. were playing . . . was pulling

PRACTICE 17, p. 22

1. 2, 1
2. 2, 1
3. 1, 2
4. 2, 1
5. 1, 2
6. 2, 1
7. 1, 2
8. 2, 1

PRACTICE 18, p. 23

1. had
2. were having
3. stopped . . . fell . . . spilled
4. served . . . came
5. looked . . . was sleeping . . . was dreaming . . . was smiling
6. was working . . . exploded
7. caused . . . dropped

PRACTICE 19, p. 23

1. 2   take . . . rains
2. 4   was riding . . . heard
3. 1   am riding . . . is repairing
4. 3   rode . . . forgot
5. 4   was having . . . crashed
6. 3   had . . . didn't eat
7. 1   is having
8. 2   has
9. 2   celebrate . . . are
10. 4   were working . . . called
11. 3   celebrated . . . was

PRACTICE 20, p. 24

1. is always complaining
2. is always talking
3. live
4. is forever leaving
5. are always interrupting
6. are always losing
7. play
8. are always studying

PRACTICE 21, p. 25

Across	Down
2. listening	1. went
5. think	3. studying
7. heard	4. ate
8. thinking	6. having
	7. have

CHAPTER 3: PERFECT AND PERFECT PROGRESSIVE TENSES

PRACTICE 1, p. 26

Part I.
1. has been . . . has remained . . . have estimated
2. has been increasing . . . have been growing
3. had been . . . had dropped
4. were
5. will be

Part II.
1. F   4. F
2. F   5. T
3. T

PRACTICE 2, p. 27
1. eaten   6. worn
2. visited   7. taken
3. worked   8. gone
4. liked   9. ridden
5. known   10. been

PRACTICE 3, p. 27
1. a. for   2. a. since
   b. for   b. for
   c. since   c. since
   d. since   d. for
   e. for   e. since
   f. since   f. since
   g. since   g. for

PRACTICE 4, p. 28
1. have already eaten
2. have won
3. have not written
4. has improved
5. has not started
6. have already swept
7. have you known
8. have made
9. have never ridden
10. Have you ever swum

PRACTICE 5, p. 29
1. the 21st of April . . . three weeks . . . April 1st . . . three weeks
2. two months ago . . . January 1st . . . two months
3. two weeks . . . February 14th
4. nine years . . . nine years . . . October, 2000

PRACTICE 6, p. 29

Answers will vary.
1. a. We have known Mrs. Jones for one month.
   b. We have known Mrs. Jones since last month.
2. a. They have lived there for (____) years.
   b. They have lived there since 2001.
3. a. I have liked foreign films since 200(____).
   b. I have liked foreign films for five years.
4. a. Jack has worked for a software company for one year.
   b. Jack has worked for a software company since last year.

PRACTICE 7, p. 30
1. is   6. is
2. has   7. has
3. is   8. is
4. is   9. has
5. has

PRACTICE 8, p. 30
1. became   5. lived
2. has been   6. have lived
3. has been   7. worked
4. has rained   8. haven't worked

PRACTICE 9, p. 30
1. knew . . . have known
2. agreed . . . have agreed
3. took . . . has taken
4. has played . . . played
5. wrote . . . has written
6. sent . . . have sent
7. has flown . . . flew
8. overslept . . . has overslept

PRACTICE 10, p. 31
1. have been talking   4. have you been sitting
2. have spoken   5. have sat
3. has won

PRACTICE 11, p. 31
1. have been playing   6. has slept
2. has played   7. have been flying
3. has raised   8. has been sleeping
4. has been lecturing   9. have been searching
5. has never missed

PRACTICE 12, p. 32
1. have never understood   6. have been traveling
2. have met   7. has grown
3. has been standing   8. wanted
4. has been painting   9. have already spent
5. have never heard   10. has been cooking

PRACTICE 13, p. 33

Sample answers
1. In 1999, Janet moved to Canada.
2. In 2000, Janet joined Lingua Schools as a teaching assistant.
3. Janet has been living / has lived in Canada since 1999.
4. Janet has been a teacher since 2001.
5. Janet has been teaching / has taught her own class since 2001.
6. Janet has been working / has worked at Lingua Schools since 2000.

PRACTICE 14, p. 33
1. We had driven only two miles = 1
   we got a flat tire = 2
2. Alan told me = 2
   he had written a book = 1
3. we arrived at the airport = 2
   the plane had already left = 1
4. The dog had eaten the entire roast = 1
   anyone knew it was gone = 2

5. We didn't stand in line for tickets = 2
   we had already bought them by mail = 1
6. Carl played the guitar so well = 2
   he had studied with a famous guitarist = 1
7. the movie ended = 2
   everyone had fallen asleep = 1
8. the professor had corrected the third paper = 1
   he was exhausted from writing comments on the
   student's papers = 2
9. I had just placed an order at the store for a new
   camera = 1
   I found a cheaper one online = 2

PRACTICE 15, p. 34
1. had not gotten
2. had not met
3. had not taken
4. had not eaten
5. had not had

PRACTICE 16, p. 34
1. b. had already finished
2. a. turned on
3. b. had burned
4. b. had never spent
5. a. helped
6. b. had never visited
7. b. had traveled

PRACTICE 17, p. 34
1. went . . . had never been . . . didn't take . . . was
2. ate . . . had never eaten
3. A: saw . . . did . . . Had you ever acted
   B: started

PRACTICE 18, p. 35
1. have been studying
2. had been studying
3. have been waiting
4. had been waiting
5. had been working
6. has been working

PRACTICE 19, p. 35
1. had been listening . . . have been dancing . . . singing
2. have been waiting
3. had been waiting
4. has been training
5. had been running
6. had been trying . . . has been teaching
7. has been performing
8. have been working . . . had been building

PRACTICE 20, p. 36
1. I've **seen** it ten times.
2. I've **been** reading it . . .
3. Our guests **left** . . .
4. We **have been** studying . . . .
5. I've been having . . .
6. . . . **had** eaten.
7. . . . , so I **ran** . . .
8. She **left** . . .
9. . . . , I **had** celebrated . . .
10. B: . . . I **have been** holding for more than half an hour!

CHAPTER 4: FUTURE TIME

PRACTICE 1, p. 37
1. He **will** be
2. will **stay** open
3. **will be**

4. Correct.
5. Our teacher **won't be**
6. Correct.

PRACTICE 2, p. 37
1. is going to visit
2. is going to win
3. are you going to take
4. is not going to be
5. Are they going to join
6. am not going to lie . . . I am going to tell

PRACTICE 3, p. 38
1. a. will set
   b. is going to set
2. a. will arrive
   b. is going to arrive
3. a. will rain
   b. is going to rain
4. a. will bloom
   b. are going to bloom
5. a. will end
   b. is going to end
6. a. will . . . buy
   b. are . . . going to buy
7. a. will . . . take
   b. am . . . going to take

PRACTICE 4, p. 38
1. Willingness
2. Prediction
3. Prediction
4. Prior plan
5. Willingness
6. Prior plan
7. Prediction

PRACTICE 5, p. 39
1. a. prior plan
2. b. decision of the moment
3. b. decision of the moment
4. a. prior plan
5. a. prior plan
6. b. decision of the moment

PRACTICE 6, p. 39
1. I'll call him
2. She's going to be / She'll be
3. I'm going to fly
4. We're going to the game
5. I'll open it
6. I'm going to teach / I will teach

PRACTICE 7, p. 39
1. will
2. are going to
3. will
4. A: Are you going to
   B: are going to
5. am going to
6. will
7. will
8. is going to
9. A: am going to
   B: will
10. B: am going to . . . will

PRACTICE 8, p. 40
Time Clauses
1. when you (return) from your trip
2. After the train (stops)
3. until it (gets) dark
4. As soon as the baby (is born)
5. When he (retires)
6. when you (are) eighteen years old
7. as soon as the late news (is) over
8. when the new semester (begins)

PRACTICE 9, p. 41
1. retire
2. rings
3. finish
4. take
5. arrives
6. graduates
7. is
8. hear
9. leave
10. get

PRACTICE 10, p. 41
1. b
2. a
3. b
4. a
5. a
6. a
7. a
8. b
9. a
10. a

PRACTICE 11, p. 42
1. will not / are not going to return . . . get
2. gets . . . will / is going to be
3. is not going to / won't be . . . learns . . . comes . . . asks
4. returns . . . is going to / will start
5. is going to / will build . . . is going to / will be . . . complete
6. hear . . . will let
7. will lend . . . finish
8. A: will / is going to be
   B: will / am going to be

PRACTICE 12, p. 43
1. 'm seeing
2. is having
3. is opening
4. is working
5. 're having
6. are attending

PRACTICE 13, p. 43
1. a, b, c
2. c
3. a, b
4. a, b, c
5. a, b
6. a

PRACTICE 14, p. 44
1. I'm sending
2. NC
3. I'm having
4. A: are you doing
   B: I'm studying
5. NC
6. are they getting
7. NC
8. we're moving
9. Is he teaching
10. A: I'm not sending
    B: I'm coming

PRACTICE 15, p. 45
1. will be sitting
2. will be flying
3. will be sleeping
4. will be snowing
5. will be watching

PRACTICE 16, p. 45
1. heals . . . will be playing
2. clear . . . will be standing
3. start . . . will be attending
4. have . . . will be shopping
5. will be attending . . . return

PRACTICE 17, p. 46
1. will already have risen
2. will have been riding
3. will already have landed
4. will have been listening
5. will have drunk
6. will have been flying
7. will have saved
8. will have taught

PRACTICE 18, p. 46
Note: *be going to* is also possible in place of *will*.
1. gets . . . will be shining
2. will brush . . . shower . . . will make
3. eats . . . will get
4. gets . . . will have drunk
5. will answer . . . will plan
6. will have called
7. will be attending
8. will go . . . will have
9. finishes . . . will take . . . returns
10. will work . . . . goes
11. leaves . . . will have attended
12. gets . . . will be playing . . . will be watching
13. will have been playing
14. will have . . . will talk
15. will watch . . . will put
16. goes . . . will have had . . . will be

CHAPTER 5: REVIEW OF VERB TENSES

PRACTICE 1, p. 48
1. has never flown
2. have been waiting . . . hasn't arrived
3. are . . . reach
4. didn't own . . . had owned
5. are having . . . has been
6. will have left . . . get
7. went . . . got . . . were dancing . . . were talking . . . was standing . . . had never met . . . introduced
8. was sitting . . . heard . . . got . . . looked . . . had just backed

PRACTICE 2, p. 48
1. am taking . . . leave . . . 'm going . . . leave . . . am going to go . . . is studying . . . has lived . . . knows . . . has promised . . . have never been . . . am looking
2. had been raining . . . dropped . . . is going to be . . . changes . . . wake . . . will be snowing

PRACTICE 3, p. 49

1. had been
2. met
3. had missed
4. was
5. got
6. took
7. was
8. had grown
9. was
10. was wearing
11. had changed
12. was still
13. asked
14. had gained
15. had turned
16. looked
17. were

PRACTICE 4, p. 49

Note: *be going to* is also possible in place of *will*.

1. will have been
2. will meet
3. will have missed
4. will be
5. get
6. will take
7. will no longer be
8. will have grown
9. will be
10. will probably wear
11. will have changed
12. will still be
13. will ask
14. will probably have gained
15. will have turned
16. will look
17. will be

PRACTICE 5, p. 50

Part I.

1. haven't seen
2. recuperating
3. happened
4. broke
5. was playing
6. is
7. doing
8. has
9. will / is going to be

Part II.

1. sent
2. haven't received
3. is not functioning
4. are trying
5. will / is going to start

PRACTICE 6, p. 51

1. used
2. use
3. does it consist
4. do teachers use
5. doesn't give
6. doesn't make
7. knows
8. sounds
9. talked
10. fell
11. agree
12. think
13. 'm taking
14. always asks
15. has been using
16. didn't realize / hadn't realized

PRACTICE 7, p. 52

1. a. is waiting
   b. has been waiting
   c. will have been waiting
2. a. is standing
   b. has been standing
   c. will have stood / will have been standing
   d. will have been standing

PRACTICE 8, p. 52

1. d. am waiting
2. c. has appeared
3. a. is in her room studying
4. b. do you think
5. c. has been working
6. c. 'm going to make
7. a. find
8. c. is
9. b. was watching
10. d. have existed
11. a. has been ringing
12. d. depends
13. a. 'm staying
14. b. has made
15. c. stepped
16. d. had been waiting
17. b. isn't going to exist
18. d. had never won
19. c. will have been studying

PRACTICE 9, p. 54

1. a. is seeing
2. a. I've talked
3. b. will be sleeping
4. c. have been boiling
5. c. had been making
6. a. don't believe
7. b. 'll help
8. b. has been
9. d. speaks
10. c. are becoming
11. a. hadn't been getting
12. a. reaches
13. a. lasted
14. c. have been working
15. c. will find
16. d. were sleeping
17. b. had lost
18. a. turn

CHAPTER 6: SUBJECT-VERB AGREEMENT

PRACTICE 1, p. 57

1. wears
2. are
3. beats
4. need
5. knows
6. magazines . . . years
7. are
8. subjects
9. There **are** . . . kinds
10. is
11. has
12. takes
13. like . . . get . . . workers . . . **don't** fit

PRACTICE 2, p. 58

1. floats	Verb	Singular
2. Boats	Noun	Plural
3. lives	Verb	Singular
4. friends	Noun	Plural
5. eats	Verb	Singular
6. Donuts	Noun	Plural
7. Babies	Noun	Plural
8. cries	Verb	Singular

PRACTICE 3, p. 58

1. bal**ls**	/z/
2. wish**es**	/əz/
3. aunt**s**	/s/
4. flowers	/z/

5. parks /s/
6. touches /əz/
7. months /s/
8. trees /z/
9. dresses /əz/
10. valleys /z/
11. industries /z/
12. swallows /z/
13. cliffs /s/
14. baths /s/
15. bathes /z/

PRACTICE 4, p. 58
1. is
2. are   6. is
3. has   7. are
4. barks   8. is
5. bark   9. are
              10. is

PRACTICE 5, p. 59
1. is
2. are   6. are
3. is   7. are
4. are   8. is
5. is . . . is 9. is
              10. are

PRACTICE 6, p. 59
1. has
2. were   6. is
3. was   7. has
4. was   8. has
5. is   9. has (informal : have)

PRACTICE 7, p. 59
1. is
2. are   6. was
3. are   7. aren't
4. is   8. isn't
5. weren't   9. has
              10. have

PRACTICE 8, p. 60
1. are
2. is   8. are
3. is   9. are
4. is   10. is
5. is . . . is . . . is   11. are
6. isn't   12. are
7. isn't   13. are
              14. are

PRACTICE 9, p. 60
1. is
2. like . . . drive
3. is
4. are . . . are
5. are . . . contains . . . are
6. costs
7. is . . . is . . . are
8. is . . . reminds . . . makes

PRACTICE 10, p. 61
1. has   9. is
2. takes   10. is
3. are . . . have 11. is
4. was . . . were 12. is . . . have
5. take   13. is
6. is   14. speak
7. are . . . is 15. use
8. has . . . are . . . were

PRACTICE 11, p. 62
1. vote
2. have participated
3. was
4. knows
5. speak . . . understand
6. are
7. do . . . broadcast
8. are
9. have been
10. has received . . . have gone
11. confirms
12. is . . . is
13. are
14. has
15. Aren't
16. is
17. begin   *4 states begin with the letter A:
    Alabama, Arkansas, Alaska, Arizona.
18. consists
19. have
20. is
21. Was

CHAPTER 7: NOUNS

PRACTICE 1, p. 63
1. cars   9. classes
2. women   10. feet
3. matches   11. heroes
4. mice   12. pianos
5. cities   13. videos
6. donkeys   14. bases
7. halves   15. bacteria
8. chiefs   16. series

PRACTICE 2, p. 63
1. potatoes   5. teeth
2. monkeys   6. beliefs
3. thieves . . . radios   7. fish
4. children   8. species . . . kilos

PRACTICE 3, p. 64
1. cares . . . feathers
2. occupations . . . Doctors . . . Pilots . . . airplanes . . .
   Farmers . . . crops . . . Shepherds . . .
3. designs buildings . . . digs . . . objects . . .
4. computers . . . Computers
5. factories . . . employs
6. Kangaroos . . . animals . . . continents . . . zoos
7. Mosquitos / Mosquitoes
8. tomatoes

PRACTICE 4, p. 64

1. a. parents'
   b. two
   c. parents + house
2. a. parent's
   b. one
   c. parent + concern
3. a. cats'
   b. many
   c. cats + eyes
4. a. cat's
   b. one
   c. cat + eyes
5. a. Mary's
   b. brother
   c. Mary + brother
6. a. Mary's
   b. brothers
   c. Mary + brothers
7. a. brothers'
   b. more than one
   c. brothers + team
8. a. brother's
   b. one
   c. brother + team

PRACTICE 5, p. 65

1. one
2. more than one
3. more than one
4. one
5. more than one
6. more than one
7. one
8. one

PRACTICE 6, p. 65

1. secretary's
2. secretaries'
3. cats'
4. cat's
5. supervisors'
6. supervisor's
7. babies'
8. baby's
9. child's
10. children's
11. people's
12. actors'
13. actor's

PRACTICE 7, p. 66

1. mother's
2. grandmothers'
3. teacher's
4. boss'
5. employee's . . . employees'
6. men's . . . women's . . . children's . . . girls' . . . boys'

PRACTICE 8, p. 66

Adjectives

1. ____ expensive
2. ✓ theater
3. ____ small
4. ✓ movie
5. ✓ family
6. ✓ family
7. ✓ computer
8. ✓ hair
9. ✓ window
10. ✓ gas

PRACTICE 9, p. 66

1. groceries . . . grocery
2. chickens . . . chicken
3. tomato . . . tomatoes
4. pictures . . . picture
5. flower . . . flowers
6. drugs . . . drug
7. eggs . . . egg
8. two lanes . . . two-lane
9. five-minute . . . five minutes
10. sixty-year-old . . . sixty years old
11. truck . . . truck
12. computers . . . computer

PRACTICE 10, p. 67

1. a. kitchen table
2. c. bedroom tables
3. b. home office
4. a. home offices
5. b. office phone
6. c. bathroom sinks
7. a. vegetable garden
8. b. cherry trees

PRACTICE 11, p. 67

1. student handbook
2. birthday party
3. government check
4. airplane seats
5. cotton pajamas
6. hotel rooms
7. ten-month-old baby
8. three-day-trip
9. three-room-apartment
10. five-page paper
11. opera singer
12. stamp collector

PRACTICE 12, p. 68

Count	Noncount
1. eggs . . . bananas	food . . . bread . . . milk . . . coffee
2. letters . . . magazines . . . catalogs . . . bills	mail
3. Euros . . . pounds . . . dollars	money
4. ring . . . earrings	jewelry
5. language	vocabulary . . . grammar
6. table . . . chairs . . . umbrella	furniture

PRACTICE 13, p. 68

1. words
2. some
3. cars
4. much
5. sandwich
6. one
7. some
8. very

PRACTICE 14, p. 69

1. hair . . . eyes
2. No change.
3. No change.
4. No change.
5. No change.
6. classes
7. faxes

PRACTICE 15, p. 69

1. courage
2. some
3. shoes
4. garbage
5. glasses . . . glass
6. glasses . . . glass
7. some lost luggage . . . many
8. much . . . some
9. hills . . . lovely . . . damp
10. good

PRACTICE 16, p. 70

1. A
2. An
3. Ø Energy
4. A
5. An
6. Ø Fruit
7. Ø Sodium
8. Ø Air
9. Ø Rice
10. An
11. A
12. Ø Football
13. A
14. A

PRACTICE 17, p. 70

1.	a	8.	a
2.	some	9.	a
3.	an	10.	an
4.	some	11.	some
5.	a	12.	some
6.	some	13.	a
7.	some	14.	some

PRACTICE 18, p. 70

1.	b	4.	b
2.	a	5.	b
3.	a	6.	a

PRACTICE 19, p. 71

1. **The s**un . . . **the** sky
2. **The b**oy is about five years old, and **the** girl . . .
3. **Penguins** live in Antarctica. **Polar** bears . . .
4. Which is more important—**love** or **money**?
5. B: Do you have **a** dictionary? Look up **the** word in **the** dictionary.
6. B: . . . I didn't see **the** bee, but . . .

PRACTICE 20, p. 71

1. A: a . . . a   5. A: a
   B: a . . .   6. A: the
   A: The   B: a
2. A: the   A: the
3. A: a   B: the
4. A: a
   B: the

PRACTICE 21, p. 72

1. Ø Lightning . . . a . . . Ø
2. a . . . the
3. Ø Circles . . . Ø
4. A . . . a . . . the . . . the
5. The . . . the . . . an
6. the . . . a . . . the . . . a . . . The . . . Ø
7. a . . . The . . . Ø

PRACTICE 22, p. 73

1. a. three . . . b. several . . . f. too many . . . g. a few . . . i. a number of
2. e. too much . . . h. a little . . . j. a great deal of . . . l. no

PRACTICE 23, p. 73

1.	many computers	8.	many
2.	much	9.	is . . . much
3.	many child**ren** are	10.	much
4.	many **teeth**	11.	was . . . much
5.	many count**ries**	12.	much
6.	much	13.	many . . . volcano**es** are
7.	much . . . much	14.	many speech**es**

PRACTICE 24, p. 74

1. a. pictures b. photographs d. ceramic bowls
2. a. milk c. magazines
3. b. people c. babies
4. a. food b. cream c. coffee
5. a. food b. pizza c. drinks
6. c. bottles of soda
7. a. thoughts c. ideas
8. c. fun d. work
9. a. people b. things c. professors
10. a. intelligence b. information d. education

PRACTICE 25, p. 75

1. a. We have a little money.
2. b. They know a few people.
3. b. She has a little patience.
4. a. I speak some Spanish.
5. b. Marta asked a few questions.

PRACTICE 26, p. 75

1.	b	5.	a
2.	a	6.	c
3.	b	7.	b
4.	a		

PRACTICE 27, p. 75

1.	some	a little
2.	some	a few
3.	some	a few
4.	some	a little
5.	not many	few
6.	some	a few
7.	almost no	little
8.	some	a few
9.	some . . . some	a little . . . a little
10.	some	a little
	some	a little

PRACTICE 28, p. 76

1.	state	6.	child . . . chimpanzees
2.	states	7.	neighbors
3.	puppies	8.	man
4.	puppy	9.	goose
5.	children	10.	women

PRACTICE 29, p. 77

1. person
2. **the** rights
3. **the** states
4. Each senator
5. Correct.
6. the small states
7. the citizens . . . correct
8. citizen

PRACTICE 30, p. 77

1.	of	7.	Ø
2.	Ø	8.	Ø
3.	of	9.	Ø . . . of . . . of
4.	Ø	10.	Ø . . . of
5.	Ø	11.	of . . . Ø
6.	of		

PRACTICE 31, p. 78

Across
3. All
4. some
6. man
8. Every

Down
1. Two
2. One
3. An
5. mice
6. many
7. men

CHAPTER 8: PRONOUNS

PRACTICE 1, p. 79
1. He → Bob
2. They → Mr. and Mrs. Nobriega
3. her → teacher
4. She → baby
5. It → kind
6. them → hawks
7. him → Mr. Frank
8. They → dog and cat

PRACTICE 2, p. 79
1. I
2. me
3. them . . . They
4. them
5. my . . . yours
6. his . . . hers . . . their
7. She and I . . . Our . . . us
8. me . . . its . . . it
9. they . . . They . . . their
10. its . . . its . . . It's

PRACTICE 3, p. 80
1. b
2. a
3. a, b
4. a
5. a, b
6. a, b
7. a, b

PRACTICE 4, p. 80
1. it . . . them
2. their
3. his . . . her
4. it . . . They
5. his or her / their
6. their . . . her
7. his or her . . . its / their

PRACTICE 5, p. 81
1. ourselves
2. herself
3. himself
4. themselves
5. myself
6. yourselves
7. yourself

PRACTICE 6, p. 81
1. is angry at himself
2. introduce myself
3. help yourself
4. pat yourself
5. talks to herself
6. fix itself
7. laugh at ourselves
8. feeling sorry for himself

PRACTICE 7, p. 82
1. c. themselves
2. b. oneself
3. a. your
4. a. you
5. c. one
6. b. you
7. a. They

PRACTICE 8, p. 82
1. a. Another
2. a. other
3. a. Others
4. a. other
5. b. the other
6. c. The others
7. a. Another
8. b. other
9. b. The others
10. c. the other
11. b. the other ★
  ★Oregon, California, Alaska, Hawaii

PRACTICE 9, p. 83
1. another
2. another
3. another
4. another
5. another
6. another

PRACTICE 10, p. 84
1. d. each other
2. f. other than
3. a. every other
4. e. in other words
5. b. after another
6. c. the other day

PRACTICE 11, p. 84
(1) **Potatoes** are grown in most **countries**. They are one of the most widely grown **vegetables** in the world. They are very versatile; they can be prepared in many different **ways**.

(2) French **fries** are popular almost everywhere. Besides frying **them**, you can boil or bake **potatoes**. **Another** way people . . . and **other** kinds of dishes. **It's** . . . . from **potatoes**. There are still **other** ways . . . **processors** to make **products** such as **potato** chips and freeze-dried **potatoes**.

(3) **Potatoes** . . . where **they** were cultivated . . . 5,000 **years** ago. . . . potatoes were the **world's** first . . . the Incas carried **their** harvested **potatoes** . . . after **the** sun came up . . . the water out of them by stepping on **them**. This process **was** repeated for four or five **days** . . . stored **them** in pots. **The** Indians . . . .

CHAPTER 9: MODALS, PART 1

PRACTICE 1, p. 85
1. ~~to hear~~   hear
2. Correct.
3. ~~can heard~~   can hear
4. Correct.
5. ~~Do you can help~~   Can you help
6. Correct.
7. ~~oughts to~~   ought to
8. Correct.
9. ~~He supposed~~   He is supposed
10. Correct.
11. Correct.
12. ~~should to tell~~   should tell

PRACTICE 2, p. 85
1. c
2. a
3. f
4. e
5. b
6. d

PRACTICE 3, p. 86

1. a. cooking
   b. if I cooked
2. a. taking
   b. if we took
3. a. if I opened
   b. opening
4. a. joining
   b. if we joined
5. a. writing
   b. if I wrote

PRACTICE 4, p. 86

1. closing
2. if I closed
3. taking
4. if I went
5. leaving
6. cooking
7. if I made
8. finishing
9. if I used
10. recommending

PRACTICE 5, p. 87

	Necessity	Lack of Necessity	Prohibition
1.	✓		
2.			✓
3.	✓	✓	
4.	✓		
5.	✓	✓	
6.	✓		
7.	✓		
8.	✓		
9.			✓
10.		✓	

PRACTICE 6, p. 88

1. had to be
2. had to memorize
3. had to cancel . . . had
4. did you have to call
5. had to get
6. had to fasten

PRACTICE 7, p. 88

1. a
2. b
3. a
4. c
5. a
6. a
7. c
8. a
9. c
10. b

PRACTICE 8, p. 89

1. doesn't have to
2. had to
3. don't have to
4. had to
5. had to
6. do . . . have to
7. had to . . . didn't have to
8. do not have to
9. has to
10. have to

PRACTICE 9, p. 89

1. b
2. a
3. a
4. b
5. b
6. a
7. a
8. b

PRACTICE 10, p. 89

1. b
2. a
3. b, c
4. a
5. All are correct.
6. a

PRACTICE 11, p. 90

1. e
2. g
3. c
4. h
5. b
6. f
7. d
8. a

PRACTICE 12, p. 91

1. should have taken
2. should have turned
3. shouldn't have watched
4. should have visited
5. should have bought
6. should have ordered
7. shouldn't have come . . . should have stayed
8. shouldn't have changed . . . should have kept

PRACTICE 13, p. 91

1. should travel
2. should have gone
3. should paint . . . should be
4. shouldn't have painted
5. shouldn't have eaten
6. shouldn't drink . . . should drink
7. shouldn't have killed
8. should make

PRACTICE 14, p. 92

1. is supposed to arrive
2. am supposed to go
3. is supposed to be
4. was supposed to arrive
5. were supposed to come over
6. is supposed to run

PRACTICE 15, p. 93

1. yes
2. yes
3. no
4. yes
5. yes
6. no
7. yes
8. yes
9. no
10. no

PRACTICE 16, p. 93

1. d
2. g
3. a
4. j
5. b
6. e
7. f
8. c
9. i
10. h

PRACTICE 17, p. 93

1. Psychologist: could . . . could
   Psychologist: should
   Patient: should
2. Carl: could . . . could
   Waiter: should
   Carl: should
3. Mary: could . . . could
   Bob: should . . . should

PRACTICE 18, p. 94

Answers may vary.
1. **can speak**
2. **can** you help
3. **don't** have to come

4. **don't have to** pay
5. **must tell** the truth
6. should **get**
7. should **have** ordered
8. are suppose**d** to be
9. are suppose**d** to be
10. Why **don't you** join
11. **should** not eat
12. **Shall** we dance?
13. let's **not** dance

CHAPTER **10**: MODALS, PART 2

PRACTICE 1, p. 95

	100%	About 95%	About 50% or less
1.			✓
2.		✓	
3.	✓		
4.		✓	
5.			✓
6.	✓		
7.		✓	
8.			✓
9.			✓
10.			✓

PRACTICE 2, p. 95
1. a. must
2. b. could
3. b. may . . . may
4. a. must
5. b. may
6. a. must
7. b. may
8. b. may be
9. b. could be
10. a. am
11. b. must be
12. b. is

PRACTICE 3, p. 96
1. f. must not like
2. a. can't be him
3. c. may not be
4. d. may not speak
5. b. can't be true
6. e. must not get

PRACTICE 4, p. 97
1. b
2. a
3. b
4. a
5. a
6. b

PRACTICE 5, p. 98
1. must not have remembered
2. couldn't have been
3. may / might not have left
4. must not have heard
5. may / might not have had
6. couldn't have happened

PRACTICE 6, p. 98
1. must have driven
2. must have been / must be
3. must not have known
4. must be
5. must have left
6. must have gone
7. must need
8. must have hurt

PRACTICE 7, p. 99
1. a
2. a
3. b
4. a
5. b
6. a

PRACTICE 8, p. 100
1. e
2. j
3. a
4. f
5. b
6. d
7. i
8. c
9. h
10. g

PRACTICE 9, page 100
1. will
2. should
3. will
4. should
5. will
6. should
7. must
8. should

PRACTICE 10, p. 101
Answers may vary.
1. could be working
2. should be flying
3. might be sleeping
4. must be kidding
5. must have been kidding
6. might be hiking
7. may not be dating

PRACTICE 11, p. 102
1. c
2. c
3. b
4. b
5. c
6. c
7. b
8. c
9. b
10. b

PRACTICE 12, p. 103
Answers may vary.
1. a. It should arrive soon.
   b. It may / might / could have taken off late.
   c. We should have called the airport.
2. a. It may be for me.
   b. It's for me.
   c. It can't be for me.
3. a. He should have responded.
   b. He may not have gotten it.
   c. He must not have gotten it.
   d. He couldn't have gotten it.
4. a. The dishwasher may / might / could be leaking.
   b. It can't be the dishwasher.
   c. A pipe must be broken.
   d. You should call a plumber.
   e. You don't have to call a plumber.

PRACTICE 13, p. 103

1. can't
2. couldn't
3. can
4. couldn't
5. can't
6. could . . . can't

PRACTICE 14, p. 104

1. would fall . . . would throw
2. would always yell . . . would come
3. would always bring
4. would always wipe
5. would stay . . . would sleep
6. would tell . . . would listen

PRACTICE 15, p. 104

1. would rather not say
2. would rather have gone
3. would rather have studied
4. would rather not eat
5. would rather have
6. would rather be sailing

PRACTICE 16, p. 105

1. have to get
2. should be able to complete
3. won't have to stand
4. will you be able to leave
5. am not going to be able to graduate
6. must not have been able to get

CHAPTER 11: THE PASSIVE

PRACTICE 1, p. 106

1. are
2. is being
3. has been
4. was
5. was being
6. had been
7. will be
8. is going to be
9. will have been
10. has been
11. was
12. are being
13. will be
14. had been
15. will have been
16. are
17. is going to be
18. were being

PRACTICE 2, p. 107

		Subject	Verb
1.	A	Henry	visited
2.	P	The park	was visited
3.	A	Olga	was reading
4.	A	Philippe	has read
5.	P	Bambi	has been read
6.	A	Whales	swim
7.	P	Whales	were hunted
8.	P	The answer	won't be known
9.	A	I	know
10.	P	Two new houses	were built
11.	A	A famous architect	designed
12.	P	Television	was invented
13.	P	The World Cup	is seen
14.	A	Television	has expanded

PRACTICE 3, p. 107

1. is written
2. is being written
3. has been written
4. was written
5. was being written
6. had been written
7. will be written
8. is going to be written
9. will have been written
10. Was . . . written
11. Will . . . be written
12. Has . . . been written

PRACTICE 4, p. 107

Part I.

1. was painted by Picasso
2. are flown by experienced pilots
3. is going to be sung by a famous singer
4. has been accepted by Yale University
5. will be examined by the doctor
6. is being questioned by the defense attorney
7. was bitten by a dog
8. was being fed by the mother bird
9. won't be persuaded by his words
10. wasn't painted by me . . . painted by Laura
11. owned by Mrs. Crane
    isn't owned by her father anymore
12. weren't signed by me
    was signed by someone else

Part II.

13. is going to clean my teeth
14. Did . . . send that email
15. don't celebrate the Fourth of July
16. Has . . . sold your house yet
17. haven't caught the thief
18. are cleaning the carpets

PRACTICE 5, p. 109

	Verb	Object Of Verb	Passive Sentence
1.	will pay	the bill	The bill will be paid by Al.
2.	will arrive	Ø	Ø
3.	supplies	towels	Towels are supplied by the hotel.
4.	happen	Ø	Ø
5.	noticed	my error	My error was noticed by everyone.
6.	arrived	Ø	Ø
7.	didn't surprise	me	I was not surprised by the news.
8.	Did . . . surprise	you	Were you surprised by the news?
9.	Do . . . exist	Ø	Ø
10.	died	Ø	Ø
11.	told	the story	The story was told by an old man.
12.	hasn't rained	Ø	Ø

PRACTICE 6, p. 109

1. b. will be notified
2. b. didn't remember
3. c. was built
4. a. is visited
5. b. don't agree
6. c. will be invaded
7. c. been accepted
8. b. died
9. a. live
10. c. was felt
11. b. was ruled
12. a. walked

PRACTICE 7, p. 110

1. b
2. b
3. a
4. b
5. a

PRACTICE 8, p. 110

1. was invented . . . told
2. was established . . . was given . . . still attend
3. is known . . . is related . . . live . . . became . . . were killed . . . were saved
4. originated . . . like . . . gives . . . was valued . . . was used . . . were treated . . . is believed

PRACTICE 9, p. 111

1. The chefs prepared the food.
2. The food was prepared yesterday.
3. The rain stopped.
4. A rainbow appeared in the sky.
5. The documents were sent to you yesterday.
6. My lawyer sent the documents to me.
7. The winner of the election was announced on TV.
8. I didn't agree with you about this.
9. What happened yesterday?
10. Something wonderful happened to me.
11. The trees died of a disease.
12. The trees were killed by a disease.
13. A disease killed the trees.
14. I was accepted at the University of Chicago.
15. I was recommended for a scholarship.

PRACTICE 10, p. 112

1. can't be
2. should be washed
3. should have been washed
4. to be finished
5. must have been built
6. have to be paid . . . must be sent
7. be permitted
8. ought to be painted

PRACTICE 11, p. 112

1. should be made
2. should make
3. should have been made
4. couldn't talk
5. couldn't have talked
6. must be registered
7. must register
8. has to be paid . . . had better not send
9. must have been
10. may have been

PRACTICE 12, p. 113

1. g. locked
2. e. closed
3. a. finished
4. h. broken
5. b. lost
6. c. crowded
7. f. gone
8. d. turned on

PRACTICE 13, p. 113

1. is interested in
2. depends on
3. is married to
4. is scared of
5. bores
6. are made of
7. is composed of
8. is located in
9. are doing

PRACTICE 14, p. 113

1. in
2. for
3. about
4. in
5. to
6. of
7. with
8. with
9. with
10. with
11. of
12. to

PRACTICE 15, p. 114

1. ~~was arrived~~ — arrived
2. ~~injured~~ — were injured
3. ~~with~~ — to
4. ~~with~~ — about
5. ~~interesting~~ — interested
6. surprise — surprised
7. Correct.
8. ~~We lost.~~ — We are lost.
9. ~~might helped~~ — might be helped
10. ~~is been~~ — is being
11. ~~was happened~~ — happened
12. ~~Will be fixed the refrigerator~~ — Will the refrigerator be fixed
13. ~~must been remembers~~ — must have been remembered

PRACTICE 16, p. 114

1. crowded
2. hungry
3. lost
4. scared
5. dressed
6. hurt
7. invited
8. fat
9. stopped
10. elected

PRACTICE 17, p. 115

1. excited
2. exciting
3. shocking
4. shocked
5. exhausting . . . exhausted
6. boring . . . bored
7. confused . . . confusing
8. interesting
9. interested
10. thrilling . . . thrilled

PRACTICE 18, p. 115

1. a. fascinating
   b. fascinated
2. a. exhausting
   b. exhausted
3. a. disappointed
   b. disappointing

PRACTICE 19, p. 115

1. a, d
2. a, b
3. b, c
4. b, d
5. b, c

PRACTICE 20, p. 116

1. frustrating
2. grown . . . irritating
3. washing
4. writing
5. written
6. depressing . . . depressed
7. entertaining
8. known . . . spilt
9. comforting . . . Barking
10. inspiring . . . United . . . divided

CHAPTER 12: NOUN CLAUSES

PRACTICE 1, p. 117

Noun Clauses

1. what he said
2. None
3. what happened
4. None
5. why Dora is calling me
6. who that man is
7. where Hank lives
8. None
9. What they are doing
10. None
11. what I should say
12. None

PRACTICE 2, p. 117

1. do they want
2. what they want
3. does Stacy live
4. where Stacy lives
5. what Carl likes
6. does Carl like
7. is Lina going
8. where Lina is going

PRACTICE 3, p. 118

1. Where does Lee Live? **D**oes he live downtown?
2. I don't know <u>where he lives</u>.
3. What does Sandra want? **D**o you know?
4. Do you know <u>what Sandra wants</u>?
5. <u>What Yoko knows</u> is important to us.
6. We talked about <u>what Yoko knows</u>.
7. What do you think? **D**id you tell your professor <u>what you think</u>?
8. My professor knows <u>what I think</u>.
9. Where is the bus stop? **D**o you know where the bus stop is?
10. What did he report? <u>What he reported</u> is important.

PRACTICE 4, p. 118

1. how far it is
2. what that is on the table
3. how much it cost
4. What he said
5. when they are leaving
6. which road we should take
7. who called

8. what's happening
9. why they work at night
10. What they are trying to do
11. what kind of insects these are
12. whose keys these are

PRACTICE 5, p. 118

1. Who is that man?
   Noun clause: who that man is.
2. Where does George live?
   Noun clause: where George lives.
3. What did Ann buy?
   Noun clause: what Ann bought?
4. How far is it to Denver from here?
   Noun clause: how far it is to Denver from here.
5. Why was Jack late for class?
   Noun clause: why Jack was late for class.
6. Whose pen is that?
   Noun clause: whose pen that is.
7. Who did Alex see at the meeting?
   Noun clause: who Alex saw at the meeting.
8. Who saw Ms. Frost at the meeting?
   Noun clause: who saw Ms. Frost at the meeting?
9. Which book does Alice like best?
   Noun clause: which book Alice likes best.
10. What time is the plane supposed to land?
    Noun clause: what time the plane is supposed to land?

PRACTICE 6, p. 119

1. b
2. c
3. e
4. a
5. f
6. d
7. g, h

PRACTICE 7, p. 120

1. a, b, c, d, f
2. a, b
3. b, e

PRACTICE 8, p. 120

1. how much this book costs?
2. when Flight 62 is expected?
3. where the nearest phone is?
4. if this word is spelled correctly?
5. what time it is?
6. if this information is correct?
7. how much it costs to fly from Toronto to London?
8. where the bus station is?
9. whose pen this is?
10. if this bus goes downtown?

PRACTICE 9, p. 121

1. g	5. f
2. a	6. b
3. e	7. d
4. c	8. h

PRACTICE 10, p. 121
1. proud
2. angry
3. disappointed
4. aware
5. lucky
6. confident
7. worried . . . relieved

PRACTICE 11, p. 122
1. a. It is surprising that . . . .
   b. . . . nobody stopped to help Sam . . . is surprising
2. a. It is unfortunate that . . .
   b. That people in modern cities are . . . is unfortunate
3. a. It is still true that people . . . .
   b. That people in my village . . . help . . . . is still true.
4. a. It is undeniably true that . . .
   b. That people need each other . . . is undeniably true
5. a. It seems strange to . . . that people in cities live
   b. The fact that people in cities . . . don't know their neighbors

PRACTICE 12, p. 122
1. Millie said, "There's an important meeting at 3:00 o'clock today."
2. "There's an important meeting at 3:00 o'clock today," she said.
3. "There is," said Millie, "an important meeting at 3:00 o'clock today."
4. "There is an important meeting today. It's about the new rules," said Millie.
5. "Where is the meeting?" Carl asked.
6. Robert replied, "It's in the conference room."
7. "How long will it last?" asked Ali.
8. "I don't know how long it will last," replied Millie.
9. "I'll be a little late," said Robert. "I have another meeting until 3:00 P.M. today."
10. "Who is speaking at the meeting?" asked Robert.
11. "I am not sure who is speaking," said Millie, "but you'd better be there. Everybody is supposed to be there."

PRACTICE 13, p. 123
(1) "You are so slow, Mr. Turtle," said the rabbit, "and I am very fast."
(2) "I don't know about that," said the turtle. "Let's have a race. We will run for five miles and see who wins."
(3) "I agree," said the rabbit.
(4) "I am so far ahead of the turtle. I am going to take a little nap right here. It is going to take a long time before that turtle can catch up with me."
(5) The turtle looked back at the rabbit and exclaimed, "Slow but steady wins the race. Who's laughing now, Mr. Rabbit?"

PRACTICE 14, p. 123
1. was
2. needed
3. was having
4. had finished
5. had finished
6. would arrive
7. was going to be
8. could solve
9. might come
10. might come
11. had to leave
12. had to leave
13. should go
14. to stay

PRACTICE 15, p. 124
1. if / whether she was planning
2. what time the movie begins
3. if / whether we could still get
4. how he can help
5. if / whether he could help
6. when the final decision would be made
7. where she had been
8. what Kim's native language is
9. if / whether I was doing
10. what time he had
11. who she should give this message
12. why I hadn't called

PRACTICE 16, p. 125
Conversation 1.
1. was going
2. was
3. asked
4. would like
5. had
6. had
7. was
8. could
9. were

Conversation 2.
1. asked
2. was
3. told
4. was
5. said
6. was
7. had heard
8. had
9. was
10. had been
11. asked
12. had been
13. had not
14. told
15. had gone
16. was

PRACTICE 17, p. 126
1. whenever
2. wherever
3. whatever
4. however
5. whichever
6. whomever
7. whichever
8. whoever
9. whatever
10. wherever

CHAPTER 13: ADJECTIVE CLAUSES

PRACTICE 1, p. 127
1. person — who fixes computers
2. man — who lives on a boat
3. woman — who speaks four languages
4. people — who are bilingual in the office
5. office — that is in an old building
6. building — which we work in
7. trees — that were over two hundred years old
8. trees — which were nearby
9. truck — that had broken down
10. truck — which caused the problem

PRACTICE 2, p. 127
1. a, b
2. a, b
3. c, d
4. a, b
5. b, c
6. b, c

PRACTICE 3, p. 128

Adjective Clauses

1. man	that I met last night
2. woman	that Sandro is going to marry
3. people	whom we invited
4. book	which I just read
5. program	that Jason installed
6. house	we built in 1987
7. cake	I left on the table
8. book	my professor wrote

PRACTICE 4, p. 128
1. a, b, c, f
2. a, c, e, f
3. c, d, e
4. a, b, c, e
5. a, c, d, e
6. a, b, c, f

PRACTICE 5, p. 128
1. . . . I read was good
2. . . . I saw was very sad
3. . . . can live a long time
4. . . . we photographed
5. . . . does many things at the same time
6. . . . can trust
7. . . . the thieves stole was valuable

PRACTICE 6, p. 129
1. c, d, g, i
2. a, b, f, h

PRACTICE 7, p. 129
1. that / who / whom / Ø
2. who / that
3. that / which / Ø
4. which
5. that / who / Ø
6. who / that
7. whom
8. that / which

PRACTICE 8, p. 130
1. ~~it~~
2. ~~he~~
3. ~~it~~
4. ~~to~~
5. for ~~who~~ whom
6. ~~who~~ that which
7. People **who** have
8. ~~him~~
9. ~~she~~
10. ~~which~~ who / that

PRACTICE 9, p. 130
1. b		5. b
2. a		6. b
3. b		7. a, c
4. a		

PRACTICE 10, p. 131
1. **His** refers to **man**.
   Do you know the man whose car is parked over there?

2. **His** refers to **doctor**.
   I know a skin doctor whose name is Dr. Skinner.
3. **Their** refers to **people**.
   The people whose home we visited were very hospitable.
4. **Her** refers to **Mrs. Lake**.
   Mrs. Lake is the teacher whose class I enjoy the most.
5. **Their** refers to **parents**.
   The teacher asked the parents whose children were failing to confer with her.

PRACTICE 11, p. 131
1. b, c		5. a, b
2. a, c		6. b
3. c		7. a, c
4. a, c		

PRACTICE 12, p. 132
1. a. where I grew up		b. in which I grew up
2. a. I lived in		b. where I lived
3. a. where I lived		b. on which I lived
4. a. where I played		b. in which I played

PRACTICE 13, p. 132
1. a. that I go
   b. on which I go
   c. when I go
2. a. when I play tennis
   b. that I play tennis
   c. on which I play tennis

PRACTICE 14, p. 133
1. e
2. c
3. f
4. d
5. a
6. h
7. g
8. b

PRACTICE 15, p. 133
1. a, d
2. b
3. c, d
4. a, b, c
5. d
6. b, c
7. c, d
8. a

PRACTICE 16, p. 134
1. c
2. h
3. a
4. f
5. g
6. b
7. e
8. d

PRACTICE 17, p. 134

1. no
2. yes   I made an appointment with Dr. Raven, **who is an expert on eye disorders.**
3. yes   Bogota, **which is the capital of Columbia,** is a cosmopolitan city.
4. no
5. yes   South Beach, **which is clean, pleasant, and fun,** is known as a party town.
6. yes   The name Bogota comes from the word *Bacata*, **which was the Indian name for the site.**
7. no
8. yes   . . . Belinda Jones, **who wrote a touching essay** . . .
9. yes   . . . Nairobi, **which is near several fascinating game reserves,** . . .
10. no
11. no
12. no
13. no
14. yes   A typhoon, **which is a violent tropical storm,** can cause . . .
15. no
16. yes   Hurricane Katrina, **which destroyed parts of New Orleans,** occurred in 2005.

PRACTICE 18, p. 135

1. a   3. a   5. b   7. b
2. b   4. b   6. a   8. a

PRACTICE 19, p. 136

1. I received two job offers, neither of which I accepted.
2. I have three brothers, two of whom are professional athletes.
3. Jerry is engaged in several business ventures, only one of which is profitable.
4. The two women, both of whom began their studies at age 40, have almost completed law school.
5. Eric is proud of his success, much of which has been due to hard work, but some of which has been due to good luck.
6. We ordered an extra-large pizza, half of which contained meat and half of which didn't.
7. The scientist won the Nobel Prize for his groundbreaking work, most of which was on genomes.
8. The audience gave a tremendous ovation to the Nobel prize winners, most of whom were scientists.

PRACTICE 20, p. 136

1. Mike was accepted at the state university, which is surprising.
2. Mike did not do well in high school, which is unfortunate.
3. The university accepts a few students each year with a low grade-point average, which is lucky for Mike.
4. The university hopes to motivate these low-performing students, which is a fine idea.
5. Mike might actually be a college graduate one day, which would be a miracle!

PRACTICE 21, p. 137

1. ~~who is wearing a green hat~~   wearing a green hat
2. ~~who is in charge of this department~~   in charge of this department
3. ~~which was painted by Picasso~~   painted

4. ~~who are doing research~~   doing research
5. ~~which are in progress~~   in progress
6. ~~which are scheduled to begin in September~~ scheduled to begin in September
7. ~~which is the largest city in Canada~~   the largest city in Canada
8. ~~that orbit the sun~~   orbiting the sun
9. ~~which was formerly known as a planet~~   formerly known as a planet
10. ~~which means to "devalue someone or something"~~ meaning to "devalue someone or something"

PRACTICE 22, p. 137

1. Brasilia, **officially inaugurated in 1960,** is the capital of Brazil. ~~It was officially inaugurated in 1960~~.
2. Rio de Janeiro, **the second largest city in Brazil,** used to be its capital. ~~It is the second largest city in Brazil~~.
3. Two languages, Finnish and Swedish, are spoken in Helsinki, **the capital of Finland.** ~~It is the capital of Finland~~.
4. In Canada, you see signs, **written in both English and French.** ~~They are written in both English and French~~.
5. Libya, **a country in North Africa,** is a leading producer of oil. ~~It is a country in North Africa~~.
6. Simon Bolivar, **a great South American general,** led the fight for independence in the nineteenth century. ~~He was a great South American general~~.
7. Five South American countries, **liberated by Bolivar,** are Venezuela, Colombia, Ecuador, Panama, and Peru. ~~They were liberated by Bolivar~~.
8. We need someone, **holding a degree in electrical engineering,** to design this project. ~~He or she holds a degree in electrical engineering~~.
9. The project **being built in Beijing** will be finished next year. ~~It is being built in Beijing~~.
10. A lot of new buildings were constructed in Beijing in 2008, **the site of the summer Olympics that year.** ~~Beijing was the site of the summer Olympics in that year~~.

PRACTICE 23, p. 138

Sample answers:

1. . . . a lot of people **waiting** in . . .
2. Students **who are** living on . . . OR Students **living** on . . .
3. . . . the librarian **who sits** . . . OR the librarian **sitting** . . .
4. . . . Anna **whose** birthday . . .
5. . . . Sapporo, **which** is . . .
6. Patrick, who is my oldest brother, is married and has one child.
7. The person **sitting** next to me is someone I've never **met.**
8. . . . is a small **city located** on . . .
9. . . . person to **whom** I wanted . . .
10. There are eighty **students from** all over the world **studying** English at this school.
11. The people who we **met on** our trip last May . . .
12. Dianne Baxter, **who** used to teach Spanish, has organized . . .
13. . . . since I came here, **some of whom** are from my country.
14. People **who** can speak English . . .
15. Grandpa is getting married again, **which** is a big surprise.

CHAPTER 14: GERUNDS AND INFINITIVES, PART 1

PRACTICE 1, p. 139
Gerunds:
1. Driving
2. driving
3. None
4. singing
5. Singing
6. None

PRACTICE 2, p. 139
1. taking
2. going
3. improving
4. flying
5. lowering
6. buying
7. drinking
8. hearing

PRACTICE 3, p. 140
Part I.
1. in
2. of
3. of
4. for
5. from

Part II.
6. of
7. for
8. to
9. to
10. of

PRACTICE 4, p. 140
1. b
2. b
3. c
4. c
5. a
6. c
7. a
8. c
9. c
10. b

PRACTICE 5, p. 141
1. about leaving
2. for being
3. from completing
4. about having
5. of studying
6. for not wanting
7. for washing . . . drying
8. of stealing
9. to eating . . . sleeping
10. for lending

PRACTICE 6, p. 141
1. about taking
2. in buying
3. to living
4. for not answering
5. about failing
6. about changing
7. for cleaning
8. from arriving
9. for writing
10. in saving . . . from wasting

PRACTICE 7, p. 142
1. playing
2. smoking
3. driving
4. paying
5. arguing
6. selling
7. having
8. reading

PRACTICE 8, p. 142
Part I.
1. go hiking
2. go sailing
3. go skiing
4. went birdwatching
5. went canoeing

Part II.
6. go dancing
7. go bowling
8. will go sightseeing
9. will go window shopping

PRACTICE 9, p. 143
1. playing
2. lying
3. locating
4. looking
5. doing
6. watching

PRACTICE 10, p. 144
1. a, c
2. a
3. a, c
4. c
5. a
6. a, c

PRACTICE 11, p. 144
1. to work
2. me to work
3. to work
4. to work / me to work
5. to work
6. to work
7. to work
8. me to work
9. me to work
10. to work / me to work
11. to work / me to work
12. to work
13. to work / me to work
14. me to work

PRACTICE 12, p. 144
1. permitted me to leave early
2. asked me to give this note to Sue
3. advised me to take Biology 109
4. ordered me to pay a fine
5. warned Greg to keep his eyes on his own paper
6. warned Greg not to look at his neighbor's paper
7. told the children to be quiet
8. allowed me to stay up late on Saturday night
9. encouraged the students to speak slowly and clearly
10. expects the students to come to class on time

PRACTICE 13, p. 145
1. The teacher allowed the children to go outside and play.
   The children were allowed to go outside and play.
2. The doctor warned my father not to eat high-cholesterol foods.
   My father was warned not to eat high-cholesterol foods.
3. The sergeant ordered the soldiers to march in formation.
   The soldiers were ordered to march in formation.
4. The soccer coach encouraged the girls to play hard and win.
   The girls were encouraged to play hard and win.
5. Mary reminded her roommate to wake her up at 7:00.
   Mary's roommate was reminded to wake her up at 7:00.
6. The police officer permitted the drivers in our lane of traffic to go ahead.
   The drivers in our lane of traffic were permitted to go ahead.
7. The letter told me to complete this form by November 15th.
   I was told to complete this form by November 15th.

PRACTICE 14, p. 145

1. a	7. a
2. a	8. a
3. b	9. b
4. b	10. a
5. b	11. a
6. b	12. b

PRACTICE 15, p. 146

1. living	8. exercising
2. to be	9. me to exercise
3. to show	10. to exercise
4. making	11. to exercise
5. to be	12. my friend to consult
6. being	13. to consult
7. humming	14. to recommend

PRACTICE 16, p. 147

Part I.

1. to stay	6. him to stay
2. to stay	7. to stay
3. him to stay	8. to stay
4. him to stay	9. him to stay
5. staying	10. to stay

Part II.

1. traveling	6. traveling
2. traveling	7. traveling
3. to travel	8. traveling
4. traveling	9. traveling
5. to travel	10. traveling

Part III.

1. working	6. working
2. to work	7. him to work
3. to work	8. to work
4. to work	9. to work
5. to work	10. working

PRACTICE 17, p. 147

1. to turn	7. speaking
2. meeting	8. buying
3. to stop	9. to tell
4. seeing	10. to learn
5. telling	11. talking
6. to talk	

PRACTICE 18, p. 148

1. b	4. a
2. a	5. b
3. b	

PRACTICE 19, p. 148

1. a, b
2. a
3. a, b
4. a
5. a, b
6. a, b
7. a, b
8. b
9. b
10. a, b

PRACTICE 20, p. 149

1. It's	6. It's
2. is	7. is
3. is not	8. to jump
4. Is it	9. To see
5. Going	10. Is

PRACTICE 21, p. 149

1. a, b, d, g, i, k, l
2. a, d, f, h, j, k, l

PRACTICE 22, p. 150

1. b	8. b
2. a	9. a
3. b	10. a
4. b	11. b
5. a	12. a
6. a	13. a
7. b	14. b

PRACTICE 23, p. 151

1. camping	7. reading
2. to operate	8. to end
3. getting	9. using . . . speaking
4. applying	10. watching
5. to turn	11. running
6. sleeping	

PRACTICE 24, p. 152

1. . . . enjoy **watching** . . .
2. . . . spend time **playing** . . .
3. . . . important **to keep** . . .
4. . . . avoid **becoming** . . . by **exercising**
5. **Playing** word games **is** . . .
6. In addition, **it** is . . .
7. . . . people **to eat** . . .
8. . . . try **to eat** . . .
9. . . . interested **in learning** . . .
10. . . . wants **to live** . . .
11. . . . excited about **attending** . . .
12. . . . struggling **to learn** . . .
13. . . . hard time **pronouncing** . . .
14. He keeps on **studying** and **practicing**.
15. . . . in bed **listening** to . . .
16. . . . dreams **about / of** traveling . . .

CHAPTER 15: GERUNDS AND INFINITIVES, PART 2

PRACTICE 1, p. 153

1. ~~for~~ to	5. ~~for~~ to
2. Correct.	6. ~~to~~ for
3. Correct.	7. ~~for see~~ to see
4. Correct.	8. Correct.

PRACTICE 2, p. 153

1. a
2. a, b
3. a, b
4. a, b
5. a
6. a
7. a, b
8. a, b
9. a, b

PRACTICE 3, p. 154

1. d
2. c
3. b
4. a
5. f
6. e

PRACTICE 4, p. 154

1. very
2. too
3. too
4. too
5. very
6. very
7. very . . . too
8. too
9. too
10. very

PRACTICE 5, p. 155

1. very . . . enough
2. too
3. enough
4. very . . . enough
5. very . . . enough
6. too . . . enough
7. too . . . enough
8. very . . . enough
9. very
10. enough

PRACTICE 6, p. 155

1. to be accepted
2. to be given
3. to be picked
4. being petted
5. to be held
6. being invited
7. being noticed
8. being invited

PRACTICE 7, p. 155

1. b
2. a
3. b
4. b
5. a
6. b
7. a
8. b

PRACTICE 8, p. 156

1. b
2. a
3. b
4. b
5. a
6. b
7. b
8. a

PRACTICE 9, p. 156

1. to be called
2. being called
3. to be elected
4. to be elected
5. to be re-elected
6. being understood
7. to be left
8. to be loved . . . needed

PRACTICE 10, p. 157

1. a, c, d
2. a, c, d
3. a, c, d
4. a, c, d
5. a, c
6. b, c

PRACTICE 11, p. 157

1. practice / practicing
2. pass / passing
3. cry / crying
4. leave
5. win
6. arrive
7. rocking / rock
8. doing / do
9. talking / talk
10. reaching / reach

PRACTICE 12, p. 158

1. a
2. b
3. c
4. a, b
5. c
6. a
7. a, c
8. a

PRACTICE 13, p. 158

1. stand
2. fixed
3. beat
4. to stop
5. to clean
6. look
7. call
8. made . . . put

PRACTICE 14, p. 159

1. b
2. b, c
3. c
4. b
5. a
6. c
7. b, c
8. b
9. a

PRACTICE 15, p. 159

1. b
2. a
3. b
4. c
5. c
6. d
7. d
8. b
9. a
10. b
11. a
12. c
13. d
14. a
15. d

PRACTICE 16, p. 160

1. to buy
2. opening
3. being asked
4. having
5. to wear . . . dressing
6. jumping . . . falling
7. being taken
8. to stop delivering . . . to fill
9. gazing . . . to cheer
10. having

PRACTICE 17, p. 161

1. b
2. b
3. b
4. b
5. a
6. b
7. a
8. a
9. a
10. b
11. b
12. a
13. c
14. a
15. b
16. a
17. b
18. c
19. a
20. a
21. c

PRACTICE 18, p. 162

1.	~~playing~~	play
2.	~~to cry~~	crying
3.	~~take~~	taking
4.	~~being~~	to be
5.	~~signing~~	to sign
6.	~~to notify~~	notifying
7.	~~calling~~	call
8.	~~translated~~	to translate
9.	~~look~~	looking
10.	~~understanding~~	understand
11.	~~for~~	to
12.	~~to fish~~	fishing
13.	~~taking~~	to take
14.	~~eating~~	to eat
15.	~~eat~~	eating
16.	~~to burn~~	burning

CHAPTER 16: COORDINATING CONJUNCTIONS

PRACTICE 1, p. 163

1.	b	5.	c
2.	c	6.	c
3.	c	7.	a
4.	b	8.	b

PRACTICE 2, p. 163

1. Conjunction: and
   <u>sweet</u> and <u>fresh</u>   a. adjective
2. Conjunction: and
   <u>apples</u> and <u>pears</u>   b. noun
3. Conjunction: and
   <u>washed</u> and <u>dried</u>   c. verb
4. Conjunction: and
   <u>washing</u> and <u>drying</u>   c. verb
5. Conjunction: and
   <u>happily</u> and <u>quickly</u>   d. adverb
6. Conjunction: but
   <u>delicious</u> but <u>expensive</u>   a. adjective
7. Conjunction: and
   <u>Apples</u>, <u>pears</u>, and <u>bananas</u>   b. noun
8. Conjunction: or
   <u>apple</u> or a <u>banana</u>   b. noun
9. Conjunction: and
   <u>red</u>, <u>ripe</u>, and <u>juicy</u>   a. adjective

PRACTICE 3, p. 164

1. c
2. e
3. a
4. g
5. f
6. d
7. h
8. b

PRACTICE 4, p. 165

1. None.
2. calm, quiet, and serene.
3. the ball, and they ran. . . .

4. kicking, throwing, and running.
5. None.
6. sit down, be quiet, and open. . .
7. None.
8. None.
9. two cups of coffee, three glasses of water, one glass of orange juice, and three orders of eggs
10. strict, but fair OR strict but fair

PRACTICE 5, p. 165

1.	I	~~he is honest~~	, and honesty
2.	C		
3.	I	~~quiet~~	quietly
4.	C		
5.	C		
6.	I	~~to tour~~	touring
7.	C		
8.	I	~~summarizing~~	summarize
9.	C		
10.	C		
11.	I	~~they require~~	
12.	C		

PRACTICE 6, p. 166

1.	knows	7.	like
2.	know	8.	has
3.	knows	9.	agrees
4.	know	10.	are
5.	know	11.	realizes
6.	wants	12.	are

PRACTICE 7, p. 166

1. Both Mary and her parents drink coffee.
   Neither Mary nor her parents drink coffee.
2. Either John or Henry will do the work.
   Neither John nor Henry will do the work.
3. Not only our school but also the restaurants in town recycle trash.
   Both our school and the restaurants in town recycle trash.

PRACTICE 8, p. 166

Part I.
1. both her mother and her father
2. both the nurses and the doctor arrive
3. both bananas and mangos originated
4. both whales and dolphins are

Part II.
5. exports not only coffee but also oil
6. Not only Air Greenland but also Icelandair fly
7. not only a green jacket but also green pants
8. not only attended Harvard University but also Harvard Law School.

Part III.
9. Either Ricky or Paula knows
10. either to Mexico or Costa Rica
11. Either Jim or Taka's parents will take her
12. She's buying either salmon or tuna

Part IV

13. neither Fred nor his children
14. neither she nor her children have
15. Luis has neither a family nor friends
16. neither hot nor cold

PRACTICE 9, p. 167
1. stopped. The birds . . .
2. stopped, and the birds . . .
3. stopped, . . . sang, ...
4. street. His mother . . .
5. street, and his mother . . . .
6. street. His mother . . . .
7. coffee, and
8. coffee. It is . . . .
9. ice cream, but . . . .

PRACTICE 10, p. 168
My brother is visiting me for a couple of days. We spent yesterday together in the city, and we had a really good time.

First I took him to the waterfront. We went to the aquarium. We saw fearsome sharks, some wonderfully funny marine mammals, and all kinds of tropical fish. After the aquarium, we went downtown to a big mall and went shopping.

I had trouble thinking of a place to take him for lunch because he's a strict vegetarian, but I remembered a restaurant that has vegan food. We went there, and we had a wonderful lunch of fresh vegetables and whole grains. I'm not a vegetarian, but I must say that I really enjoyed the meal.

In the afternoon, it started raining. We decided to go to a movie. It was pretty good but had too much violence for me. I felt tense when we left the theater. I prefer comedies or dramas. My brother loved the movie.

We ended the day with a delicious home-cooked meal and some good conversation in my living room. It was an excellent day. I like spending time with my brother.

PRACTICE 11, p. 168
1. John will call either Mary or Bob.
2. Sue saw not only the mouse but also the cat.
3. Both my mother and father talked to the teacher
4. . . . is going . . .
5. I enjoy reading not only novels but also magazines.
6. Both smallpox and malaria are dangerous diseases.
7. . . . compact car. She is saving . . . .
8. . . . snow tonight. The roads . . . .
9. . . . we attended an opera, ate at marvelous restaurants, and visited . . . .

PRACTICE 12, p. 169
Across	Down
3. but	1. Neither
4. only	2. Both
6. Either	3. and
7. nor	

CHAPTER 17: ADVERB CLAUSES

PRACTICE 1, p. 170
Adverb Clauses
1. as she was leaving the store
2. before we have breakfast
3. Since Douglas fell off his bicycle last week
4. Because I already had my boarding pass
5. if the workplace is made pleasant
6. After Ceylon had been independent for 24 years
7. as soon as she receives them
8. once he becomes familiar with the new computer program

PRACTICE 2, p. 170
1. . . . calm. Tom . . . .
2. . . . calm, Tom . . . .
3. . . . calm. He . . . .
4. . . . fishing, the lake was calm. He . . .
5. . . . calm, so Tom went fishing. He . . . .
6. . . . quiet, Tom . . . .
7. . . . calm, quiet, and clear . . . .
8. . . . poor, he . . . .
9. . . . poor. He . . . .
10. Microscopes, automobile dashboards, and cameras . . . people to use. They are designed . . . people. When "lefties" use these items, ...

PRACTICE 3, p. 171
1. b	7. b
2. c	8. c
3. d	9. b
4. c	10. a
5. c	11. d
6. d	12. a

PRACTICE 4, p. 171
1. 1, 2	5. 2, 1
2. 2, 1	6. 1, 2
3. 1, 2	7. S
4. 2, 1	8. 1, 2

PRACTICE 5, p. 172
1. d	6. j
2. i	7. c
3. a	8. e
4. f	9. b
5. h	10. g

PRACTICE 6, p. 172
1. My registration was cancelled because I didn't pay the registration fee on time.
2. I'm late because there was lot of traffic.
3. Because he was on a good weight-loss diet, Harry lost 35 pounds.
4. Since Mario's is closed on Sundays, we can't have lunch there tomorrow.
5. Now that Jack has a car, he drives to work.
6. Natalie should find another job since she is very unhappy in this job.
7. David will lead us because he knows the way.
8. Frank is looking for a job in a law office now that he has graduated from law school.

PRACTICE 7, p. 173
1. even though
2. because
3. Because
4. Even though
5. Because
6. Even though
7. even though
8. because

PRACTICE 8, p. 173
1. even though
2. because
3. Because
4. Even though
5. even though
6. because
7. because
8. even though

PRACTICE 9, p. 174
1. c
2. a
3. b
4. b
5. a
6. c
7. b
8. a

PRACTICE 10, p. 175
1. if it ~~will rain~~ tomorrow — rains
2. If my car doesn't start tomorrow morning — no change
3. If I have any free time during my work day — no change
4. if I ~~will have~~ some free time tomorrow — have
5. If we don't leave within the next ten minutes, we ~~are~~ late — will be
6. If we ~~will leave~~ within the next ten minutes — leave
7. if the population ~~will continue~~ to grow at the present rate — continues

PRACTICE 11, p. 175
1. a. so   b. does
   Meaning: If Tom lives near you
2. a. so   b. are
   Meaning: If you are a resident of Springfield
3. a. not   b. don't
   Meaning: If you don't have enough money
4. a. so   b. are
   Meaning: If you are going to do the laundry
5. a. so   b. did
   Meaning: If I left the water running in the sink

PRACTICE 12, p. 176
1. doesn't approve . . . approves
2. can afford . . . can't afford
3. is raining . . . isn't raining
4. don't understand . . . understand
5. don't want to . . . whether you want to

PRACTICE 13, p. 176
1. unless you can stand the heat
2. unless it is broken
3. unless you cooperate with your opponents

PRACTICE 14. p. 177
1. he wants something
2. she runs out of clean clothes
3. the temperature outside goes below 50 degrees F
4. it is absolutely necessary to get somewhere quickly
5. will you get into Halley College
6. could I afford a big house like that

PRACTICE 15, p. 177
1. pass
2. not going to go
3. rains
4. in case
5. only if
6. always eat
7. even if
8. whether
9. won't
10. don't wake
11. if
12. can we

PRACTICE 16, p. 178
1. h
2. g
3. a
4. f
5. b
6. d
7. e
8. c

PRACTICE 17, p. 178
1. b
2. b
3. d
4. a
5. b
6. c
7. d
8. b
9. c
10. a

CHAPTER 18: REDUCTION OF ADVERB CLAUSES TO MODIFYING ADVERBIAL PHRASES

PRACTICE 1, p. 180
1. While they were riding in the car for six hours
2. While riding in the car for six hours
3. Before taking our long car trip across the country
4. While watching the exciting basketball game on TV
5. While they were watching the exciting basketball game on TV
6. Before leaving for the airport
7. while we were walking on the beach this afternoon
8. while walking on the beach this afternoon
9. While I was trying to get a taxi
10. Before getting into a taxi

PRACTICE 2, p. 180
Grammatically correct items:
2, 3, 4, 6, 8, 10

PRACTICE 3, p. 181
1. ~~he opened~~ — opening
2. ~~I left~~ — leaving
3. ~~I had met~~ — meeting / having met
4. ~~I searched~~ — searching
5. ~~he was herding~~ — herding
6. ~~they marched~~ — marching
7. ~~she was flying~~ — flying
8. ~~they imported~~ — importing

PRACTICE 4, p. 181

1. a. leaving
   b. left
2. a. invented / had invented
   b. inventing / having invented
3. a. working
   b. was working
4. a. flies
   b. flying
5. a. studied
   b. studying
6. a. learning
   b. learned
7. a. taking
   b. take
8. a. was driving
   b. driving

PRACTICE 5, p. 182

Subjects

1. Adv. clause: Sam   Main clause: car   (no change)
2. Adv. clause: Sam   Main clause: he
   While driving to work, Sam had a flat tire.
3. Adv. clause: Nick   Main clause: son   (no change)
4. Adv. clause: Nick   Main clause: he
   Before leaving on his trip, Nick gave his itinerary to his secretary.
5. Adv. clause: Tom   Main clause: he
   After working in the garden all afternoon, Tom took a shower and then . . .
6. Adv. clause: Sunita   Main clause: they   (no change)
7. Adv. clause: a friend   Main clause: American (no change)
8. Adv. clause: she   Main clause: Emily
   Emily always straightens her desk before leaving the office at the end of the day.

PRACTICE 6, p. 183

Modifying Adverbial Phrases

1. Riding his bicycle to school   a
2. Being seven feet tall   b
3. Driving to work this morning   a
4. Running five miles on a very hot day   a, b
5. Having run for 26 miles in the marathon   b
6. Drinking a tall glass of soothing iced tea   a, b
7. Clapping loudly at the end of the game   a
8. Speaking with her guidance counselor   a
9. Knowing that I was going to miss the plane because of heavy traffic   b
10. Having missed my plane   b
11. Waiting for my plane to depart   a

PRACTICE 7, p. 184

1. h
2. i
3. j
4. b
5. d
6. a
7. c
8. f
9. e
10. g

PRACTICE 8, p. 184

1. b, c
2. a, b,c
3. a, b
4. a, b
5. a, c
6. b, c
7. a, c

PRACTICE 9, p. 185

1. a. Upon receiving her acceptance letter for medical school, Sarah
   b. On receiving her acceptance letter for medical school, Sarah
2. a. Upon hearing the sad news,
   b. When she heard the sad news,
3. a. On looking at the accident victim,
   b. When they looked at the accident victim,

PRACTICE 10, p. 185

1. (d) arriving at the airport.
2. (e) reaching the other side of the lake
3. (c) discovering a burnt-out wire
4. (a) learning that the problem was not at all serious
5. (b) being told she got it

PRACTICE 11, p. 186

1. d
2. a
3. f
4. i
5. j
6. h
7. g
8. b
9. e
10. c

CHAPTER 19: CONNECTIVES THAT EXPRESS CAUSE AND EFFECT, CONTRAST, AND CONDITION

PRACTICE 1, p. 187

1. b, c, f
2. a, d, e
3. a, c, e
4. b, d, f

PRACTICE 2, p. 187

1. because
2. because
3. due to / because of
4. because
5. due to / because of
6. because
7. because
8. due to / because of

PRACTICE 3, p. 188

1. heavy traffic
2. there was heavy traffic
3. he is getting old
4. his age
5. she is afraid of heights.
6. her fear of heights
7. a cancellation
8. there was a cancellation today

PRACTICE 4, p. 188

1. . . . headache,
2. No change
3. . . . headache,
4. No change
5. . . . headache. **T**
6. . . . headache. **She,** therefore, . . .
7. . . . headache. **She** . . . , therefore.
8. . . . headache, . . .

PRACTICE 5, p. 188

Sentence 1.

1. a
2. b
3. c

Sentence 2.

1. a
2. b
3. a
4. b

PRACTICE 6, p. 189

1. a. I bought lemonade . . . didn't have any orange juice
   b. the store didn't have any orange juice, I bought lemonade
   c. The store didn't have any orange juice. . . . I bought lemonade.
   d. The store didn't have any orange juice. . . . I bought lemonade.
2. a. Mel has excellent grades. Therefore, he will go to a top university.
   b. Mel has excellent grades. He, therefore, will go to a top university.
   c. Mel has excellent grades. He will go to a top university, therefore.
   d. Mel has excellent grades, so he will go to a top university.
3. a. there had been no rain for several months, the crops died.
   b. There had been no rain for several months. . . . the crops died.
   c. There had been no rain for several months. The crops, therefore, died.
   d. There had been no rain for several months, so the crops died.

PRACTICE 7, p. 190

Part I.

1. Because
2. Therefore,
3. because of
4. Therefore,
5. Therefore,
6. because of
7. Because . . . town,
8. Because of

Part II.

9. Due to
10. Since . . . eyesight,
11. . Consequently,
12. . . . heights. Consequently,
13. due to
14. . Consequently,
15. Since

PRACTICE 8, p. 190

1. . . . **Therefore,** . . .
2. No change.
3. . . . **He simply** . . .
4. . . . reservation,
5. . **Therefore,** . . .
6. . . . orders, . . .
7. No change.
8. . . . . **The button** . . . years ago. **The zipper** . . .
9. . . . unique. **No two zebras** . . .
10. No change.

PRACTICE 9, p. 191

Sentence 1.

a. Because she ate some bad food, Kim got sick.
b. Because of some bad food, Kim got sick.
c. Kim ate some bad food, so she got sick.
d. Due to some bad food, Kim got sick.

Sentence 2.

a. Adam had driven for thirteen hours. Therefore, he was exhausted.
b. Since Adam had driven for thirteen hours, he was exhausted.
c. Due to the fact that Adam had driven for thirteen hours, he was exhausted.
d. Adam had driven for thirteen hours, so he was exhausted.

PRACTICE 10, p. 191

1. such	4. such	7. so	10. so
2. so	5. such	8. such	
3. so	6. so	9. so	

PRACTICE 11, p. 192

1. It was such a nice day that we took a walk.
2. The weather was so hot that you could fry an egg on the sidewalk.
3. She talked so fast that I couldn't understand her.
4. It was such an expensive car that we couldn't afford it.
5. There were so few people at the meeting that it was canceled.
6. Ted was so worried about the exam that he couldn't fall asleep last night.
7. The tornado struck with such great force that it lifted automobiles off the ground.
8. Joe's handwriting is so illegible that I can't figure out what this sentence says.
9. David has so many girlfriends that he can't remember all of their names.
10. There were so many people at the meeting that there were not enough seats for everyone.

PRACTICE 12, p. 192
Sentences 1, 3, 4, 5, 7, 8 express purpose

PRACTICE 13, p. 193
1. d
2. i
3. a
4. f
5. j
6. c
7. e
8. g
9. h
10. b

PRACTICE 14, p. 193
1. 1   5. 2
2. 1   6. 2
3. 1   7. 1
4. 2   8. 2

PRACTICE 15, p. 193
1. Rachel turned on the TV so that she could watch the news.
2. Alex wrote down the time and date of his appointment so that he wouldn't forget to go.
3. Nancy is taking extra courses every semester so that she can graduate early.
4. Sue lowered the volume on the TV set so that she wouldn't disturb her roommate.
5. Ed took some change from his pocket so that he could buy a newspaper.
6. I turned on the TV so that I could listen to the news while I was making dinner.
7. I turned off the phone so that I wouldn't be interrupted while I was working.
8. It's a good idea for you to learn keyboarding skills so that you'll be able to use your computer more efficiently.
9. Lynn tied a string around her finger so that she wouldn't forget to take her book back to the library.
10. The Parks Department has placed wastebaskets in convenient places in the park so that people won't litter.

PRACTICE 16, p. 194
1. is   6. isn't
2. is   7. is
3. isn't   8. isn't
4. is   9. isn't
5. is   10. is

PRACTICE 17, p. 194
1. a. Even though
   b. Despite
   c. Despite
   d. Despite
   e. Even though
2. a. In spite of
   b. Although
   c. Although
   d. In spite of
   e. In spite of
3. a. Despite
   b. Although
   c. Despite
   d. Although
   e. Despite
4. a. In spite of
   b. Even though
   c. in spite of
   d. even though
   e. in spite of
   f. even though
   g. even though
   h. in spite of

PRACTICE 18, p. 196
1. e   6. i
2. c   7. d
3. b   8. j
4. g   9. h
5. a   10. f

PRACTICE 19, p. 196
1. a. Even though it was night, we could see the road very clearly.
   b. Although it was night, we could see the road very clearly.
   c. It was night, but we could see the road very clearly.
2. a. Despite the fact that Helen has a fear of heights, she enjoys skydiving.
   b. Despite her fear of heights, Helen enjoys skydiving.
   c. Helen has a fear of heights; nevertheless, she enjoys skydiving.
3. a. Though Millie has the flu, she is working at her computer.
   b. Millie has the flu, but she is working at her computer anyway.
   c. Millie has the flu, but she is still working at her computer.

PRACTICE 20, p. 197
Possible answers
1. Red is bright and lively, while gray is a dull color. OR While red is bright and lively, gray is a dull color.
2. Jane is insecure and unsure of herself. Her sister, on the other hand, is full of self-confidence.
3. While a rock is heavy, a feather is light. OR A rock is heavy, while a feather is light.
4. Some children are unruly. Others, however, are quiet and obedient. OR Some children are unruly; others, however, are quiet and obedient. OR Some children are unruly. Others are quiet and obedient, however.
5. Language and literature classes are easy and enjoyable for Alex. On the other hand, math and science courses are difficult for him. OR Language and literature classes are easy and enjoyable for Alex; on the other hand, math and science courses are difficult for him.
6. Strikes can bring improvements in wages and working conditions; however, strikes can also cause loss of jobs and bankruptcy. OR Strikes can bring improvements in wages and working conditions. Strikes can also cause loss of jobs and bankruptcy, however.

PRACTICE 21, p. 197

Modals in the answers may vary.

1. I am going to have to (should / had better / must) call my mother. Otherwise, she'll start worrying about me.
2. The bus had better come soon. Otherwise, we'll be late for work.
3. You should make a reservation. Otherwise, you won't get seated at the restaurant.
4. Beth should stop complaining. Otherwise, she will lose the few friends she has.
5. You have to have a government-issued ID. Otherwise, you can't get on the plane.
6. Louis has to apply for his driver's license in person. Otherwise, he can't replace it.
7. You have to be a registered voter. Otherwise, you can't vote in the general election.
8. You should clean up the kitchen tonight. Otherwise, you'll have to clean it up early tomorrow.

PRACTICE 22, p. 198

1. e
2. h
3. d
4. g, h
5. b
6. f
7. a
8. c

PRACTICE 23, p. 198

1. exports
2. doesn't export
3. uses
4. is
5. originated
6. is

PRACTICE 24, p. 198

1. passes
2. doesn't pass
3. passes
4. passes
5. doesn't pass
6. passes
7. doesn't pass

PRACTICE 25, p. 199

1. the flowers bloomed
2. I took good care of the garden
3. my care
4. my care
5. , the flowers didn't bloom
6. . . . ; therefore, the flowers didn't bloom
7. ; however, the flowers bloomed
8. . . . garden. **N**evertheless, the flowers did not bloom
9. . . . garden, so the flowers did not bloom
10. . . . garden, the flowers bloomed
11. . . . garden, the flowers didn't bloom
12. the flowers bloomed anyway
13. . . . garden, the flowers will bloom
14. . . . garden, the flowers will not bloom
15. . . . garden. **O**therwise, the flowers will not bloom
16. . . . garden. **C**onsequently, the flowers did not bloom
17. . . . garden. **N**onetheless, the flowers bloomed
18. the flowers will bloom
19. will the flowers bloom
20. , yet the flowers did not bloom
21. the flowers won't bloom
22. or not you take good care of the garden

CHAPTER 20: CONDITIONAL SENTENCES AND WISHES

PRACTICE 1, p. 200

1. a. yes
   b. no
2. a. yes
   b. no
3. a. no
   b. yes
4. a. no
   b. no
   c. yes
5. a. no
   b. no
   c. yes
   d. no

PRACTICE 2, p. 200

Group 1
1. c
2. a
3. b

Group 2
1. c
2. a
3. b

Group 3
1. c
2. b
3. a

Group 4
1. a
2. c
3. b

PRACTICE 3, p. 201

1. heat . . . boils
   heat . . . will boil
2. forget . . . look
   forget . . . will look
3. pet . . . purrs
   pet . . . will purr
4. have . . . will call
   have . . . call
5. eat . . . will get
   eat . . . get
6. is . . . are
   is . . . will be

PRACTICE 4, p. 202

1. b
2. a
3. b
4. a
5. b
6. b

PRACTICE 5, p. 202

1. were . . . would be
2. had . . . would travel
3. had . . . would like
4. liked . . . would cook
5. weren't . . . could have
6. didn't have . . . would go / 'd go

PRACTICE 6, p. 203

1. h
2. d
3. b
4. j
5. i
6. c
7. a
8. e
9. g
10. f

PRACTICE 7, p. 203

1. b
2. a
3. a
4. a
5. b
6. b

PRACTICE 8, p. 204

1. had not taken . . . would not have met
2. had not forgotten . . . could have paid
3. had known . . . would have visited
4. had paid . . . would not have cut off
5. had been . . . would not have been canceled
6. had not discovered . . . would not have developed

PRACTICE 9, p. 204

1. c
2. a
3. b
4. e
5. f
6. d

PRACTICE 10, p. 205

1. had . . . could fly
2. could fly . . . would arrive
3. get . . . will have / 'll have
4. have . . . will tell / 'll tell
5. had had . . . would have told him
6. had told . . . would not have been

PRACTICE 11, p. 205

1. If I hadn't been sick yesterday, I would have gone to class.
2. If Alan ate breakfast, he wouldn't overeat at lunch.
3. If his watch had not been slow, Kostas would not have been late to his own wedding.
4. If the bus were not always so crowded, I would ride it to work every morning.
5. If Sara had known that Highway 57 was closed, she would have taken an alternative route.
6. If someone had been there to help her, Camille could have finished unloading the truck.

PRACTICE 12, p. 206

1. If the wind weren't blowing so hard, we could go sailing.
2. If the wind had not been blowing so hard, we could have gone sailing.

3. If the water weren't running, I could hear you.
4. If the water had not been running, I could have heard the phone.
5. If the baby were not hungry, she wouldn't be crying.
6. If Dick had not been sleeping soundly, he would have heard his alarm clock.
7. If I had not been watching an exciting mystery on TV, I would have answered the phone.
8. If I weren't trying to concentrate, I could talk to you now.

PRACTICE 13, p. 206

1. a, c
2. b, d
3. a, d
4. b, c
5. a, d
6. a, d

PRACTICE 14, p. 207

1. If it weren't raining, we would finish the game.
2. If I had eaten lunch, I wouldn't be hungry now.
3. If Bob hadn't left his wallet at home, he would have money for lunch now.
4. If Bruce were not always daydreaming, he would get his work done.
5. If I hadn't played basketball for three hours last night, my muscles wouldn't hurt today.
6. If the band had not been playing so loud, I could have heard what you said.
7. If Diane had not asked the technician a lot of questions, she wouldn't understand how to use her computer now.
8. If Olga and Ivan had been paying attention, they would have seen the exit sign on the highway.
9. If the doctor had explained the test results to me, I would know what they mean.
10. If we had not been sleeping last night, we would have heard the thunder and lightning.

PRACTICE 15, p. 208

1. Were I
2. Should you need
3. Had I known
4. Had I been offered
5. Should anyone call
6. Should the pizza need reheating
7. Should you feel
8. Were you really a lawyer

PRACTICE 16, p. 208

1. c
2. b
3. c
4. b

PRACTICE 17, p. 209

1. I hadn't forgotten to tell him that she needed a ride.
2. you hadn't helped
3. I had opened the door quickly
4. he could have gotten time off from work
5. he had told his boss about the problem

PRACTICE 18, p. 209

1. d
2. a
3. c
4. d
5. c
6. d
7. c
8. b
9. d
10. a
11. c
12. d
13. b
14. d
15. c
16. b
17. b
18. b
19. a
20. c

PRACTICE 19, p. 211

1. b
2. b
3. a
4. b
5. b
6. b

PRACTICE 20, p. 211

1. were shining
2. had gone
3. had driven
4. could swim
5. had won
6. had gotten
7. hadn't quit
8. were winter
9. would sing

PRACTICE 21, p. 212

1. had gone . . . could paint
2. hadn't moved . . . had taken
3. would stop
4. hadn't invited
5. hadn't paid
6. A. . . . would hurry . . .
   B. . . . would relax
7. A. . . . hadn't been elected
   B. . . . hadn't voted
8. A. . . . weren't . . . were
   B. . . . were . . . . were
9. had told
10. would go

PRACTICE 22, p. 213

1. would get
2. would snow
3. would leave
4. would hang up
5. would end
6. would order

PRACTICE 23, p. 213

1. would look
2. had had
3. hadn't been driving
4. would not have slid
5. steps
6. had known

7. would not have crashed
8. had not taken
9. would not have lost
10. had not lost
11. would have had
12. had had
13. would not have to pay
14. hadn't been driving
15. would not have run into
16. would not be
17. were
18. would take
19. stay
20. would stay
21. were not
22. could go
23. will fly
24. will take
25. could drive
26. would be
27. had

APPENDIX: SUPPLEMENTARY GRAMMAR UNITS

PRACTICE 1, p. A1

1.   **S**   **V**   **O**
   <u>Airplanes</u> <u>have</u> <u>wings</u>.

2.   **S**   **V**   **O**
   The <u>teacher</u> <u>explained</u> the <u>problem</u>.

3.   **S**   **V**   **O**
   <u>Children</u> <u>enjoy</u> <u>games</u>.

4.   **S**   **V**   **O**
   <u>Jack</u> <u>wore</u> a blue <u>suit</u>.

5.   **S**   **V**   **O**   **S**   **V**
   Some <u>animals</u> <u>eat</u> <u>plants</u>. Some <u>animals</u> <u>eat</u>
       O
   other <u>animals</u>.

6.   **S**
   According to an experienced waitress, <u>you</u>
     V   **O**
   <u>can carry</u> full <u>cups</u> of coffee without spilling

   them just by never looking at them.

PRACTICE 2, p. A1

1.   **VI**
   Alice <u>arrived</u> at six o'clock.

2.   **VT**
   We <u>drank</u> some tea.

3.   **VI**
   I <u>agree</u> with you.

4.   **VI**
   I <u>waited</u> for Sam at the airport for two hours.

5.   **VI**
   They're <u>staying</u> at a resort hotel in San Antonio,
   Texas.

6.   **VT**
   Mr. Chan <u>is studying</u> English.

7. The wind <u>is blowing</u> hard today. [VI]

8. I <u>walked</u> to the theater, but Janice <u>rode</u> her bicycle. [VI] [VT]

9. Crocodiles <u>hatch</u> from eggs. [VI]

10. Rivers <u>flow</u> toward the sea. [VI]

PRACTICE 3, p. A2

1. Jack opened the <u>heavy</u> door <u>slowly</u>. [ADJ] [ADV]

2. <u>Chinese</u> jewelers carved <u>beautiful</u> ornaments from jade. [ADJ] [ADJ]

3. The <u>old</u> man carves <u>wooden</u> figures <u>skillfully</u>. [ADJ] [ADJ] [ADV]

4. A <u>busy</u> executive <u>usually</u> has <u>short</u> conversations on the telephone. [ADJ] [ADV] [ADJ]

5. The <u>young</u> woman had a <u>very</u> <u>good</u> time at the picnic <u>yesterday</u>. [ADJ] [ADV] [ADJ] [ADV]

PRACTICE 4, p. A2

1. quickly
2. quick
3. polite
4. politely
5. regularly
6. regular
7. usual
8. usually
9. well
10. good
11. gentle
12. gently
13. bad
14. badly

PRACTICE 5, p. A3

1. Sue **always takes** a walk in the morning.
2. Tim **is always** a hard worker.
3. Beth **has always worked** hard.
4. Jack **always works** hard.
5. **Do you always work** hard?
6. Taxis **are usually** available . . . .
7. Yusef **rarely takes** a taxi . . . .
8. I **have often thought** about . . . .
9. Yuko **probably needs** some help.
10. **Have you ever attended** the show . . . ?
11. Al **seldom goes** out . . . .
12. The students **are hardly ever** late.
13. **Do you usually finish** your . . . ?
14. In India, the monsoon season **generally begins** . . .
15. . . . Mr. Singh's hometown **usually receives** around . . . .

PRACTICE 6, p. A3

1. Jim came to class <u>without</u> his books.
2. We stayed <u>at</u> home <u>during</u> the storm.
3. Sonya walked <u>across</u> the bridge <u>over</u> the Cedar River.
4. When Alex walked <u>through</u> the door, his little sister ran <u>toward</u> him and put her arms <u>around</u> his neck.
5. The two <u>of</u> us need to talk <u>to</u> Tom too.
6. Animals live <u>in</u> all parts <u>of</u> the world. Animals walk or crawl <u>on</u> land, fly <u>in</u> the air, and swim <u>in</u> the water.
7. Scientists divide living things <u>into</u> two main groups: the animal kingdom and the plant kingdom.
8. Asia extends <u>from</u> the Pacific Ocean <u>in</u> the east <u>to</u> Africa and Europe <u>in</u> the west.

PRACTICE 7, p. A4

1. <u>Jack</u> <u>put</u> the <u>letter</u> <u>in the mailbox</u>. [S] [V] [O] [PP]

2. The <u>children</u> <u>walked</u> <u>to school</u>. [S] [V] [PP]

3. <u>Mary</u> <u>did</u> her <u>homework</u> <u>at the library</u>. [S] [V] [O] [PP]

4. Chinese <u>printers</u> <u>created</u> the first paper <u>money</u> <u>in the world</u>. [S] [V] [O] [PP]

5. Dark <u>clouds</u> <u>appeared</u> <u>on the horizon</u>. [S] [V] [PP]

6. <u>Mary</u> <u>filled</u> the <u>shelves</u> <u>of the cabinet</u> <u>with boxes</u> <u>of old books</u>. [S] [V] [O] [PP] [PP] [PP]

PRACTICE 8, p. A4

	L.VERB	+	ADJ
1.	Ø (no linking verb in the sentence)		
2.	looked		fresh
3.	Ø		
4.	Ø		
5.	tasted		good
6.	grew		quiet
7.	Ø		
8.	Ø		
9.	Ø		
10.	smells		delicious
11.	Ø		
12.	got		sleepy
13.	became		rough
14.	Ø		
15.	Ø		
16.	sounded		happy
17.	turns		hot
18.	Ø		
19.	Ø		
20.	appears		certain
21.	seems		strange

PRACTICE 9, p. A5

1. clean
2. slowly
3. safely
4. anxious
5. complete
6. wildly
7. honest
8. thoughtfully
9. well
10. fair
11. terrible
12. good
13. light
14. confidently
15. famous
16. fine

PRACTICE 10, p. A6

	Question word	Auxiliary verb	Subject	Main verb	Rest of question
1a.	Ø	Can	Bob	live	there?
1b.	Where	can	Bob	live	Ø?
1c.	Who	can	Ø	live	there?
2a.	Ø	**Is**	**Ron**	**living**	there?
2b.	Where	**is**	**Ron**	**living**	Ø?
2c.	Who	**is**	Ø	**living**	there?
3a.	Ø	**Does**	**Sue**	live	there?
3b.	Where	**does**	**Sue**	live	Ø?
3c.	Who	Ø	Ø	**lives**	there?
4a.	Ø	**Will**	**Ann**	live	there?
4b.	Where	**will**	**Ann**	live	Ø?
4c.	Who	**will**	Ø	live	there?
5a.	Ø	**Did**	**Jack**	live	there?
5b.	**Where**	**did**	**Jack**	live	Ø?
5c.	**Who**	Ø	Ø	**lived**	there?
6a.	Ø	**Has**	**Mary**	**lived**	**there?**
6b.	**Where**	**has**	**Mary**	**lived**	Ø?
6c.	**Who**	**has**	Ø	**lived**	**there?**

PRACTICE 11, p. A7

1. When are you going to the zoo?
2. Are you going downtown later today?
3. Do you live in an apartment?
4. Where does Sue live?
5. Who lives in that house?
6. Can you speak French?
7. Who can speak Arabic?
8. When did Olga arrive?
9. Who arrived late?
10. What is Ann opening?
11. What is Ann doing?
12. What did Mary open?
13. Who opened the door?
14. Has the mail arrived?
15. Do you have a bicycle?
16. What does Alex have in his hand?
17. Do you like ice cream?
18. Would you like an ice cream cone?
19. What would Joe like?
20. Who would like a soft drink?

PRACTICE 12, p. A8

1. How do you take your coffee?
2. What kind of dictionary do you have? (have you? / have you got?)
3. What does he do for a living?
4. Who was Margaret talking to? / To whom was Margaret talking?
5. How many people showed up for the meeting?
6. Why could none of the planes take off?
7. What was she thinking about? / About what was she thinking?
8. How fast / How many miles per hour (OR: an hour) were you driving when the police officer stopped you?
9. What kind of food do you like best?
10. Which apartment is yours?
11. What is Oscar like? *(also possible:* What kind of person / man is Oscar?)
12. What does Oscar look like?
13. Whose dictionary fell to the floor?
14. Why isn't Abby here?
15. When will all of the students in the class be informed of their final grades?
16. How do you feel?
17. Which book did you prefer?
18. What kind of music do you like?
19. How late is the plane expected to be?
20. Why did the driver of the stalled car light a flare?
21. Which pen do you want?
22. What's the weather like in July?
23. How do you like your steak?
24. How did you do on the test?
25. How many seconds are there in a year?

PRACTICE 13, p. A9

1. How much money do you need?
2. Where was Roberto born? / In what country/city was . . .? / What country/city was Roberto born in?
3. How often do you go out to eat?
4. Who(m) are you waiting for? *(very formal and seldom used:* For whom are you waiting?)
5. Who answered the phone?
6. Who(m) did you call?
7. Who called?
8. How much gas/How many gallons of gas did she buy?
9. What does *deceitful* mean?
10. What is an abyss?
11. Which way did he go?
12. Whose books and papers are these?
13. How many children do they have? [*British or regional American:* How many children have they?]
14. How long has he been here?
15. How far is it / How many miles is it to Madrid?
16. When / At what time can the doctor see me?
17. Who **is** her roommate?
18. Who **are** her roommates?
19. How long / How many years have your parents been living there?
20. Whose book is this?
21. Who's coming over for dinner?
22. What color **is** Ann's dress?
23. What color **are** Ann's eyes?
24. Who can't go . . . ?
25. Why **can't** Bob go? / How come **Bob can't** go?

26. Why **didn't you** / How come **you didn't** answer . . .
    ? *(formal and rare:* Why **did you not** answer the
    phone?)
27. What kind of music do you like?
28. What don't you understand?
29. What **is** Janet **doing** right now?
30. How do you spell *sitting*? [*you* = impersonal
    pronoun]
31. What **does** Tom **look like**?
32. What **is** Tom **like**?
33. What does Ron do (for a living)?
34. How far / How many miles is Mexico from here?
35. How do you take / like your coffee?
36. Which (city) is farther north, Stockholm or
    Moscow? / Of Stockholm and Moscow, which
    (city/one) is farther north?
37. How are you getting along?

PRACTICE 14, p. A10
1. Haven't you seen . . . ? No.
2. Don't you feel . . . ? No.
3. Wasn't he . . . ? No.
4. Didn't Mary tell . . . ? No.
5. Don't Janet and you work . . . ? Yes.
6. Isn't that . . . ? Yes.
7. Wasn't she . . . ? No.
8. Isn't she . . . ? Yes.

PRACTICE 15, p. A11
1. don't you
2. have you
3. didn't she
4. aren't there
5. have you
6. don't you (*also possible but less common:* haven't you)
7. won't you
8. doesn't he
9. shouldn't we
10. can they
11. are they
12. isn't it
13. didn't they
14. aren't I
15. isn't it

PRACTICE 16, p. A11
1. He's
2. Ø
3. He's
4. Ø
5. She'd
6. Ø
7. She'd
8. Ø
9. We'll
10. They're
11. It's
12. It's
13. Ø
14. Ø
15. We're
16. Ø

17. She's
18. She'd
19. She'd . . . we'd
20. Ø . . . he'd

PRACTICE 17, p. A12
1. I don't have any problems. I have no problems.
2. There wasn't any food on the shelf. There was no
   food on the shelf.
3. I didn't receive any letters from home. I received no
   letters from home.
4. I don't need any help. I need no help.
5. We don't have any time to waste. We have no time
   to waste.
6. You shouldn't have given the beggar any money. You
   should have given the beggar no money.
7. I don't trust anyone. I trust no one.
8. I didn't see anyone. I saw no one.
9. There wasn't anyone in his room. There was no one
   in his room.
10. She can't find anybody who knows about it. She can
    find nobody who knows about it.

PRACTICE 18, p. A13
1. We **have no** time to waste. OR We **don't have any**
   time to waste.
2. I **didn't have any** problems. OR I **had no**
   problems.
3. I **can't do anything** about it. OR I **can do
   nothing** about it.
4. You **can hardly ever understand** her when she
   speaks.
5. I **know neither** Ann **nor** her husband. OR I **don't
   know either** Ann **or** her husband.
6. **Don't ever drink** water from . . . . OR **Never
   drink** water from . . . .
7. . . . I **could barely hear** the speaker.

PRACTICE 19, p. A13
1. **Hardly had I stepped** out of bed . . . .
2. **Never will I say** that again.
3. **Scarcely ever have I enjoyed** myself more . . . .
4. **Rarely does she make** a mistake.
5. **Never will I trust** him again because . . . .
6. **Hardly ever is it** possible to get . . . .
7. **Seldom do I skip** breakfast.
8. **Never have I known** a more . . . .

PRACTICE 20, p. A13
1. honesty, fairness
2. school, class
3. her illness, her husband's death
4. jail, prison
5. ghosts, UFOs
6. my cousin, a friend
7. mathematics, sports
8. you, your children
9. smoking, cigarettes
10. magazines, a newspaper, websites

PRACTICE 21, p. A14

1. of	6. of
2. at	7. to
3. from	8. for
4. in	9. on
5. at	10. from

PRACTICE 22, p. A14

Situation 1:

1. to	5. with
2. to	6. to
3. of	7. to
4. to	

Situation 2:

1. with/by	4. of
2. with	5. of
3. with	6. of, by

PRACTICE 23, p. A15

1. c	5. a
2. e	6. g
3. b	7. d
4. f	

PRACTICE 24, p. A15

1. to	7. about
2. for	8. with
3. from	9. on
4. on	10. with
5. about	11. on
6. for	12. of

PRACTICE 25, p. A16

1. for	8. for . . . to
2. for	9. about
3. of	10. of
4. to . . . for	11. of
5. with	12. to / with
6. to	13. with
7. on	14. to

PRACTICE 26, p. A16

Sample answers:

1. be	5. write
2. arrive	6. see
3. tell	7. become
4. talk	8. be

PRACTICE 27, p. A17

1. take
2. be named
3. stay
4. be postponed
5. be admitted
6. be controlled . . . (be) eliminated
7. have
8. be
9. know
10. be
11. be permitted
12. not be
13. return
14. be built
15. not tell
16. be told

PRACTICE 28, p. A18

1. raised	9. lies
2. rises	10. raises
3. sat	11. rose
4. set	12. lays
5. lay	13. laid
6. lying	14. set
7. laid	15. sat
8. lie	16. lies

SPECIAL WORKBOOK SECTION: PHRASAL VERBS

PRACTICE 1, p. A21

1. a. after
   b. over
   c. up
   d. into
2. a. out
   b. into
   c. out
   d. out of
3. a. over
   b. through with
   c. out of
   d. back from
   e. off
4. a. off
   b. up
   c. on
   d. back
   e. in

PRACTICE 2, p. A22

1. passed out
2. Pick out
3. takes after
4. think . . . over
5. puts up with
6. passed away
7. show up
8. get along with
9. turn in
10. pass out

PRACTICE 3, p. A23

1. our assignment?
2. a lie. / a story.
3. the city. / the banks.
4. your cigarette. / the lights. / the fire.
5. the war? / the crisis?
6. the problem? / the puzzle?
7. the lights? / the music? / the printer?
8. his classmate. / a girl.
9. chocolate. / smoking.
10. a friend. / a classmate.
11. high school. / college.

PRACTICE 4, p. A23

1. into	6. up
2. off	7. into . . . out
3. on	8. up
4. back	9. up
5. out	10. on

PRACTICE 5, p. A24

1. away / out
2. up
3. off / out
4. up
5. off
6. up
7. about, on
8. out of
9. off
10. off . . . in

PRACTICE 6, p. A25

1. out
2. back
3. by / in
4. on . . . off
5. put . . . out
6. up
7. up . . . away / out
8. out . . . back
9. up
10. on

PRACTICE 7, p. A27

1. up
2. over
3. after
4. up
5. out
6. down
7. up
8. out
9. off
10. up
11. out

PRACTICE 8, p. A28

1. back
2. up
3. out
4. over
5. on . . . off
6. in . . . out
7. on . . . off
8. on . . . off
9. up with
10. A: about / on
    B: along with
11. A: over . . . in
    B: over

NOTES

NOTES

NOTES

NOTES